Data Scient Pocket Guide

Over 600 Concepts, Terminologies, and Processes of Machine Learning and Deep Learning Assembled Together

Mohamed Sabri

www.bpbonline.com

FIRST EDITION 2021
Copyright © BPB Publications, India
ISBN: 978-93-90684-97-7

All Rights Reserved. No part of this publication may be reproduced, distributed or transmitted in any form or by any means or stored in a database or retrieval system, without the prior written permission of the publisher with the exception to the program listings which may be entered, stored and executed in a computer system, but they can not be reproduced by the means of publication, photocopy, recording, or by any electronic and mechanical means.

LIMITS OF LIABILITY AND DISCLAIMER OF WARRANTY

The information contained in this book is true to correct and the best of author's and publisher's knowledge. The author has made every effort to ensure the accuracy of these publications, but publisher cannot be held responsible for any loss or damage arising from any information in this book.

All trademarks referred to in the book are acknowledged as properties of their respective owners but BPB Publications cannot guarantee the accuracy of this information.

Distributors:

BPB PUBLICATIONS
20, Ansari Road, Darya Ganj
New Delhi-110002
Ph: 23254990/23254991

DECCAN AGENCIES
4-3-329, Bank Street,
Hyderabad-500195
Ph: 24756967/24756400

MICRO MEDIA
Shop No. 5, Mahendra Chambers,
150 DN Rd. Next to Capital Cinema,
V.T. (C.S.T.) Station, MUMBAI-400 001
Ph: 22078296/22078297

BPB BOOK CENTRE
376 Old Lajpat Rai Market,
Delhi-110006
Ph: 23861747

To View Complete
BPB Publications Catalogue
Scan the QR Code:

Published by Manish Jain for BPB Publications, 20 Ansari Road, Darya Ganj, New Delhi-110002 and Printed by him at Repro India Ltd, Mumbai

www.bpbonline.com

Dedicated to

My father and our Sundays…

About the Author

Mohamed Sabri, the author of this book, completed his graduation in Mathematics and Economics from the University of Ottawa. He is a Managing Partner and Consultant in the field of Data Science and MLOps, and is working with the North American organizations in the Banking, Retail, and Gaming sector. With an irrefutable passion for Data Science, he is driven to do more for the domain by being involved in a range of innovative AI projects that help him deliver end-to-end solutions in the field of AI.

He drives his professional journey with his excellent communication skills and his expertise in Tech popularisation for complex projects. Building upon his commitment towards ensuring work and team cohesiveness, he has successfully executed several AI projects.

In his book, "Data Scientist Pocket Guide", he has interestingly poured his secrets of becoming a benevolent data scientist.

His secret passion for connecting and networking with people and professionals is channelled through this book, that attempts to connect and reach several data scientists and make their everyday job enriching and easier.

About the Reviewer

Prateek Gupta is a Data Enthusiast and loves data-driven technologies. Prateek has done his B.Tech in Computer Science & Engineering and currently working as a Data Scientist in an IT company. Prateek has a total of 10 years of experience in the software industry, and currently, he is working in the Computer Vision area. Prateek is also author of the book "Practical Data Science with Jupyter" 2 nd Edition published by the BPB Publications.

Acknowledgments

The completion of this book could not have been possible without the support of BPB Publications. I would like to thank all the team members of BPB Publications; despite the COVID crisis, they extended their full support with access to all the resources that were critical in completing this book. I would like to thank my family for their support and encouragement while writing this book, with a special mention to my parents for being an incredible source of inspiration in my life. A huge thanks to my father for teaching me how to be patient and resilient in life. Lastly, I would like to underline the importance of patience in writing a book or facing any challenge in life.

Preface

At the beginning of my career as a data scientist, I use to go on search engines and use various sources to find explanations about a concept in data science. This was time consuming and the answers to my questions where not always reliable. It is hard for any data scientist to find quickly all the answers to his questions and sometimes answers vary from a source to another. Also, some concepts are hard to understand so you have to find a source that explains clearly what a concept means. This book is a first of a kind dictionary or glossary that regroups the most popular terms in data science. It helps data scientist from beginners to senior to look for definitions very quickly and have reliable answers to their questions. Usually books in data science focuses on coding and on practical use cases, whereas this book goal is to explain concepts and give a better idea to data scientist about what the words means. It's good to be able to code in data science and build machine learning models but if the data scientist doesn't understand the logic and the mechanism behind each concept it is hard for him to provide good results and explain its work. I hope you will keep this book as your Bible for data science and use it each time you have doubt about a concept's meaning. Have fun!

This book is separated into two sections. The first section is composed of 26 chapters, each chapter correspond to a letter in the alphabet and a set of definitions in each chapter. The second section is an FAQ or frequently asked questions and it contains all the questions that a data scientist might have when it comes to data science, the questions covers some theorical parts and others are more practical such as "should I learn R or Python?".

This book objective is not be read all at once but to become your data science Bible, so each time you might have a question about a concept and wondering how it works or what does it mean you might look at the book for answers. Also, this book is a good support for beginners that are always confused around all the concepts that they might find in data science. So, the lecture of this book is not linear you might start to read wherever you want and jump to any chapter based on the answers you are looking for. This book is a first of a kind in data science as no other book regroup as much terms in the field as this book does.

Downloading the code bundle and coloured images:

Please follow the link to download the
Code Bundle and the *Coloured Images* of the book:

https://rebrand.ly/i9waffm

Errata

We take immense pride in our work at BPB Publications and follow best practices to ensure the accuracy of our content to provide with an indulging reading experience to our subscribers. Our readers are our mirrors, and we use their inputs to reflect and improve upon human errors if any, occurred during the publishing processes involved. To let us maintain the quality and help us reach out to any readers who might be having difficulties due to any unforeseen errors, please write to us at:

errata@bpbonline.com

Your support, suggestions and feedbacks are highly appreciated by the BPB Publications' Family.

Did you know that BPB offers eBook versions of every book published, with PDF and ePub files available? You can upgrade to the eBook version at www.bpbonline.com and as a print book customer, you are entitled to a discount on the eBook copy. Get in touch with us at **business@bpbonline.com** for more details.

At **www.bpbonline.com**, you can also read a collection of free technical articles, sign up for a range of free newsletters, and receive exclusive discounts and offers on BPB books and eBooks.

BPB is searching for authors like you

If you're interested in becoming an author for BPB, please visit **www.bpbonline.com** and apply today. We have worked with thousands of developers and tech professionals, just like you, to help them share their insight with the global tech community. You can make a general application, apply for a specific hot topic that we are recruiting an author for, or submit your own idea.

The code bundle for the book is also hosted on GitHub at **https://github.com/bpbpublications/Data-Scientist-Pocket-Guide**. In case there's an update to the code, it will be updated on the existing GitHub repository.

We also have other code bundles from our rich catalog of books and videos available at **https://github.com/bpbpublications**. Check them out!

PIRACY

If you come across any illegal copies of our works in any form on the internet, we would be grateful if you would provide us with the location address or website name. Please contact us at **business@bpbonline.com** with a link to the material.

If you are interested in becoming an author

If there is a topic that you have expertise in, and you are interested in either writing or contributing to a book, please visit **www.bpbonline.com**.

REVIEWS

Please leave a review. Once you have read and used this book, why not leave a review on the site that you purchased it from? Potential readers can then see and use your unbiased opinion to make purchase decisions, we at BPB can understand what you think about our products, and our authors can see your feedback on their book. Thank you!

For more information about BPB, please visit **www.bpbonline.com**.

Table of Contents

1. FAQ 1

How to fine tune a machine learning algorithm? 1
How to build deep neural network architecture? 2
How to train a machine learning algorithm faster? 3
Why do we normalize the input data in deep neural network? 4
When can we consider that we did a good job in a machine learning project? 4
When should we use deep learning instead of the traditional machine learning models? 5
How much time does it take to become a good data scientist? 6
How to evaluate the performance of a model? 6
In case of a large dataset, should I sample my data or use distributed computing? 7
How much time should I spend in data transformation? 7
How to select the right machine learning algorithm? 8
Should I learn R or Python? 8
What's the trade-off between bias and variance? 8
What is the difference between supervised and unsupervised machine learning? 9
What is the difference between L1 and L2 regularizations? 9
What's the difference between type I and type II error? 9
What's the difference between probability and likelihood? 10
What's the difference between a generative and discriminative model? 10
Which is more important model accuracy, or model performance? 11
How would you handle an imbalanced dataset? 11
How do you ensure that you're not overfitting with a model? 12
What's the "kernel trick" and how is it useful? 13
How do you handle missing data in a dataset? 13
What are the origins of machine learning? 14
What is the difference between a classifier and a model? 14
What is the difference between a parametric learning algorithm and a non-parametric learning algorithm? 15
What is the difference between a cost function and a loss function in machine learning? 15

What is the difference between covariance and correlation? 15
Why did it take so long for deep networks to be invented? 16
What are some good books/papers for learning machine learning? 16
What are the advantages of semi-supervised learning over supervised and
unsupervised learning? 17
When should I apply data normalization/standardization? 17
How do you deal with a machine learning problem with a large number of
features? 17
When should one use median as opposed to the mean or average? 18
Why is "Naive" Bayes called naive? 18

2. A 19
    A/B testing 19
    Accuracy 20
    Action 21
    Activation function 21
    Active learning 22
        AdaBoost 23
        AdaDelta 24
        AdaGrad 25
        Adam 25
    Adaptive learning rate 26
    Affine layer 26
    Agent 27
    Agglomerative clustering 27
    AlexNet 27
        Algorithm 28
    Anaconda 29
    Anchor box 29
    Annotator 30
    ANOVA 30
    Apache Spark 31
    ARIMA 31
    Artificial general intelligence (AGI) 33
        Artificial intelligence 33
        Artificial narrow intelligence (ANI) 33
        Artificial super intelligence (ASI) 34

- Association learning 34
  - *Association rules*... 34
- Attention mechanism 34
- Attribute 35
- Area under the ROC Curve (AUC) 35
- Autocorrelation 36
- Autoencoder 36
- Automatic summarization 37
- Automation bias 38
- Autoregression 38
- Average pooling 38
- Average precision 39

3. B 41

- Backpropagation 41
  - *Backpropagation through time (BPTT)* 42
- Bag of words 42
- Bagging 42
- Bar chart 43
- Base learner 44
- Baseline 44
- Batch 44
- Batch gradient descent 45
- Batch normalization 45
- Bayes' theorem 46
  - *Bayesian inference* 46
  - *Bayesian statistics* 47
- Bellman equation 47
- Bernoulli distribution 48
- Bias 49
  - *Bias-variance trade-off* 49
- Bidirectional Recurrent Neural Network 49
  - *Big Data* 50
  - *Big O notation* 50
- Binarization 51
  - *Binary classification* 51
  - *Binary variables* 52

- Binning 52
- Binomial distribution 52
- Black box model 53
- BLEU score 54
- Boosting 54
  - *Bootstrapping* 55
- Bottleneck layer 55
- Bounding box 55
- Box plot 55
- Bucketing 56
- Business analytics 56
  - *Business intelligence* 57

4. C 59

- Caffe 59
- Calibration 59
- Candidate generation 60
- Candidate sampling 60
- Categorical cross-entropy 60
  - *Categorical variable* 61
- Centroid 61
  - *Centroid-based algorithm* 61
- Chain rule 62
  - *Chainer* 62
- Channel 63
- Checkpoints 63
- Chi-square test 63
  - *Chi-squared distribution* 63
- CIFAR: 64
- Classification 64
  - *Classification threshold* 65
  - *Classifier* 65
- Clipping 66
- Cloud 66
- Clustering 66
- CNN 67
- CNTK 68

Co-adaptation 68
COCO 69
Coefficient of determination 69
Cohen's kappa 69
Collaborative filtering 70
Complexity 71
Computer vision 71
Concordant-discordant ratio 72
Confidence interval 72
Confusion matrix 73
Connectivity-based algorithm 73
Continuous learning 74
Continuous variable 75
Contrastive divergence 75
Convenience sampling 75
Convergence 75
Convex function 76
Convolution 76
    Convolutional layer 76
    Convolutional neural network 77
    Correlation 77
Cosine similarity 77
Cost function 78
Covariance 78
Coverage bias 78
CPU 79
Cross-entropy 79
Cross validation 79
CUDA 80

5. D 81

Dashboard 81
Data analysis 82
Data augmentation 82
Data engineering 82
Data mining 83
Data parallelism 83

Data preparation 83
Data science 83
Data transformation 84
Data wrangling 84
Database 85
Databricks 85
DataFrame 85
Dataset 85
Davies-Bouldin index 86
DBSCAN 86
Decile 87
Decision boundary 87
    Decision tree 88
    Deduction 89
    Deep belief network 89
    Deep dream 90
Deep learning 91
    Deep Q-network 92
    Deeplearning4j 92
    Degree of freedom 92
    Dense feature 92
Dense layer 92
Density-based algorithm 93
Dependent variable 93
    Deployment as API 93
Deployment in batch 94
Depth 94
Depth-wise separable convolutional neural network 94
Descriptive statistics 94
Device 95
Dimensionality reduction 95
Discounted cumulative gain 95
Discrete variable 96
Discriminative model 96
    Discriminator 96

Divisive clustering 96
Downpour stochastic gradient descent 97
Downsampling 98
Dplyr 98
DropConnect 98
   Dropout regularization 99
Dummy variable 99
Dunn index 99
Dynamic model 100
Dynamic programming 100

6. E 101

Early stopping 101
EDA 101
ELU 102
Embedding space 102
   Embeddings 103
Ensemble learning algorithm 103
Ensemble models: 103
Entropy 103
Episode 104
Epoch 104
Epsilon greedy policy 104
ETL 105
Euclidean distance 105
Evaluation metric 105
   Example 106
   Experimentation 106
Expert system 106
Exploding gradient problem 106
Exploration vs. exploitation 107
Exponential family distribution 107
Exponential loss 107
   Exponential smoothing 108
Extrapolation 108
Extreme values 109

7. F 111

- F1 Score 111
- Face recognition 111
- Facet 112
- Factor analysis 113
- False negative 114
- False positive 114
- Feature 114
  - *Feature cross* 115
  - *Feature engineering* 115
  - *Feature hashing* 115
- Feature learning 115
  - *Feature reduction* 116
  - *Feature selection:* 117
- Federated learning: 117
- Feedback loop 118
- Feedforward 118
- Few-shot learning 119
- Fine-tuning 119
- Flume 120
- Focal loss 120
- Forget gate 120
- Frechet inception distance 121
- Frequentist statistics 121
- F-score 121
- Full softmax 121
- Fully connected layer 121

8. G 123

- Gain and Lift Charts 123
- Gated Recurrent Unit (GRU) 124
- Gaussian distribution 125
- General AI 126
- Generalization 126
- Generalization curve 126
- Generalized Linear Model (GLM) 127

Generative adversarial neural network (GAN) 127
Generative classification 128
    Generator *128*
Genetic algorithm 128
Ggplot2 128
Gini coefficient 129
GloVe 130
Go 130
Goodness of fit 130
GoogleNet 130
GPU 131
Gradient accumulation 131
Gradient descent 131
Greedy policy 131
Grid search 132
Ground truth 132

9. H 133

Hadoop 133
Hashing 133
Heuristic 134
Hidden layer 134
Hidden Markov model 134
Hierarchical clustering 135
Highway layer 136
Highway network 136
Hinge loss 136
Histogram 137
Hive 138
Holdout sample 138
Holt-Winters forecasting 138
Huber loss 139
Hyperparameter 139
    Hyperparameter tuning *139*
Hyperplane 139
Hypothesis 140

10. I 141

International Conference on Machine Learning (ICML) 141
Integrated Development Environment (IDE) 141
ImageNet Large Scale Visual Recognition Challenge (ILSVRC) 142
Image recognition 142
ImageNet 143
Imbalanced dataset 143
Implicit bias 143
Imputation 143
Inception 144
    Inception module 144
Independent and identically distributed (i.i.d.) 145
Independent Component Analysis (ICA) 145
Induction 145
Inferential statistics 145
Input gate 146
Input layer 146
Instance 147
Instance-based learning 147
Interpretability 147
Intersection over Union (IoU) 148
    Intersection over Union (IoU) 148
    Interquartile Range (IQR) 148
Item matrix 149
Iteration 149

11. J 151

Jacobian 151
Julia 151
Jupyter notebook 152

12. K 153

Keras 153
Kernel 153
Kernel support vector machine 154
KL divergence 154
K-means 154
K-median 155

K-nearest neighbors (kNN) 155
Kolmogorov Smirnov chart 155
Kurtosis: 156

13. L 157

L1 Loss 157
    L1 regularization 157
L2 loss 158
    L2 regularization 158
Labeled data 159
Lasso regression 159
Latent variable 159
Layer 159
Leaky ReLU 160
Learning rate 160
Least squares regression 160
Line chart 161
Linear activation function 161
Linear discriminant analysis 162
Linear model 162
    Linear regression 162
Log loss 163
    Log-Cosh loss 163
Logistic regression 164
    Logits 164
    Log-odds 164
Long Short-Term Memory (LSTM) 164
    Loss curve 165
Loss function 165
Loss surface 166

14. M 167

Machine Learning 167
Machine translation 167
Magnet loss 168
Mahout 168
Majority class 168

Manhattan distance...168
MapReduce 168
Market basket analysis...169
Market mix modeling 169
Markov chain..169
 Markov decision process..*169*
  Markov property *169*
Matplotlib..170
Matrix factorization 170
Max pooling..170
Maximum likelihood estimation..171
Mean 171
 Mean absolute error *171*
 Mean reciprocal rank *171*
 Mean squared error..*172*
Median 172
Memory-based learning 172
Mini-batch...172
 Mini-batch gradient descent *173*
 Minimax loss *173*
 Minority class *173*
Management Information System (MIS) 173
Machine learning (ML) 173
ML-as-a-service (MLaaS) 174
MLOps...174
MNIST...174
Mode 174
Model capacity..175
Model parallelism...175
Model selection 175
Model...175
Momentum 175
Monte Carlo simulation 176
Moving average..176
Multi-agent reinforcement learning 176
Multi-class classification..176

Multilayer perceptron	177
Multinomial classification	177
Multivariate analysis	177
Multivariate regression	*177*
MXNet:	177

15. N 179

Naïve Bayes	179
NaN	179
Nash equilibrium	179
Natural language generation	180
Natural language processing	180
Natural Language Understanding (NLU)	*181*
Negative class	*181*
Negative log likelihood	*181*
Nesterov accelerated gradient	181
Neural Machine Translation (NMT)	181
Neural network	*182*
Neural Turing machine (NTM)	182
Neuron	183
N-gram	183
No free lunch theorem	183
Node	183
Noise	*183*
Noise contrastive estimation	*184*
Nominal variable	184
Nonlinear transform function	184
Normal distribution	184
Normalization	185
Normalized discounted cumulative gain	185
NoSQL	186
Notebook	186
Null	186
Null accuracy:	186
Numerical data	187
Numpy	187
NVIDIA	187

16. O 189
Object Detection 189
Objective 190
Objective function 190
One hot encoding 190
One shot learning 191
One vs all 191
Online inference 191
Online learning 191
Oozie 192
OpenCV 192
Optimizer 192
Ordinal variable 193
Outlier 193
Output gate 194
Output layer 194
Overfitting 195

17. P 197
Pandas 197
Parallel processing 197
Parameter update 198
Parameters 198
Part of speech tagging 198
Partial derivative 198
Participation bias 198
Partitioning 199
Pattern recognition 199
Peak signal-to-noise ratio: 199
Perceptron: 199
Performance 200
Perplexity 200
Pie chart 200
Pig 201
Pipeline 201
Poisson distribution 202
Polynomial regression 202

Pooling 203
Population 203
Positive class: 204
Post-processing 204
Precision and recall 204
Prediction 204
Predictive model 205
    Predictor variable *205*
    Pre-processing *205*
    Pre-trained model *205*
Principal Component Analysis (PCA) 205
Prior belief 206
Probability density 206
Proxy label 206
P-value 206
Python 207
    PyTorch *207*

18. Q 209
Q-function 209
Q-learning 209
Quadratic loss 210
Quantile 210
    Quantile loss *210*
Quartile: 210
Question answering (NLP) 211

19. R 213
R 213
Radial basis function network 213
Random-Access Memory (RAM) 214
Random forest 214
Random initialization 215
    Random policy *215*
    Random search *216*
    Range *216*
Rank 216

Rater 216
Recommendation engine 216
Reconstruction entropy 217
Rectified linear unit 217
Recurrent neural network 217
Recursive neural network 217
    Regression *218*
    Regression spline *218*
    Regularization *218*
Reinforcement learning 218
Relationship extraction 219
Relative entropy 219
    Rectified linear unit (ReLU) *219*
Replay buffer 219
Representation 219
Representation learning 220
Residual 220
ResNet 220
Response variable 220
Restricted Boltzmann Machine (RBM) 221
Reward 221
Ridge regression 221
Ridge regularization 221
Risk 221
Root Mean Square Propagation (RMSProp) 222
Recurrent Neural Network (RNN) 222
Robotic Process Automation (RPA) 222
ROC-AUC 222
Root Mean Squared Error (RMSE) 222
    Root Mean Squared Logarithmic Error (RMSLE) *223*
    Rotational invariance *223*
    R-squared/Adjusted R-squared *223*

20. S 225
Sampling 225
Sampling bias 225
SAS 226

Scala 226
Scalar 226
Scaling..226
Scikit-learn 226
Scoring 227
Seasonality...227
Selection bias 227
    Self-supervised learning 227
    Semi-supervised learning..228
Sensitivity 228
Sentiment analysis..228
Sequence to sequence 228
Serialization 229
Shape of a tensor...229
Siamese neural network 229
Sigmoid function...229
Signal processing..229
Silhouette coefficient 230
Similarity learning..230
Single shot object detector 230
Singularity..230
Skewness..231
Skipgram 231
Smooth mean absolute error: 231
SMOTE 231
Softmax 232
Sparse feature 232
    Sparse representation 232
    Sparse vector..232
    Sparsity..232
Spatial pooling 233
Spatial-temporal reasoning 233
Specificity 233
Speech recognition...233
Speech segmentation 233
Splitting data 234

SPSS 234
Structured Query Language (SQL) 234
Squared hinge loss 234
Squared loss 235
Stacking 235
Standard deviation 235
Standard error 235
Standardization 235
Stata 236
State 236
State-action value function 236
    Static model 236
Stationary 236
    Statistical inference 236
Statistics 237
STD decomposition: 237
Stochastic gradient descent 238
Stratified sampling 238
Stride 238
Strong AI 238
Strong classifier 239
Structural SIMilarity (SSIM) 239
    Structured data 239
Subsampling 239
Supervised learning 239
Support vector machine (SVM) 240
    SVM 240
Synthetic feature 240

21. T 241

Tanh 241
Target variable 241
T-distribution 242
Tensor 242
Tensorflow 242
Test set 243
Text-to-speech: 243

Theano 243
Time series analysis 243
Tokenization: 243
Topic modeling 244
Torch 244
Tensor Processing Unit (TPU) 244
Training 244
    Training set 244
Translational invariance 245
Transfer learning 245
Transformer 245
Trend analysis 245
Triplet loss 246
True negative 246
True positive 246
Truncated SVD 246
T-test 246
Turing test 247
Type I error 247
Type II error 247

22. U 249
Underfitting 249
Univariate analysis 249
Universal function approximation theorem 250
Unlabeled data 250
Unstructured data 250
Unsupervised learning 250
Upweighting 251
User matrix 251

23. V 253
Validation set 253
Vanishing gradient problem 253
Variance 254
Variational autoencoder 254
VC dimension 254

Vector	254
VGG	255

24. W 257

Wasserstein loss	257
Watson studio	257
Weak classifier	258
Weight decay	258
Weight sharing	258
Weighted alternating least squares	*258*
Weighting	259
Width	259
Word embedding	259
Word segmentation	259
Word2vec	259

25. X 261

Xavier initialization	261
Xception	261
XGboost	262

26. Y 263

You only look once (YOLO)	263

27. Z 265

Zero shot learning	265
Z-test	265

Index **267-278**

CHAPTER 1
FAQ

How to fine tune a machine learning algorithm?

Fine tuning refers to a technic in machine learning where the goal is to find the optimal parameters. Fine tuning helps in increasing model performance and accuracy. Obviously, fine tuning is performed on training data and tested on validation data or test data. Usually, before fine tuning an algorithm, it is important to try several algorithms to find the better one. Fine tuning comes at the end of the training phase.

Note that fine tune also refers to an approach in transfer learning. Fine tuning can mean training a neural network algorithm using another trained neural network parameters. This is done by initializing a neural network algorithm with a parameter from another neural network model and usually in the same domain problem.

Fine tuning is the last step in the training phase as it comes after trying multiple machine learning algorithms and selecting the best ones. Fine tuning is considered as a non-necessary phase as it is possible to create a machine learning model without fine tuning it. However, if the idea is to increase accuracy, fine tuning is the best way.

Fine tuning can also be called hyperparameter optimization and there are multiple technics to perform the optimization. Manual search is a technic that uses the data scientist's experience to select the best parameters and find the optimal ones. For example, a data scientist can decide to reduce the value of the batch size in training a neural network algorithm to help get a faster converges. Manual search is not the most optimal technic but can be combined with other technics. Random search is a technic that creates a grid of hyperparameters and tries different random combination of hyperparameters. Random search is usually used in combination with cross validation as each combination of hyperparameters is tested with a specific fold from the dataset. Grid search is a technic that sets up a grid of hyperparameters and trains the model on each possible combination. The parameters to be used in the grid search are usually selected from a prior random search. Bayesian optimization is considered to be the best technic over the others as it uses probabilities to find the optimal search spaces for the hyperparameters.

So, fine tuning is a set of technics that can help in improving the performance. When it refers to hyperparameter tuning it can be is used at the end of the training phase and can make a difference between a good model and a very good model. When it refers to transfer learning it can help improve deep neural network model performance.

How to build deep neural network architecture?

Today, deep learning is one of the most promising machine learning algorithms, especially for image recognition and unstructured data. A deep neural network is basically a neural network with more than two hidden layers. Hidden layers are layers between the input layer and the output layer in a neural network, its role is to learn features from input layer. While increasing the number of hidden layers, it helps the neural network to learn more complex features from the input data.

Building a state-of-the-art deep neural network first depends on the type of problem that has to be solved. A problem in image classification doesn't require the same architecture as a problem in anomaly detection or forecasting. In image classification, the most common type of layers that are used is convolutional layers as they are most suitable for images as input. In anomaly detection, it is preferable to use an architecture based on encoder-decoder as the neural network will deconstruct and reconstruct the input and try to flag any input that doesn't follow the general pattern.

One of the most frequently asked question about building a deep neural network is how deep the neural network should be at the beginning of the training. The ideal situation is to start with the smallest architecture possible which means the least layers possible and then increasing the number of layers until it reaches the best possible performance.

Another frequently asked question is how to select activation functions. An activation function plays a crucial role in a deep learning model as it is capable of transforming input data to a nonlinear approximation. To make it simple, the most popular activation function for hidden layers is ReLU. It is the one that shows the best results, in most of the case. For the layer before the output layer, the selection is based on the type of problems that are being solved. For example, if the problem is a classification problem, the Softmax activation function is the one that should be used as it helps in converting the data into probabilities. Also, for the activation function usage, it is recommended to sometimes try new ones (Tanh, Leaky ReLU, etc.) and see if that increases the performance and accuracy.

Also note that every type of deep neural network architecture has its specific use case. For example, a generative adversarial neural network is a type of architecture that can be used to generate data. It can also be used for anomaly detection but it cannot be used for image classification or any other task. So, you have to consider all possible architectures of neural networks as a tool box and select the most appropriate one based on the problem that you are trying to solve.

How to train a machine learning algorithm faster?

Sometimes, when trying to train a machine learning algorithm, it can take a long time, that is, sometimes days and even weeks or more. This can be due to the amount of training of data used or the type or size of the algorithm used; obviously the performance of your machine learning model is also impacted by your computer or server capabilities like Memory and processor.

To make the training faster, there are different technics such as using GPU instead of CPU. This switch of processor helps in making the computing faster as GPU can handle more computing in parallel. Note that not all algorithms and frameworks support GPU computing. The most popular ones to support it are neural networks and XGboost.

Another technic to making the computing faster is parallel computing. This can be performed in multiple ways: either by parallelizing the data or by parallelizing the model. For example, parallelizing data can be performed by using a cluster of machines with the support of a framework like Spark MLlib.

Another option is to change the algorithm and select another one with less complexity as the complexity of an algorithm plays a crucial role in the training time. For example, a support vector machine is considered as a complex algorithm which means that that the training time can grow very fast. So, on large dataset, it is advisable to select another algorithm with less complexity.

The last option is to basically sample the data. On a large dataset, it is possible to sample the dataset using stratification which helps the dataset in keeping its original ratios and characteristics. A decade ago, sampling the data used to be the most popular technic to make the computing time faster. Nowadays, the most popular technic is GPU usage or parallelization.

Why do we normalize the input data in deep neural network?

Normalization of the input is one of the best practices in deep neural network. In general, normalization of the data helps in speeding the learning and getting to convergence faster.

Also, the data becomes more suitable for the activation function, especially the sigmoid function. Now, imagine that the inputs are of different scales (not normalized). The weight of some inputs will be updated faster or larger than the other ones. This might hurt the learning. On another side, it guarantees that there are positive and negative values available as inputs for the next layer and this makes the learning more flexible.

Note that the other type of transformations can achieve the same result than normalizing the input for a deep neural network such as standardization; linearly scale input data, and so on.

When can we consider that we did a good job in a machine learning project?

In machine learning, it is always hard to evaluate if a work or a project has been well-performed. Usually, to answer such a problem, there are an infinite number of ways to obtain a good solution. Also, a job or a project can be infinitely improved but you don't have an infinite amount of time to deliver a project.

In general, the criteria to evaluate if a job done has been good are that it is logical and follows the best practice. The best practice means that the tools and technics used have been approved by the community and are considered as a standard in the industry.

When a data scientist delivers a work, he should not be a perfectionist and should think like an engineer who is trying to solve a practical problem. As an engineer, the data scientist should be result-oriented, focusing on how to get the best outcome in the shortest amount of time.

Usually in a data science project, we apply the lean and agile style where the idea delivers a result fast and iterates to improve the work. So, this means that the data scientist will have to update his work on a regular basis by improving it at each iteration.

Sometimes, it can get very confusing while talking about whether a job has been done well in machine learning, because a good result in accuracy doesn't necessarily mean that your job is good and if you get a bad result in accuracy, it doesn't mean that our job is not good. This is directly related to the problem that you are trying to solve since sometimes, some problems are very hard and it is almost impossible, due to the data, to get good accuracy. This means that even if the accuracy is not strong, you may have done great work.

So, while evaluating a machine learning job, the focus should be on the logic and reasoning behind the work instead of focusing on the accuracy.

When should we use deep learning instead of the traditional machine learning models?

To understand when to use deep learning instead of traditional machine learning, it is important to understand the strengths of deep learning compared to traditional machine learning. Deep learning shows better results than traditional machine learning in image recognition, object detection, speech recognition, and natural language processing. This means that for any task that includes unstructured data, it is better to use deep learning. This is due to the fact that deep learning extracts its own features and patterns by itself which are then adapted to unstructured data such as images.

To treat an image with traditional machine learning, we will have to extract all the relevant features from the image prior to training which is time-consuming and can be inaccurate. So, deep learning is preferred in case it is hard to extract features from the data.

Deep learning can also show a strong advantage in case we have a large amount of data which is not the case for some machine learning algorithms. With large data, deep learning is capable of learning better and showing a better performance. So, when we have a large amount of data, deep learning is preferred over the other machine learning technics.

How much time does it take to become a good data scientist?

A good data scientist is a data scientist that has a good understanding of statistics, mathematics, computer science, and of course, machine learning. A good data scientist is capable of solving any hard problem and finding an optimal solution to any type of problem.

Becoming a good data scientist is a journey as it takes continuously learning new technics and updating your knowledge. Becoming a good data scientist doesn't necessarily require a PhD but it requires discipline and autonomy. It is also a matter of talent since to be able to solve some problems, a good scent is required.

Becoming a decent data scientist requires years of hard work, and therefore, becoming a good data scientist requires you to be a step ahead.

How to evaluate the performance of a model?

Evaluating the performance of a model is one of the most important steps in a machine learning project as it helps in discovering if the trained model is a good model that can be deployed. To evaluate a model's performance, we use what is called a metric, either a visual metric or a mathematical metric. Usually, these metrics are called performance metrics.

An evaluation metric is defined based on the type of problem that we are trying to solve. It can be a classification problem, a regression problem, an unsupervised model, image recognition, and so on.

There are several types of evaluation metrics. Some of them are as follows:
- **Classification problem**: **Area Under the Curve (AUC)**, confusion matrix, accuracy, recall, precision, and F1-score.
- **Regression problem**: Mean square error, root mean square error, mean absolute error, coefficient of determination, Adjusted R-squared.

Each evaluation metric is unique and has its own strength, so don't hesitate to use multiple evaluation metrics for the same project to evaluate the same machine learning model.

In case of a large dataset, should I sample my data or use distributed computing?

In the past, when a statistician or a data analyst was in front of a large dataset, the most popular technic was to sample the data to apply the machine learning algorithms afterwards. Nowadays, a new technic has emerged which is called distributed computing, and more precisely, data parallelism. This technic helps in using all the data in training a machine learning model.

In term of time consumption, sampling data is faster to setup than distributed computing. So, in case of a small project with limited time for delivery, it is more relevant to use sampling dataset. In cases when the project is a long-length project with a focus on the performance, using distributed computing is more relevant. On another side, if we are trying to apply the deep learning model it is more advisable to use distributed computing to be able to take advantage of the complete dataset.

Distributed computing and data parallelism require strong knowledge in data engineering and computer science. So, it's a practice that might take time to be setup for a beginner.

How much time should I spend in data transformation?

Data transformation is a process that is performed by data scientists during the data preparation step when the data can be transformed in various ways depending on the format, the type, and the purpose. The most popular data transformations are natural logarithm for continuous target variable to erase a skew in data, the one hot encoding transformation to transform categorical variables into dummies, binning transformation to create categories for continuous variables, and more.

Data transformation is the most important step in a data science project. The more time that is spent on data transformation, the higher is the model performance. The true secret of a good data science project resides in data transformation and how well it is performed. So, don't hesitate in spending as much time as possible on this step. Data transformation can also be done iteratively by doing it once, then training the model, then getting back to data transformation, and so on.

If you are wondering why data transformation is so important, it is due to the fact that a machine learning model is very sensitive to the format of the input data and the nature of the input data. A good data transformation will value the input data more, hence helping the model to find the key variables to use for training.

How to select the right machine learning algorithm?

The best practice in machine learning is at the first training phase which is to train multiple potential models without any fine tuning and comparing the performance using the test dataset. With this approach, it is possible to select the right algorithms for the fine tuning phase. In this phase, it is advised to compare as much models as possible. Also, it is advisable to create a benchmark model. It can be a simple model such as a linear regression, and its results can be used to compare the performance of the other models.

Should I learn R or Python?

Both R and Python are considered to be the most popular programing languages in data science. R is popular because it contains all the necessary statistical libraries which make the work using the libraries very easy. Also, R has its own IDE RStudio. R also has ShinyR which is a framework for software development that is directly programmable in R. On the other hand, Python is popular because it's a language that is easy to learn. It contains all the libraries for machine learning and deep learning. It is also popular because it's a fast language. Python, compared to R, can handle a larger dataset which makes it practical for big data. If you have to choose between R and Python, it's better to start learning Python because it is more standard than R and is easy to learn. Then, the second language that is advised to learn is R as it is good for statistical modeling.

What's the trade-off between bias and variance?

In statistics and machine learning, the trade-off bias and variance is the problem of minimizing the error. At the same time, there are two types of errors which avoid supervised learning algorithms from generalizing over the training sample. These are as follows:

Bias is the error from incorrect assumptions in the learning algorithm. A high bias can be linked to an algorithm which lacks relevant relationships between the input data and the expected output called underfitting.

The variance is the error due to the fact that the model captures small variation in the training set. A high variance can cause overfitting which occurs due to the model taking in consideration the random noise of the training dataset.

This compromise can be found in classification problems, regression problems, and all types of machine learning.

What is the difference between supervised and unsupervised machine learning?

Supervised and unsupervised machine learning is two popular forms of machine learning. In supervised learning, the algorithm takes in consideration the input features and tries to predict an output or a target that is also called label in classification. In unsupervised learning, the algorithm doesn't need any target or label as it creates groups or clusters based on input data, so it tries to group the training data together. Unsupervised learning can also be used to extract features and patterns from data. The popular algorithms in supervised learning are categorized as either classification or regression models. In unsupervised learning, there is clustering model, dimensionality reduction, and autoencoders.

What is the difference between L1 and L2 regularizations?

L1 and L2 regularizations are technics that help in avoiding overfitting while training a machine learning model. Both technics add up a regularization penalty term to the cost function except that L1 adds up the absolute value of the weights and L2 adds up the squared value of the weights. In a regression case, L1 regularization is called LASSO regression and L2 regularization is called ridge regression. So, regularization can be used with a deep neural network, logistic regression, and so on.

What's the difference between type I and type II error?

In a research study, the type I error, also called the alpha or false positive error, is the error made when the researcher rejects the null hypothesis, being true in the population. It is equivalent to finding a false positive result because the researcher concludes that there is a difference between the hypotheses when it does not really exist. It is related to the level of statistical significance.

In a research study, the type II error, also called the beta error or false negative, is committed when the researcher does not reject the null hypothesis, being false in the population. It is equivalent to the probability of a false negative result since the researcher concludes that he has been unable to find a difference that exists in reality.

Examples of type I errors include a test that shows a patient having an illness when the patient does not have the illness; or an experiment indicating that a treatment should cure an illness when, in fact, it does not work.

Examples of type II errors are a blood test that is not detecting the disease it was designed to detect in a patient who really has the disease; or a clinical trial of a medical treatment showing that the treatment doesn't work when it seems to.

What's the difference between probability and likelihood?

In probability and statistics, the difference between probability and likelihood is that the probability can be quantified while the likelihood cannot be quantified. Probability represents the percentage of chance that a fact has to occur. Likelihood hypothesizes that a fact could happen.

What's the difference between a generative and discriminative model?

A discriminative model models the decision boundary between the classes for classification problems. It will distinguish between the classes based on the different properties learned from the data. A discriminative model is usually opposed to a generative model which has different properties like explicitly modeling the distribution of each class instead of learning the different properties. Usually, the discriminative models perform better than the generative models if there is a large amount of data.

A generative classification or generative model is a statistical model that is based on the joint probability between the target variable and predictor. The types of generative models are Naïve Bayes classifier and linear discriminant analysis.

Which is more important model accuracy, or model performance?

Model accuracy is considered to be a subset of model performance. Model performance can include in addition to model accuracy, model training speed, model response time, model capacity to provide a response, and so on. However model accuracy can reach a paradox, as it can be a bad metric to evaluate some classification problems. For example, let say we have a binary classification problem, where we classify if it is a fraud or not a fraud. In our case, the model classifies all test data as not fraud and scored an accuracy of 99%, but we keep in mind that only 1% of test data is fraud meaning that all true fraud where classified as not fraud. So even if the accuracy is very high, the classification is very weak as it cannot detect fraud properly, this is one of the limits of model accuracy.

Overall, model accuracy is a subset of model performance, and model accuracy has its limit, so it's irrelevant to compare both of them.

How would you handle an imbalanced dataset?

Classification on unbalanced data is a classification problem where the training sample contains a large disparity between the classes that are to be predicted. This problem frequently occurs in binary classification problems and in particular, the detection of anomalies. We will present a non-exhaustive list of useful techniques to fight against this type of problem.

It may sound simplistic, but collecting additional data is almost always overlooked and can sometimes prove to be effective as the additional data can help reduce the disparity between the classes to be predicted.

It is possible to modify the dataset used before training the predictive model to have more balanced data. This strategy is called resampling and there are two main methods that you can use to equalize classes: oversampling and undersampling. Oversampling methods work by increasing the number of observations of the minority class in order to arrive at a satisfactory minority class/majority class ratio. Undersampling methods work by reducing the number of observations of the majority class in order to arrive at a satisfactory minority class/majority class ratio.

There are algorithms that are used to generate synthetic samples automatically. The most popular of these algorithms is **SMOTE (Synthetic Minority Over-sampling Technique)**. As its name suggests, SMOTE is a method of oversampling. It works by creating synthetic samples from the minority class instead of creating simple copies.

Sometimes, the resampling methods are not effective enough and in this case, the problem needs to be rethought. It may be that the algorithm used is not suitable for your data. Do not hesitate to test others, possibly combined with the resampling methods that we have seen precedingly. Tree-based ensemble models like the random forest are generally more suited to unbalanced data. Also, it is also possible to play with probabilities. If, for example, you want to be able to absolutely predict the vast majority of potential churners, even if you misclassify a few non-churners, you can modify the probability threshold beyond which the customers will be considered churners. The lower the threshold, the more the accuracy of our class will increase, but the recall will decrease.

The penalized classification makes it possible to impose an additional cost on the model for classification errors committed on the minority class during training. These penalties can bias the model so that it pays more attention to the minority class.

How do you ensure that you're not overfitting with a model?

In machine learning, overfitting is generally caused by a bad dimensioning of the structure that is used to classify or make a regression. Due to its great capacity to capture information, a structure in a situation of overfitting or over-learning will have difficulty in generalizing the characteristics of the data. It then behaves like a table that contains all the samples used during learning and loses its predictive powers on new samples.

To ensure that our model is not overfitting, we usually apply the model to test the data. If we see on the test data that the evaluation metric is dropping drastically, then this might mean that our model is overfitting as the drop may be due to the fact that the model must have lost its predictive powers.

There are several methods to avoid overfitting such as cross validation or regularization.

What's the "kernel trick" and how is it useful?

Kernel trick is a technic used while working with higher dimensions, especially with the support vector machine algorithm which uses kernel as a way to find decision boundaries between data. The kernel trick is a method that allows you to use a linear classifier to solve a non-linear problem. The idea is to transform the representation space of the input data into a larger space where a linear classifier can be used and good performance can be obtained. Linear discrimination in a large space is equivalent to non-linear discrimination in an original space.

There are different kernels such as polynomial kernel and radial basis function kernel. It can also be used with perceptron, all dimensionality reduction technics such as principal component analysis, and so on.

How do you handle missing data in a dataset?

It is important to identify missing data in a dataset before applying a machine learning algorithm. Indeed, many of these are based on statistical methods which are supposed to receive a complete data set as input. Otherwise, the algorithm may provide a poor predictive model or worse, it would simply not work. Thus, processing the missing data is a necessary phase for any data science project.

Dealing with missing data is like repairing the dataset so that it can be used by the machine learning algorithms. Repairing a dataset can take many forms such as removing the missing data or replacing the missing values with artificial values.

Drop observations consist of deleting the observations (the lines) which contain at least one missing feature. The result dataset will not contain any observations with a missing value. This is the default behavior in several statistical tools.

Missing data imputation refers to replacing missing values in the dataset with artificial values. Ideally, these replacements should not lead to a significant change in the distribution and composition of the data set such as imputation by rule, imputation by mean or mode, and imputation by regression.

What are the origins of machine learning?

The concretization of the idea of machine learning is mainly due to *Alan Turing* and to his concept of the "universal machine" in 193, which is at the base of the computers of today. He continued to lay the foundation for machine learning with his article on the computer and intelligence in 1950 in which he developed, among other things, the Turing test.

In 1943, neurophysiologist *Warren McCulloch* and mathematician *Walter Pitts* published an article describing the functioning of neurons by representing those using electrical circuits. This representation was the theoretical basis of neural networks.

Arthur Samuel, a pioneering American computer scientist in the artificial intelligence sector, was the first person to use the term "machine learning" in 1959, following the creation of his program for IBM in 1952.

A major advance in the machine intelligence sector was the success of IBM's computer, Deep Blue, which was the first to defeat the world chess champion *Garry Kasparov* in 1997. The Deep Blue project inspired many others in the context of artificial intelligence, particularly another big challenge: IBM Watson, the computer whose goal was to win the Jeopardy game. This goal was reached in 2011 when Watson won at Jeopardy by answering the questions by natural language processing.

What is the difference between a classifier and a model?

A classifier is a machine learning model that can assign classes to specific data points. So, it will map the input data to a specific category. A classifier is derived from a classification machine learning algorithm as a classifier is the resulted model of classification training.

When a machine learning algorithm is trained on data, the result is called a model. A model is considered as a mathematical equation with parameters where each parameter is learned by training the machine learning algorithm.

As you can see, the definition of a classifier and a model are similar and so, sometimes they are used interchangeably.

What is the difference between a parametric learning algorithm and a non-parametric learning algorithm?

A parametric learning algorithm is an algorithm that has a fixed number of parameters and so, it is computationally faster but makes assumptions about the data. Sometimes, the assumptions can be wrong. A type of parametric algorithm is linear regression.

A nonparametric learning algorithm is an algorithm with a changing number of parameters as the number of parameters grows with the data. It makes few assumptions about the data but is computationally slow. A type of nonparametric algorithm is a decision tree like CART.

What is the difference between a cost function and a loss function in machine learning?

Loss function and cost function have quite a close meaning except that sometimes a cost function is more general and global than a loss function.

A cost function is also called a **loss function** or an objective function. It measures the error of a machine learning model. It corresponds to the distance between the actual values vector and the predicted values vector. This cost function then tends to be minimized in order to obtain a better model. There are different types of cost functions that behave differently such as mean square error, cross-entropy, exponential cost, Hellinger cost, KL divergence, and so on.

What is the difference between covariance and correlation?

Covariance and correlation are two mathematical concepts that are commonly used in statistics. Both determine the relationship and measure the dependence between two random variables. Despite some similarities between these two mathematical terms, they are different from each other. Correlation is when the change in one item can result in the change in another item.

Correlation is considered to be the best tool to measure and express the quantitative relationship between two variables in the formula. In contrast, covariance occurs when two items vary together.

A measure that is used to indicate how much two random variables change in tandem is called covariance. A measure that is used to represent how closely two random variables are related is called a correlation.

The value of the correlation is between -1 and +1. Conversely, the value of the covariance is between $-\infty$ and $+\infty$.

Why did it take so long for deep networks to be invented?

Deep neural networks were invented in the 1960s and backpropagation was invented in the 1970s. However, by that time, it was hard and even almost impossible to train a neural network with more than three hidden layers due to the vanishing gradient descent problem. The vanishing gradient problem is an issue where there is a very rapid decrease in the values of the gradients during the backpropagation leading to the cancellation of the gradient and the stopping of learning. But the main reason why the deep neural networks were not popular during that time is the fact that people didn't have access to the computing resources like we have today.

What are some good books/papers for learning machine learning?

If you are looking for good books for beginners, some resources are as follows:
- *Machine Learning For Absolute Beginners: A Plain English Introduction (2nd Edition)*
- *Machine Learning (in Python and R) For Dummies (1st Edition)*
- *The Hundred-Page Machine Learning Book*
- *Data Science Fundamentals and Practical Approaches: Understand Why Data Science Is the Next*

For research papers with code, the best database is as follows:
- https://paperswithcode.com/

A blog with practical case studies around machine learning is as follows:
- https://machinelearningmastery.com/

What are the advantages of semi-supervised learning over supervised and unsupervised learning?

Semi-supervised learning is an approach in machine learning between unsupervised learning and supervised learning. It takes a small sample of labeled data with a large amount of unlabeled data for training. Semi-supervised learning can be used in various domains, but it is very popular in document classification as the data is abundant and doesn't contain many labels.

Semi-supervised learning is less expensive in data annotation than supervised learning. Also, compared to unsupervised learning, it creates more value than just extracting patterns from data. However, semi-supervised learning is not perfect as it can sometimes give weak performance and is always based on multiple assumptions.

When should I apply data normalization/standardization?

Standardization is the ability to rescale data with a mean of 0 and standard deviation of 1 whereas normalization means rescaling data in a range of values from 0 to 1. Usually, standardization is preferred over normalization.

If the data doesn't follow a Gaussian distribution or we don't know the distribution, it's better to use normalization. If we know that the distribution is Gaussian, then it's better to use standardization.

How do you deal with a machine learning problem with a large number of features?

A problem with a large number of features can cause some problems such as computational high complexity; or if the number of features is higher than the number of observations, some algorithms cannot be used. To deal with this, we can apply regularization if it is allowed by the algorithm to avoid overfitting due to a high number of features. We can also apply feature selection as we select the best features by variance or any other technic. With this technic, we reduce the number of features and increase the performance. The last technic would be to use dimensionality reduction such as principal component analysis that helps in reducing the number of features.

When should one use median as opposed to the mean or average?

The mean represents the average of a variable over a certain number of observations. The median represents the middle value of a variable over a certain number of observations, splitting the data into 50% higher and 50% lower.

The mean is the most used descriptive statistics in general but sometimes, it's better to use the median. For example, if the data is skewed, it is always better to use the median instead of the mean. The more that the data is skewed, the less representative is the mean and the more accurate is the median.

Why is "Naive" Bayes called naive?

If Naïve Bayes is called naïve, it is due to the assumption made that the presence of a certain feature in the data is not related to the presence of any other feature. This assumption is actually never true as all these components are always dependent on each other, and that's why it is considered as naïve.

CHAPTER 2
A

A/B testing

A/B testing is a statistical test that helps in evaluating the performance of two versions from the same concept. A/B testing is very popular in marketing for comparing the performance of different versions of a visual template (When we compare more than two versions, we talk about A/Z testing). To run the test, we show a specific version to a group of customers and another version to another group of customers. Then, we compare the performance of the visuals in each group. After that, we need to prove that the performance that results from our A/B testing is significant and not because of luck in the group selection. To do so, we use hypothesis testing. We will then drop a null hypothesis and try to reject it.

A/B testing is also very popular in machine learning deployment. It is used to compare the performance of two different models in production for the same problem and then show which model is better in a live environment.

Example: Let's suppose you work for the marketing department of a company that has developed a mobile app. The company wants to change the color of its app from green to orange. The idea is to use A/B testing to evaluate if the color change has an impact on the time spent by people on the application. 1000 people are randomly selected and view the app in orange (the experimental group) and another 1000 who were people randomly selected view the app in green (the status quo group). We observe that the experimental group spends 15 minutes more on the app than the status quo group. Now, we need to prove whether or not our results are statistically significant. In this case, we create a null hypothesis and test it to see if we can reject it.

A/B testing is the most popular concept for these kinds of use cases, but there are other variations of the test such as:

- **A/A testing**: For testing the same version on two different groups and check whether there is no difference.
- **A/Z testing**: For comparing more than two versions of the same concept.
- **Multivariate testing**: For comparing multiple combinations of the same concept.

See also the following definitions: Deployment as API, statistics, and t-test

Accuracy

It is also called classification accuracy. It is a popular metric for evaluating a classification model. It is the ratio of the number of correct predictions by total predictions made by using the following formula:

$$Accuracy = \frac{Number\ of\ Correct\ prediction}{Total\ prediction\ made}$$

The limits of classification accuracy come up when we have an imbalanced dataset. Suppose that we have a binary classification where 99% of the observations are from group 0 and 1% are from group 1. Our model can score 99% accuracy very easily. But if the model gets the prediction of group 1 all wrong, the score will still be 99%. In this case, a high accuracy doesn't represent the real performance of the model.

In the case of a binary classification, the formula is as follows:

$$Accuracy = \frac{True\ Positive + True\ Negative}{Total\ prediction\ made}$$

See also the following definitions: Machine learning, Area Under the ROC Curve (AUC), and evaluation metrics

Action

In the area of reinforcement learning, an agent (or robot) takes an action within an environment to maximize its reward. An action is what makes the agent move from one state to another and interact with the environment.

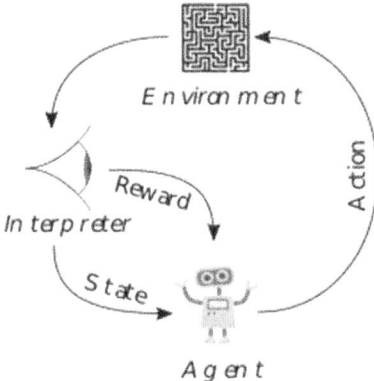

Figure 2.1: A visual representation of RL interaction
(Image source: https://en.wikipedia.org/wiki/Reinforcement_learning)

The choice of the action is supported by the policy. The above schema represents the interaction in the reinforcement learning model.

See also the following definitions: Reinforcement learning and Bellman equation

Activation function

Activation function is a key element of neural network algorithms. A neural network without activation function is more like a simple linear regression. An activation function transforms the entire input weighted sum from the previous layer to a specific value based on a non-linear function. Then, it passes it to a neuron in the next layer. The activation functions are the keys of universal approximation of functions for a neural network. The choice of the action is supported by the policy. The following schema represents the interaction in the reinforcement learning model:

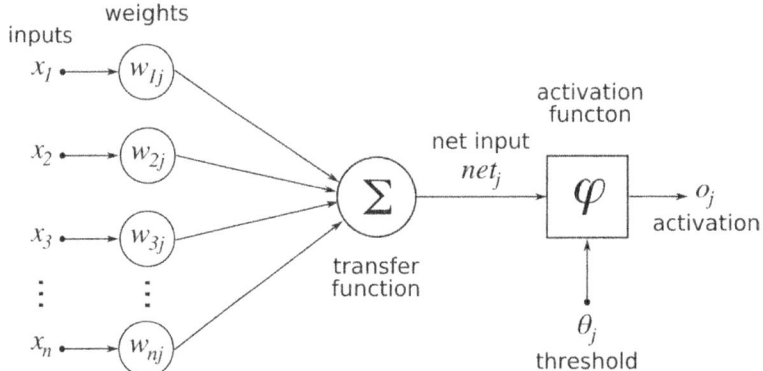

Figure 2.2: Schema of an activation function in a neural network (Image source: https://commons.wikimedia.org/wiki/File:ArtificialNeuronModel_english.png)

There are different types of activation functions. Most of them are non-linear as follows: Linear, sigmoid, Tanh, ReLU, Leaky ReLU, ELU, Softmax, and so on.

Hint: How to choose an activation function? The selection is based on the way each activation function behaves. For example, sigmoid and tanh suffer from vanishing gradient problem, whereas ReLU avoids the vanishing problem. The vanishing gradient problem is an issue where there is a very rapid decrease in the values of the gradients during the backpropagation leading to the cancellation of the gradient and the stopping of learning. The position of the activation function in layers (hidden layer or output layer) is also important in choosing the function. Softmax is very popular for output layer for classification problems and linear function for a regression problem, while ReLU or ELU are the most popular ones for hidden layers.

See also the following definitions: Neural network, ReLU, Tanh, Softmax, and hidden layer

Active learning

It is a subdomain of machine learning where the learner (the algorithm) interacts with a teacher to get the label of specific data points. The data used by the algorithm is not originally labeled and the learner chooses which data points are more interesting so the training is done on a specific part of the dataset. This technic is very useful when labeling the data is costly or difficult. The teacher that gives a hint to the learner can be a human user or another machine or system. This subdomain is close to but not the same as semi-supervised machine learning or passive supervised learning. Note that with active learning, it is possible to solve classification or regression problems. The business case for using or not using active learning is chosen based on how expensive or difficult it is to get labeled data.

Example: Let's suppose that you work for a law firm. They have a large pool of documents and they would like to be able to classify the documents based on how relevant they are for a specific court case. In this case, labeling such an amount of documents can be extremely costly as it requires a qualified lawyer to label all the pool. By using active learning, the firm can save time and money while completing the task. The learner will rank the examples according to their informativeness and ask the teacher (a lawyer) for labels only for the informative examples.

See also the following definitions: Zero shot learning, machine learning, deep learning, and continuous learning

AdaBoost

It stands for adaptive boosting and is a meta-algorithm for boosting. The idea of using a boosting approach such as AdaBoost is to enhance the general performance. Globally, AdaBoost combines multiple weak learners into one strong learner. For AdaBoost, weak learners are decision trees and a strong learner is a combination of the output results from the decision trees. Each decision tree is made a stump (only one node and two leaves) and so, AdaBoost is a forest of stumps. A stump is as follows:

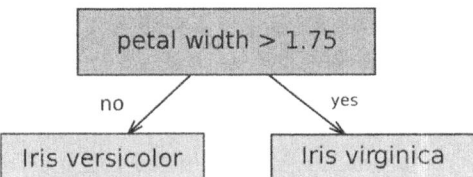

Figure 2.3: The representation of a stump, AdaBoost is a group of numerous stumps
(Image source: https://en.wikipedia.org/wiki/Decision_stump)

Each stump is weighted in the final decision. The weight for the final decision is based on the incorrect instances' prediction. The more incorrect answers a stump has, the smaller is the weight and vice-versa. The weight for the final decision is called the amount of say and has the following formula:

$$Amount\ of\ say = \frac{1}{2}\log(\frac{1 - (Sum\ of\ weights\ of\ wrong\ answers)}{Sum\ of\ weights\ of\ wrong\ answers})$$

The meta-algorithm will put more weight on instances that are difficult to predict and less weight on those that are easier to predict. So the next stump to be built will learn from the previous stump's mistakes. Before the first stump is created, all instances weights are the same (1 divided by the total number of samples). Then, after the stump is created, the weight changes based on the mistakes and the correct answer that the model had. After this, the mistakes have higher weights than the correct answers. The weights are then used to build the new dataset on which the next stump will train; this new dataset will contain more of the weighted mistakes and less of the weighted correct answer. After this is done, the process starts over with neutral weights. The way that training AdaBoost works is as follows:

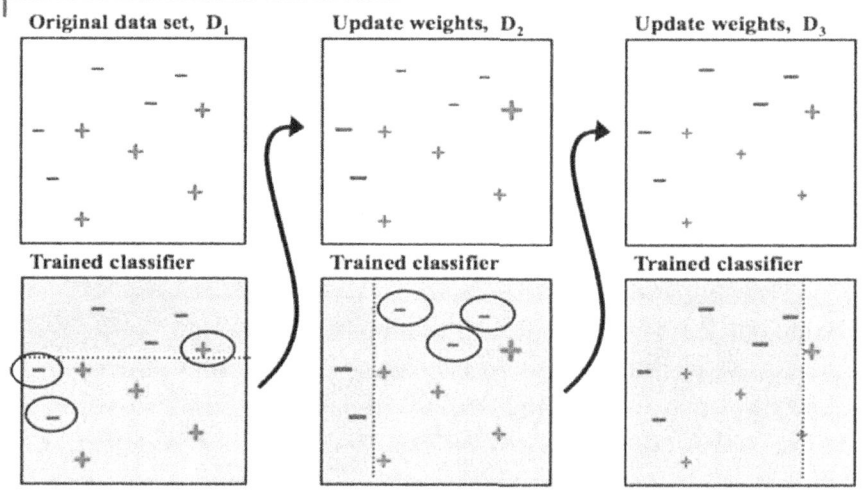

Figure 2.4: Adaboost algorithm training
(Image source: https://iq.opengenus.org/gradient-boosting/)

AdaBoost can be used for classification and regression problems. Boosting is a large domain and is very powerful for increasing performance. Other models also exist such as XGBoost, CatBoost, or LightGBM. For an explanation about the boosting algorithm, check out the definition of boosting.

See also the following definitions: AdaDelta, AdaGrad, and Adam optimization

AdaDelta

AdaDelta is an optimizer for deep learning (or deep neural network). AdaDelta is an upgrade of another optimizer called AdaGrad. The main issue with AdaGrad comes from the learning rate, as the learning rate can decay over time. This means that it is constantly decreasing, that is, until the deep learning algorithm stops learning. AdaDelta helps avoid this issue with its mathematical formula where instead of adding all the past squared gradients, AdaDelta adds only a fixed number of past gradients.

$$\Delta\theta_t = -\frac{\eta}{\sqrt{E[g^2]_t + \epsilon}} g_t$$

Here, $\Delta\theta_t$ represents the parameter update vector, η represents the learning rate, $E[g^2]_t$ is the average over past squared gradient at t, g_t is the gradient at time t, and ϵ is a term that avoids dividing by zero.

For more details about what an optimizer is, see the definition of optimizer.

See also the following definitions: AdaBoost, AdaGrad, and Adam optimization

AdaGrad

It stands for "Adaptive Gradient." It is an optimizer for deep neural network algorithms. This optimizer doesn't require fixing the learning rate prior to training as it adapts the learning rate for each parameter of the deep learning model. The optimizer will make important updates on the learning rate for less frequent parameters and small updates for frequent ones. This optimizer is very interesting for cases with scattered data such as word embedding with infrequent words. The mathematical formula for AdaGrad is as follows:

$$\theta_{t+1} = \theta_t - \frac{\eta}{\sqrt{G_t + \epsilon}} g_t$$

Here, θ_{t+1} is the parameter at t+1, θ_t is the parameter at t, η is the learning rate, G_t represents the sum of the squares of all past gradients, g_t is the gradient at time t, and a is a term that avoids dividing by zero.

The only issue with AdaGrad is that the accumulation of the term G_t in the denominator keeps growing during the training. This makes the learning rate very small and the algorithm stops learning. To avoid this issue, the AdaDelta optimizer is considered as a good alternative to AdaGrad.

For more details about what an optimizer is go to the definition of optimizer.

See also the following definitions: AdaBoost, AdaDelta, and Adam optimization

Adam

It stands for Adaptive Moment Estimation and is an optimizer for deep neural network algorithms. This optimizer is the best of both worlds. It does what AdaGrad, AdaDelta, and Momentum optimizer do at the same time. It calculates the learning rate for each parameter and also calculates the momentum changes. Adam doesn't require a lot of memory and has low computational costs. Also, it is considered to be the optimizer that outperforms the most. That's why it is the most used optimizer in the deep learning community. Technically, Adam has an adaptive learning rate for each parameter and takes into account, at the same time, the decay average of past squared gradient (like AdaDelta) and the decay average of past gradient (like Momentum). The formula for Adam is as follows:

$$\theta_{t+1} = \theta_t - \frac{\eta}{\sqrt{v'_t + \epsilon}} m'_t$$

Here, θ_{t+1} is the parameter at t+1, θ_t is the parameter at t, η is the learning rate, v'_t is the bias-free second moment of gradient at t, m'_t is the bias-free first moment of gradient at t, ϵ is a term that avoids dividing by zero.

For more details about what an optimizer is, go to the definition of optimizer.

See also the following definitions: AdaBoost, AdaDelta, and AdaGrad

Adaptive learning rate

Adaptive learning rate is opposed to the learning rate schedules where the learning rate decay is fixed in advance. In the adaptive learning rate, the learning rate changes based on performance and operate at the parameter level. Moreover, every parameter has its own independent learning rate. This method is used in the following optimizers: RMSprop, AdaGrad, AdaDelta, and Adam. The adaptive learning rate is more convenient in case we have sparse data or in case the learning rate schedules method doesn't perform well for a specific dataset and deep learning architecture.

See also the following definitions: Learning rate, RMSprop, AdaGrad, AdaDelta, and Adam

Affine layer

It is also known as a fully connected layer. It is the way that a layer is connected to another in the neural network architecture where all the inputs of a layer are connected to each activation function of another layer. They are used in the convolutional neural network and recurrent neural network but are more popular with the convolutional net.

Hint: If the fully connected layer is located at the last layers of your neural network architecture, it will help sum up the extracted features from the previous layers to deliver the last output layer for a classification problem. If the affine layer is located at the beginning of the neural network, it will be useful for abstract features extraction. A neural network with only fully connected layers is called a multilayer perceptron. Note that in TensorFlow, a fully connected layer is called a dense layer.

See also the following definitions: Dense layer, convolutional neural network, and recurrent neural network

Agent

An agent in reinforcement learning is the active part that makes the decision regarding the actions that are to be taken. To take a decision, the agent uses observations from the environment (states) and the associated rules (policies). The agent is optimized using a reward that is maximized for a future event with a trade-off between short-term and long-term rewards. This is shown as follows:

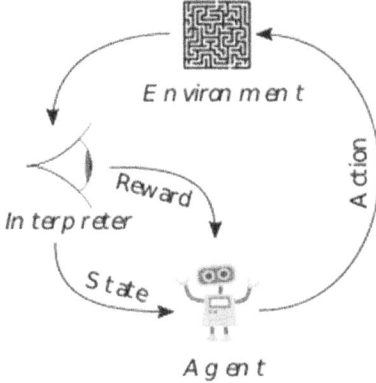

Figure 2.5: A visual representation of agent interaction
(Image source: https://en.wikipedia.org/wiki/Reinforcement_learning)

Also, during the training, the agent switches between exploitation and exploration. In exploitation, it defines an action based on its own experience; and in exploration, it will randomly try different types of actions to learn new patterns. The interaction within reinforcement learning is represented in the preceding image.

See also the following definitions: Reinforcement learning and Bellman equation

Agglomerative clustering

For more details, see the definition of connectivity-based algorithm.

See also the following definitions: Hierarchical clustering, clustering, and divisive clustering

AlexNet

AlexNet is a deep learning architecture for image recognition that was the winner model in ILSVRC 2012, a visual recognition competition. With a Top-5 error rate of 15.3%, the model far outperformed all the others. AlexNet has significantly influenced the computer vision community and is considered to be one of the turning points for deep learning adoption.

AlexNet is constructed of five convolutional layers and three fully connected layers. It contains an overlapping max pooling after the first convolutional layers. The ReLU activation function is applied after all the layers. The AlexNet architecture has been represented in the preceding section.

See also the following definitions: VGG, deep learning, ILSVRC, and deep dream

Algorithm

An algorithm is a term that regroups all types of mechanisms that describe how to perform tasks (such as calculation, reasoning, data processing, classification, and so on) based on a set of rules or instructions.

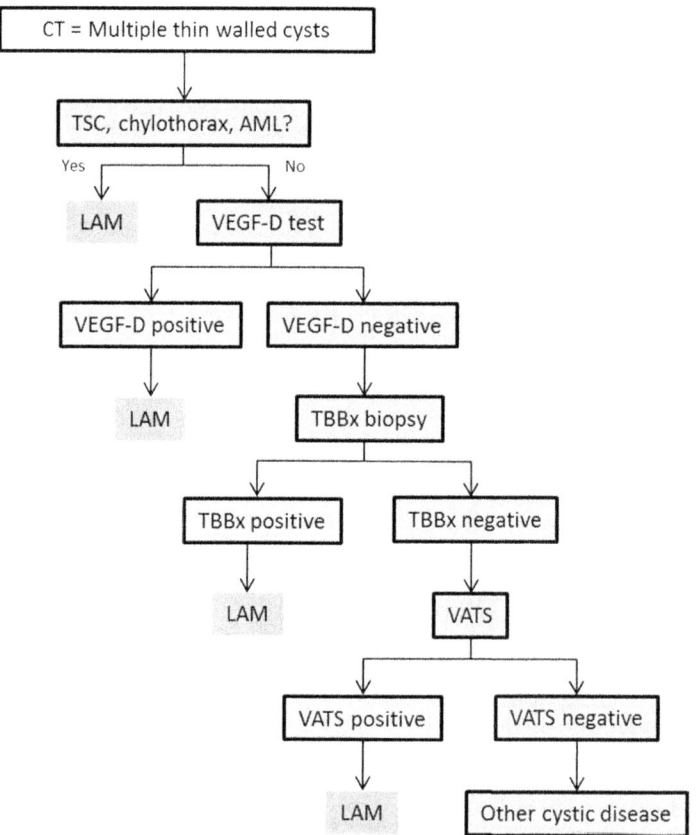

Diagram 1. Proposed algorithm for the diagnosis of LAM.
CT: computed tomography; TSC: tuberous sclerosis complex; AML: angiomyolipoma; VEGF-D: vascular endothelial growth factor D; TBBx: transbronchial biopsy; VATS: video-assisted thoracoscopic surgery.

Figure 2.6: An example of a mathematical algorithm (Source image: https://commons.wikimedia.org/wiki/File:Flow_chart_for_SIMPLE_Algorithm.jpg)

One type of algorithms that are very popular are machine learning algorithms. However, these algorithms are based on an implicit set of rules (the algorithm is not shown how to perform a task based on explicit instructions, but based on data). The preceding image is a representation of an algorithm.

See also the following definitions: Machine learning and artificial intelligence

Anaconda

Anaconda is the most popular data science platform for Python and R. Anaconda is an open source distribution platform. This platform is well-suited for data processing, machine learning engineering, data visualization, and so on. It simplifies the data scientists' job as it manages libraries, dependencies, and environment with Conda. It also provides access to several development tools such as Jupyter Notebook, Spyder, and Orange. The platform is available on Windows, Linux, and macOS.

See also the following definitions: Jupyter Notebook and Notebook

Anchor box

Anchor boxes or bounding boxes are manually created boxes that are used in object detection in computer vision. They help identify a single or multiple objects of different shapes. Anchor boxes have four coordinates and are added to the output of the object detection algorithm and so, the algorithm predicts the class of the object and the coordinates of the box that includes the shape. Usually, there are numerous anchor boxes for one object detection task.

Figure 2.7: *Anchor boxes representation as an output of a model*

YOLO algorithm (**You Only Look Once**) which is a real time object detection framework uses an anchor box for object detection. Anchor boxes have to be manually labeled by a human annotator prior to training. The preceding image represents the shape and positioning of an anchor box.

See also the following definitions: Deep learning and image recognition

Annotator

Annotator is the individual which is in charge of labeling data. It is used more often to describe the image annotations. Annotation is the label generated for every raw data. The annotation is usually done by a human. Annotation is a crucial process in machine learning since supervised machine learning algorithms require the data to be labeled. The most popular data annotations are the following: text annotation, image annotation, video annotation, and audio annotation. Data annotation is a fastidious process that requires a lot of time and resources. Some third-party companies offer their own annotation service.

See also the following definitions: Deep learning

ANOVA

ANOVA is short for analysis of variance and its goal is to compare population means. To do so, the analysis is based on samples from the populations. In other words, ANOVA is the study of the dependence of one quantitative variable on one or two qualitative variables (called factors). With one factor, it is called a bivariate analysis and with two factors, it is called a multivariate analysis. We use hypothesis testing to know if the population means are the same. The null hypothesis is that all the populations' means are equal. The test F is then applied to compare the inter-sample variance to the intra-sample variance to be able to reject the null hypothesis.

Example:

We would like to study the dependence of the exams performance score (quantitative variable) of all the schools in our city area (factor or qualitative variable). Now, we want to find out if the dependence between the two variables is significant.

See also the following definitions: Chi-square test, t-test, and z-test

Apache Spark

Apache Spark is an open source cluster computing framework. It is designed to perform batch processing, streaming, interactive queries, and machine learning. Apache Spark has a higher performance as it can perform queries 100 times faster than Hadoop. It allows interacting with different tools and programming languages such as Java, Scala, Python, R, and SQL. Spark gives access to powerful libraries such as Spark SQL, Spark Streaming, MLlib, and GraphX. Apache Spark can run on several environments like Hadoop, Kubernetes, standalone, and so on. Spark is very popular in the data science community as it allows faster computing and helps in dealing with large datasets.

See also the following definitions: Big data and machine learning

ARIMA

It stands for Auto Regressive Integrated Moving Average and is a very popular forecasting technic. It will predict a time series using its previous values. To be able to use ARIMA, the time series has to be non-seasonal, except when you are using SARIMA or Seasonal ARIMA.

ARIMA has 3 parameters:

- (p) is the order of the auto regressive which is the number of lags as a predictor.
- Then (d) is the order of the integrated which is the amount of differencing that will make the time series stationary.
- (q) is the order of the moving average that represents the lagged forecast error that will be used in the ARIMA model.

Note that if the time series is already stationary, then (d) should be equal to 0. The equation of ARIMA regroups the equation of the auto regressive model, differentiating (or integrated) and moving average. It is as follows:

$$Z_t = \beta_0 + \beta_1 Z_{t-1} + \ldots + \beta_n Z_{t-n} + \varepsilon_t + \theta_1 \varepsilon_{t-1} + \ldots + \theta_n \varepsilon_{t-n}$$

Here, is the difference between the actual value and the lag value, is the parameter of the auto regressive equation, is the forecast error, and is the parameter of the moving average equation.

Hint: How do we find the order of differencing (d)? based on the autocorrelation and ACF plot to see what the right differencing order is? How do we find the order of the auto regressive term (p)? By inspecting the **partial autocorrelation (PACF)** plot. The order of the auto regressive will be equal to the lags that cross the significance limit in the PACF plot. How do we find the order of the moving average (q)? By using the **autocorrelation plot (ACF)** and seeing what the lags that cross the significance limit are.

In Python:

```
import pmdarima as pm

model = pm.auto_arima(df.value, start_p=1, start_q=1,
                      test='adf',       # use adftest to find optimal 'd'
                      max_p=3, max_q=3, # maximum p and q
                      m=1,              # frequency of series
                      d=None,           # let model determine 'd'
                      seasonal=False,   # No Seasonality
                      start_P=0,
                      D=0,
                      trace=True,
                      error_action='ignore',
                      suppress_warnings=True,
                      stepwise=True)
```

Code source: https://www.machinelearningplus.com/time-series/arima-model-time-series-forecasting-python/

In R:

```
from pyramid.arima import auto_arima

model = auto_arima(train, trace=True, error_action='ignore', suppress_warnings=True)

model.fit(train)
```

Code source: https://www.analyticsvidhya.com/blog/2018/08/auto-arima-time-series-modeling-python-r/

Also, in Python or R, there are packages that automatically find the optimal parameters of the ARIMA models as previously described.

See also the following definitions: Time series analysis

Artificial general intelligence (AGI)

Artificial general intelligence can also be referred to as strong AI that can perform the full range of human intelligence abilities. The strong AI can perform the following tasks at the same time: reasoning, knowledge representation, learning, communicating, and achieving a goal using all the available skills. It is hard for a human researcher to classify any AI as strong AI, but one of the most popular tests for this purpose is the Turing test. The Turing test consists of a machine and human conversing with another human. If the last human is not capable of distinguishing between the machine and the human, the test is successful and the machine can be called as Artificial General Intelligence. Note that as of now, no AI has reached the level of a strong AI.

See also the following definitions: Artificial intelligence, artificial narrow intelligence (ANI), and artificial super intelligence

Artificial intelligence

It describes a machine that can mimic some specific human cognitive capabilities such as reasoning, learning, problem solving, vision, communicating, and so on. Today, AI is capable of understanding human speech, translating human speech, driving a car autonomously, winning a strategic game (AlphaGo), and so on. A popular sub-field in artificial intelligence is machine learning. This field consists of a machine that is capable of learning from data and doesn't require to be explicitly coded.

See also the following definitions: Artificial general intelligence (AGI), artificial narrow intelligence (ANI), and artificial super intelligence

Artificial narrow intelligence (ANI)

It is also known as narrow AI or weak AI. It is a machine capable of performing a single and specific task very well such as speech to text, translation, object recognition, and so on. Narrow AI is not conscious and does not have emotions like a human; it acts in a pre-determined way.

See also the following definitions: **Artificial general intelligence (AGI)**, artificial intelligence, and artificial super intelligence

Artificial super intelligence (ASI)

It is a hypothetical concept where machine intelligence far surpasses human intelligence and capabilities. Superintelligence is usually associated with the concept of technological singularity where the result of an superintelligence will consist of drastic changes in humanity.

See also the following definitions: **Artificial general intelligence (AGI)**, artificial intelligence, and **artificial narrow intelligence (ANI)**

Association learning

For more details, see the definition of association rules.

Association rules

It is a popular machine learning algorithm for market basket analysis. It helps in choosing the most relevant items for a customer based on the items that they have already selected. Association rules mainly find the relationship between the selected items by customers. The analysis is done at a transactional level and it analyzes all the items contained in one transaction.

See also the following definitions: Market basket analysis

Attention mechanism

Attention mechanism is a very popular concept in deep neural network that has helped in increasing the performance of different neural network architecture. The attention mechanism helps in focusing on some specific factors rather than the others when processing the data. The mechanism is very popular in machine translation. There are different types of attention mechanism: soft attention, self-attention, general attention, and so on.

See also the following definitions: Deep learning and machine translation

Attribute

Attribute has the same meaning as feature and it represents the characteristic of an observation. It can be referred to in a table as a column name.

See also the following definitions: Variable and training set

Area under the ROC Curve (AUC)

AUC Or AUC-ROC stands for "Area under the Curve Receiver Operating Characteristics." It is a visual tool to help evaluate the performance of a classification model. It maps the true positive rate in function of a false positive rate. It shows how much the model can distinguish between classes.

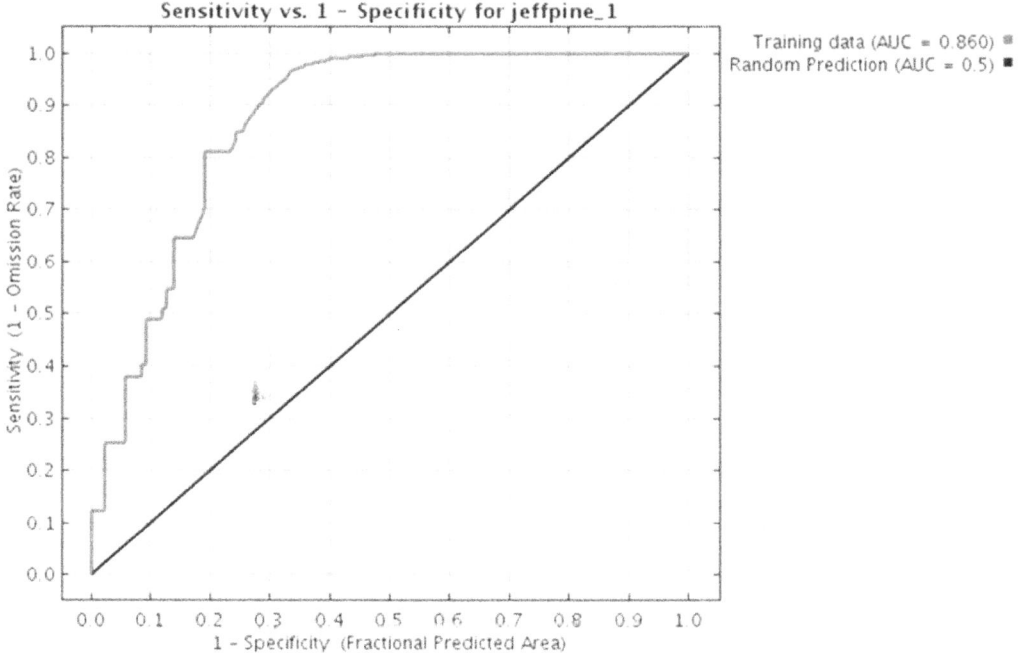

*Figure 2.8: Area under the ROC Curve comparison
(Source image: https://commons.wikimedia.org/wiki/File:ROC_curve_of_the_maxent_model_of_
Jeffrey_pine_trees_in_relation_to_annual_precipitation.png)*

The higher the area under the curve is, the better is the model performance. An AUC equal to 1 is a perfect model and an AUC equal to 0 is a model that cannot distinguish between classes at all. An AUC greater than 0.5 is better than a random classifier. The preceding figure is a representation of an AUC ROC curve.

See also the following definitions: Accuracy, machine learning, and evaluation metrics

Autocorrelation

Autocorrelation measures the linear relationship between a time series and the lagged version of the series at different time intervals. This measurement is similar to regular correlation between two series except that we apply it to the series and its lags.

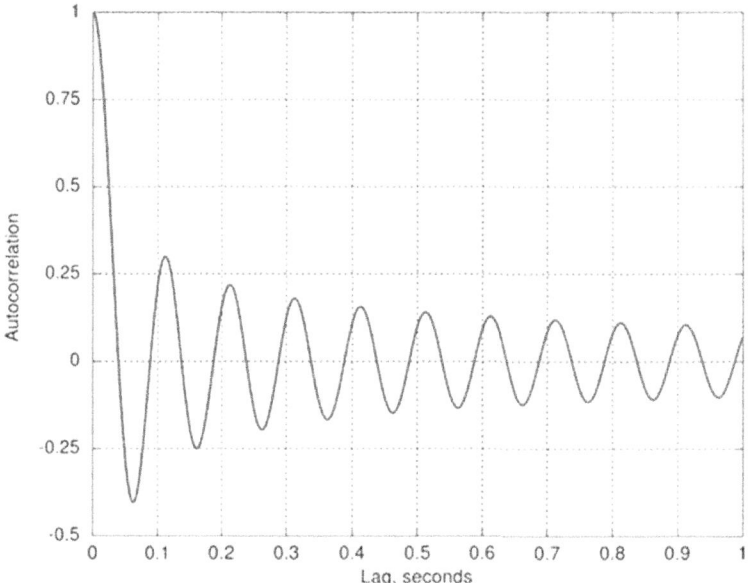

Figure 2.9: *Graphical representation of autocorrelation*
(Source image: https://commons.wikimedia.org/wiki/File:Jakes_rayleigh_autocorr_10Hz_doppler.svg)

The autocorrelation varies between -1 and 1 where -1 is negatively correlated, 1 is positively correlated, and 0 has no correlation. A plot of autocorrelation is called the **autocorrelation function** (**ACF**). It is represented in the preceding image.

See also the following definitions: Correlation

Autoencoder

An autoencoder is a deep neural network used in an unsupervised machine learning task and representation learning. Like PCA, an autoencoder is a dimensionality reduction technic except that autoencoders are good for non-linear representations.

The autoencoder will compress the input to a lower-dimensional representation through a bottleneck layer (encoder) and then reconstruct it from the lower representation to the original higher-dimensional data (decoder). This means that an autoencoder predicts its own input based on a layer (bottleneck) that will learn the representation from the input. Adding noise to the input helps the model in learning to predict the data without noise. It is useful in building models that are specialized in data denoising. Note that a large neural network that does not have a diverse dataset may tend to memorize the dataset instead of learning the pattern, especially if the bottleneck layer is missing.

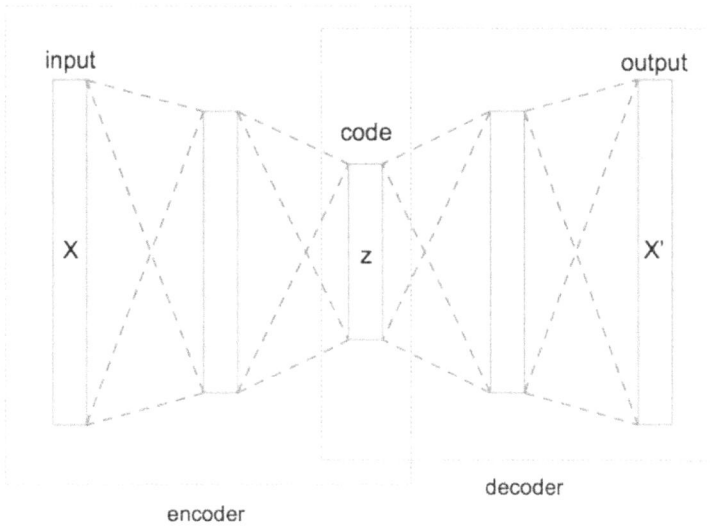

Figure 2.10: A representation of an autoencoder with a bottleneck
(Source image: https://fr.wikipedia.org/wiki/Fichier:Autoencoder_structure.png)

Some use cases are dimensionality reduction, image denoising, image or data generation, feature extraction, and anomaly detection. A visual representation of an autoencoder is represented in the preceding image.

See also the following definitions: Deep learning

Automatic summarization

It is an automatic process that helps in creating a summary that contains the most important information from a larger content. Automatic summarization can be applied to text, audio, and images. This technic is becoming more and more familiar and accessible thanks to deep learning. There are two types of summarization: extractive summarization and abstractive summarization.

"Automatic text summarization is the task of producing a concise and fluent summary while preserving key information content and overall meaning"

— *Text Summarization Techniques: A Brief Survey, 2017*

See also the following definitions: Machine translation

Automation bias

Automation bias is when a human decision maker favors recommendations made by an automated system over a non-automated system even if the automated system provides an error. The automated system can be a machine learning model and the decision maker can favor the recommendations from the machine learning model instead of common sense which can be caused by over trusting the machine learning model.

See also the following definitions: Bias, bias-variance trade-off, coverage bias, implicit bias, and sampling bias

Autoregression

Autoregression is a regression that is applied in a time series forecasting and analysis where the model output variable is dependent linearly on the lagged version of itself. Autoregression is very similar to a linear regression except that the independent variables are lagged values of the output.

$$Y_t = \beta_0 + \beta_1 Y_{t-1} + \varepsilon$$

Here, Y_t represents the time series at time t, Y_{t-1} represents the time series at time t-1, β_1 and β_0 are the parameters, and ε represents the error.

See also the following definitions: Regression and machine learning

Average pooling

Average pooling is a pooling technic used in convolutional neural network as it compresses the input matrix in a lower dimension. The manipulation performed by average pooling is represented as follows:

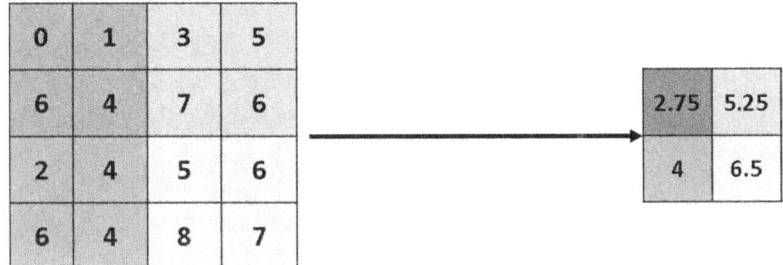

Figure 2.11: Average pooling

In contrary to max pooling, average pooling takes the average of the values in the rolling window instead of taking the maximum ones.

See also the following definitions: Convolutional neural network and max pooling

Average precision

Average precision is a metric used to evaluate the performance of classification models. Average precision corresponds to the area under the precision recall curve. The value of the average precision is between 0 and 1.

See also the following definitions: Evaluation metrics and precision

CHAPTER 3

B

Backpropagation

It is a popular algorithm for updating weights and biases (parameters) in a feedforward neural network model. It is named as backpropagation since it propagates from output to input the weights' updates using chain rules. The updates of the weights are done to minimize the loss function (or objective function). Backpropagation is usually complementary to a gradient descent algorithm where the gradient descent updates the weights and biases, and backpropagation computes the variation of the error based on the weight's changes. Backpropagation updates the weights using the partial derivative of the total error (loss) and the weights by using the following equation:

$$\delta_j = \frac{\partial C}{\partial w_j}$$

Here, δ_j is the error of neuron j and $\frac{\partial C}{\partial w_j}$ is the derivative of the cost functions in the function of the weight w of the neuron j (or simply the variation of the cost function based on the changes in the weight of the neuron j).

See also the following definitions: Neural network and gradient descent

Backpropagation through time (BPTT)

BPTT is an algorithm that calculates the gradient or updates the weights in **recurrent neural network** (**RNN**) applied to the sequential data. The most common sequential data using BPTT to train an RNN is time series or natural language processing. The recurrent neural network is shown one input and one output pair at each timestep. The timestep errors are calculated and accumulated through each timestep. Then, the network updates its weights. BPTT has several disadvantages. The gradient descent can vanish or explode frequently. If the timesteps increase, the computational cost will increase very quickly. Truncated backpropagation through time is another version of BPTT that avoids these issues.

See also the following definitions: Backpropagation and neural network

Bag of words

It is a technic to extract text features from a raw document. The extracted features can later be used by the machine learning algorithm. It solves problem like document classification and language modeling. It will measure the frequency of words and vocabulary present in the raw document. It is named as a "bag" because it doesn't take into consideration the meanings of the words, the syntax, or the position in the text. It's a raw way of structuring data. This technic transforms the data into large dummy vectors.

See also the following definitions: Structured data

Bagging

It is also called bootstrap aggregating. It is an ensemble algorithm in machine learning. It helps in improving the performance and stability, and in avoiding underfitting of the underlaying machine learning algorithms. It is usually applied to decision trees algorithms. The most popular bagging algorithm is random forest. Bagging can be used to solve regression or classification problems. The bagging algorithm creates a lot of weak learners from decision trees based on training from samples. The samples are created by sampling with replacement. The learners are combined to create one strong learner that performs better than the individual weak learners.

Hint: What is the difference between bagging and boosting? In bagging, all the input data has the same weight before sampling with replacement while in boosting, the input data is weighted based on the performance of the previous learner. Also, bagging builds weak learners in parallel while boosting builds models sequentially (one after the other). At the end, for bagging, the output is computed by the average responses or by voting while in boosting, each weak learner is weighted based on its performance.

When do we use bagging and when do we use boosting? Bagging will help make the variance low while boosting will help make the bias low. This means that if there is a case where we have to face overfitting (high variance), it's better to use bagging, and if there is a performance issue (high bias), it's better to use boosting.

See also the following definitions: Boosting, ensemble model, and base learner

Bar chart

It is a graphical representation for categorical variables. The rectangular bars are proportional to the values of each category in the categorical variable. The graphic can be horizontal or vertical. An example of a bar chart is as follows:

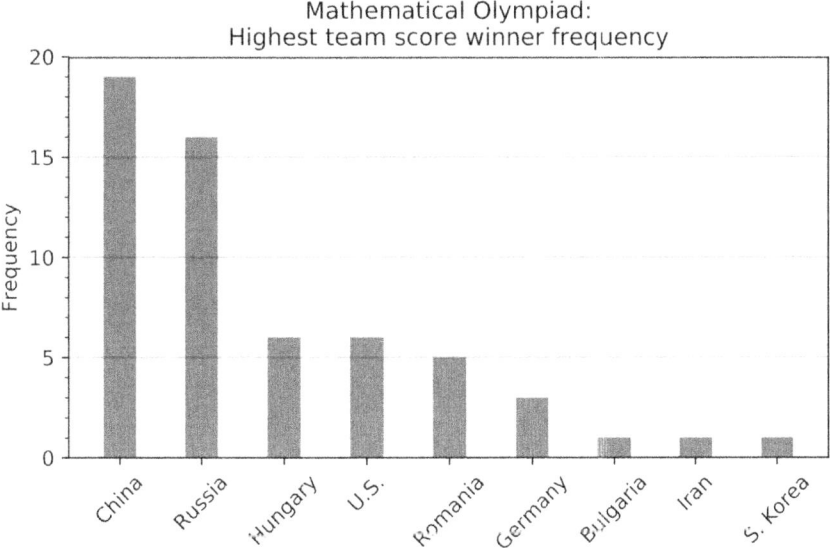

Figure 3.1: A representation of a stacked bar chart
(Source image: https://commons.wikimedia.org/wiki/File:International_Mathematical_Olympiad_highest_team_score_bar_chart.svg)

A bar chart can be used for more complex visualization in a grouped way with more than two bars per category or in a stacked way with more than a categorical variable per bar.

See also the following definitions: Line chart, pie chart, and box plot

Base learner

A base learner can also be referred to as a weak learner. An ensemble model contains several learners. These learners are called base learners. It is a machine learning model that usually performs poorly (just above luck). The base learners combined create a strong learner that generally performs well. A base learner can be of decision trees algorithm (for example, stumps) or any kind of algorithm (like SVM, Logistic Regression, and so on).

See also the following definitions: Decision tree, boosting, XGboost, and random forest

Baseline

A baseline is the benchmark against which any further results can be compared with. In machine learning, a baseline model is a simple model that is first trained, and then its performance becomes the benchmark for any future algorithm training and performance. Randomness can also be designated as a baseline. A visual representation of a baseline is as follows:

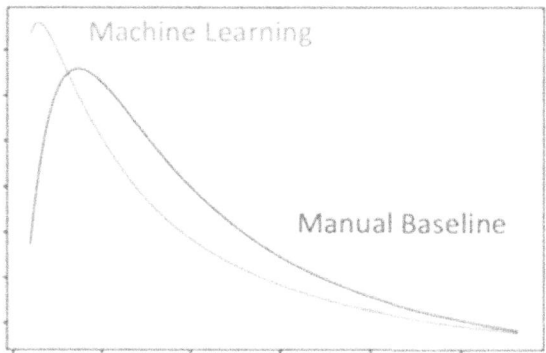

Figure 3.2: Representation of error between baseline and machine learning model

Without a baseline, a model performance can become meaningless.

See also the following definitions: Loss curve and evaluation metrics

Batch

A batch size is a hyperparameter that can be defined before training a model. Batches are small amount of samples from the initial datasets; the dataset is entirely divided into batches. Technically, a batch represents the number of observations that the algorithm will see before updating its parameters (parameters don't have the same meaning as hyperparameters). A batch is not to be confused with an epoch. An epoch is the number of times an algorithm sees the entire dataset while a batch is the subdivision of the entire dataset into smaller groups that is presented to the model. Both epoch and batch can be defined at the beginning, prior to training.

See also the following definitions: Batch normalization and gradient descent

Batch gradient descent

Batch gradient descent is a technic that is used to minimize the cost function in a neural network. The batch technic will uses all the training data at once to make a single update of the parameters. This means that each epoch consists of one single batch that includes all the training data. The gradient descent moves directly to the local or global minimum which is interesting in case if the convex or smooth error manifolds. It can increase the speed by processing all the data at once. The gradient descent has a more stable convergence. It has less oscillations when it comes close to the global minima. However, the batch gradient descent can lead to local minima instead of a global one. Processing the data at once can lead to computing memory issues.

See also the following definitions: Batch normalization and gradient descent

Batch normalization

It is a normalization technic that is applied within neural network hidden layers. A batch normalization normalizes the output from a previous activation function by subtracting the output and the mean of a batch of data and dividing it by the standard deviation of the batch. Batch normalization solves the internal covariate shift as small updates of parameters of one layer affect the previous layers' updates parameters by backpropagation a lot. So, batch normalization reduces this shift which results in speeding the training and improving the performance. Batch normalization allows having a higher learning rate without vanishing gradient issues and helps in avoiding overfitting. The batch normalization has the following formula:

$$x_i = \frac{x_i - \mu_B}{\sqrt{\sigma_b + \epsilon}}$$

It is similar to an ordinary normalization where x_i is the output from the activation function, μ_B is the mean of the batch, σ_b is the standard deviation of the batch, and ϵ is a term that avoids dividing by zero.

See also the following definitions: Batch and gradient descent

Bayes' theorem

Bayes' theorem provides a formula for finding the probability of a hypothesis given an evidence following conditional probability. The Bayes' theorem is used in several machine learning algorithms such as Naive Bayes classifier which can be used for spam filtering. The formula of Bayes theorem is as follows:

$$P(H|E) = \frac{P(E|H)\,P(H)}{P(E)}$$

Here, $P(H|E)$ is the probability of the hypothesis given the evidence, $P(E|H)$ is the probability of the evidence given the hypothesis, $P(H)$ is the probability of the hypothesis, $P(E)$ is the probability of the evidence.

Example:

You are planning a trip tomorrow to Quebec City but a storm is forecasted for tomorrow. The odds are as follows: 0.3% chance of having an accident on the road however the weather may be, 2% chance of a storm, and also 9% of accidents occur when there are storms.

$$P(Accident|Storm) = \frac{9\% * 0.3\%}{2\%} = 1.35\%$$

So, your probability of having an accident given that there is a storm tomorrow is 1.35%.

See also the following definitions: Bayesian inference and Bayesian statistics

Bayesian inference

It is a statistical inference method used to derive population characteristics or probability distribution based on the Bayes Theorem. This calculation of probabilities is done using new data and the probabilities can be updated as much as new information is gathered. For more details, see the definition of Bayesian statistics.

See also the following definitions: Bayes theorem and Bayesian statistics

Bayesian statistics

They are opposed to the frequentist statistics that calculate the probability of an event based on a repeated experiment and only on the experiment. The following chart represents how the Bayesian statistics work:

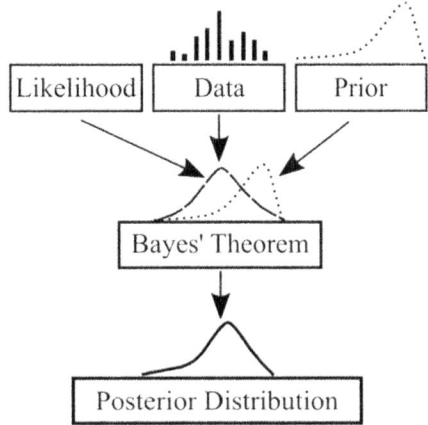

Figure 3.3: A representation of computing the distribution of probabilities using Bayesian statistics

While Bayesian statistics keep updating the probability of an event based on the new data coming from an experiment, this is called Bayesian inference as it is a way of computing the probabilities of an event using the Bayes theorem. Then, the probabilities are continuously updated based on the new data. For more details, see the definition of Bayes theorem.

See also the following definitions: Bayes theorem and Bayesian inference

Bellman equation

Bellman equation is a key concept in reinforcement learning. It helps to evaluate the expected reward relative to the advantage or disadvantage of each state. Its equation is as follows:

$$V(s) = max_a(R(s, a) + \gamma V(s'))$$

Here, $V(s)$ is the target value at s, $R(s, a)$ is the reward knowing state s and action a, γ is a gamma discount factor, and $V(s')$ is the output value of our model at the next states.

γ, the gamma factor, is a hyperparameter that can be tuned. Note that a low value of the gamma will result in short-term reward thinking and a high value will result in long-term reward thinking.

The Bellman equation is very popular in dynamic programming. For more details, see the definition of dynamic programming.

See also the following definitions: Reinforcement learning, action, and agent

Bernoulli distribution

Bernoulli distribution is a discrete probability distribution for a random variable. It can take the value of 1 with the probability p and value of 0 with probability $q = 1-p$. A simple representation of a Bernoulli distribution is as follows:

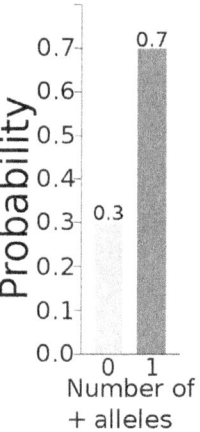

Figure 3.4: Bernoulli distribution
(Source image: https://commons.wikimedia.org/wiki/File:Bernoulli_0.7.svg)

In general, it is useful for representing any kind of experiment that has two facets (yes/true/one or no/false/zero).

See also the following definitions: Binomial distribution, chi-squared distribution, Gaussian distribution, t-distribution, exponential family distribution, normal distribution, and Poisson distribution

Bias

Bias in statistics is when the result is under or overestimates the true characteristic of a population; it represents the amount of errors between the result and the truth.

Bias in machine learning is a concept that helps in evaluating the performance of a model. A model with high bias means that it is underfitting and is not capable enough to correctly map the inputs with the output. Let's suppose that you have a dataset where the relationship between the inputs and the outputs is nonlinear and it is a complex representation. Then, using a linear regression might result in a model that has high bias. The model is not capable of finding relevant relationship between your inputs and output.

See also the following definitions: Bias-variance trade-off, automation bias, coverage bias, and sampling bias

Bias-variance trade-off

Bias-variance trade-off is a central problem in supervised machine learning. An optimal model has a low bias and a low variance, but reaching this optimal can be difficult. Usually, simple models on complex problems tend to have high bias with low variance and complex models on complex problems tend to have low bias with high variance. The ideal situation is to find a good balance between minimizing the bias and the variance.

See also the following definitions: Bias, automation bias, coverage bias, and sampling bias

Bidirectional Recurrent Neural Network

Bidirectional recurrent neural network (BRNN) consists of two independent RNNs where the information is forwarded in one neural network and backwarded in the other. The output of the two networks is concatenated together to form one output. This architecture is helpful for including future and past inputs from a sequence in the model which gives context to the information and increases the performance in specific cases. It is commonly used in speech recognition, handwritten recognition, and entity extraction.

See also the following definitions: Recurrent neural network and convolutional neural network

Big Data

It represents a set of data that is so large that traditional data extraction and analysis tools cannot process it. The interpretability and meaning of this big data is also difficult for humans as the data can come from various sources with large volumes. To describe this phenomenon, it is common to use a tri-dimensional filter that describes what big data is: Volume where the data is so large that it cannot be analyzed and extracted by using traditional tools; velocity where the data is generated on a fast rhythm, for example, Facebook generates 4 petabytes of data per day; and variety where data comes from different sources such as video content, images, IoT data, and so on.

The big data ecosystem has been revolutionized with the release of tools such as Hadoop and MapReduce that are capable of dealing with a large amount of information.

Big data is very useful and popular in data science as it allows data experts to gain access to a large amount of unstructured information that can reveal new patterns. Data science's most popular big data tool is Apache Spark that allows it to deal with a large amount of data and perform different types of analysis and modeling. For more details, see the definition of Apache Spark.

Hint: When can we start talking about big data? It is hard to quantify as to at what amount of data we can start talking about big data, but if the data respects the 3V described above and traditional tools fail in extracting and analyzing the data, we can start talking about it as big data.

See also the following definitions: Apache Spark

Big O notation

Big O notation can classify an algorithm complexity based on the running time and required space as the input size grows or the number of parameters grows. The most common representation of Big O notation is as follows:

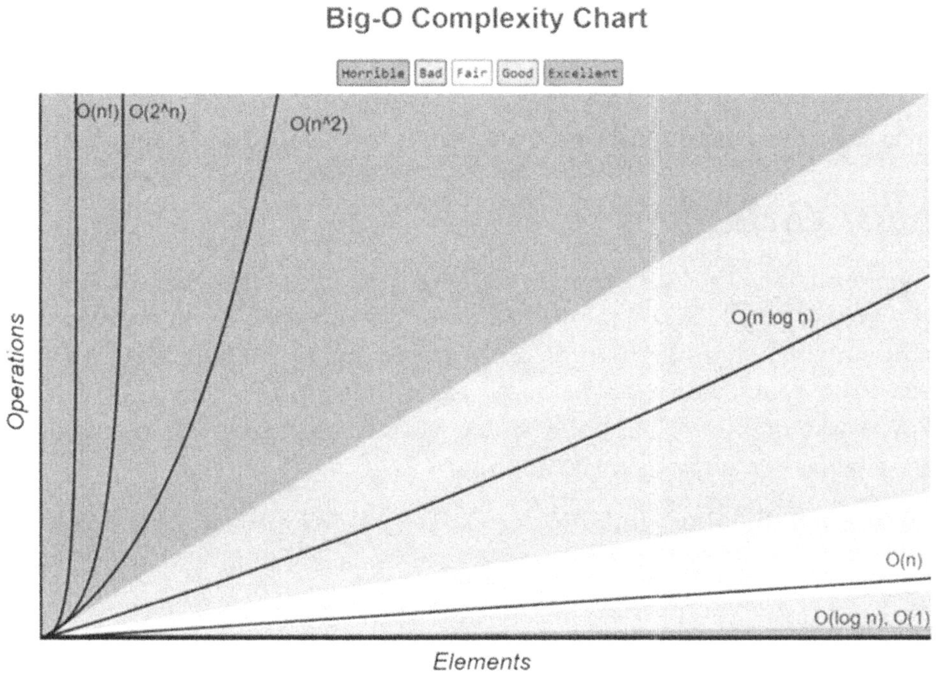

Big-O Complexity Chart

Figure 3.5: A representation of complexity shapes and their impacts

The complexity can have a shape that is constant, linear, quadratic, and so on.

See also the following definitions: Complexity

Binarization

Binarization is used in image processing for a deep neural network. It transforms a pixel image from a scale of 0-255 spectrum to a scale of 0-1 spectrum. This simple process is mandatory as neural networks are more efficient while working with normalized data.

See also the following definitions: Normalization

Binary classification

Binary classification or binomial classification is a sub-field in supervised machine learning. The target variable (dependent variable) is binary which means that it is composed of only two values (usually zero and one). To solve a binary classification problem, different models can be used such as decision trees, logistic regression, neural network, support vector machine, and so on. Also, for evaluating a binary classification, we use specific types of evaluation metrics: precision and recall, confusion matrix, and ROC curves.

See also the following definitions: Classification and multi-class classification

Binary variables

They represent the variables that only have two possible values. For example, male/female, 1/0, is fraud/is not fraud, and so on. A sub-type of binary variable is a dummy variable where the two possible values are 1 or 0. Dummy variables are derived from categorical variables with no relationship between the categories. In machine learning, binary variables are commonly used either as predictors or as target variables (c.f. binary classification).

See also the following definitions: Variable, categorical variable, continuous variable, discrete variable, dummy variable, nominal variable, and ordinal variable

Binning

Binning means regrouping a continuous or discrete variable into categories to create a new categorical variable. For example, the variable age is considered as a continuous variable (from 0 to 100). We can apply binning and create a new categorical variable where age is grouped into categories (from 0-10 years old, from 11-18, and so on)

See also the following definitions: Categorical variable, continuous variable, and discrete variable

Binomial distribution

In the theory of probability and in statistics, binomial distribution represents the modeling of the number of successes obtained from repeated and independent random experiments. The output of a binomial distribution always has to be binary (success/failure). There are two parameters in this probability distribution: n or the number of experiments and p or the probability of success. So, the probability of k success in n experiments is represented as follows:

$$P(X = k) = \binom{n}{k} p^k (1-p)^{n-k}$$

Note that each experiment is called Bernoulli trial. The experiments can be represented in a tree of probabilities. The tree of probabilities is as follows:

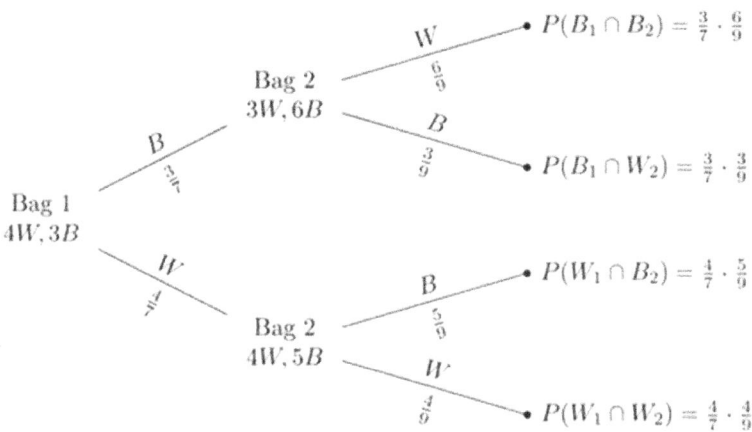

Figure 3.6: A representation of a tree of probabilities
(Source image: http://www.texample.net/tikz/examples/probability-tree/)

A visual way to represent this series of experiments is to use a probability tree. With generation of each tree, two branches leave from each node, one for success and one for failure.

See also the following definitions: Chi-squared distribution, Gaussian distribution, T-distribution, exponential family distribution, Normal distribution, Poisson distribution, and Bernoulli distribution

Black box model

A black box is a system where only the input and the output are known. The internal mechanism including the type of model and the entire engineering are unknown. Black box models are using offered as software as a service by several vendors for visual recognition, classification problem, AutoML, and so on. Even if the usage of the black box model is popular, in some cases, it can be an issue as it is not possible to understand what impacts the output and how the input is processed. It is possible to "hack" black boxes using reverse engineering; with multiple outputs predicted and their inputs, it is possible to rebuild the models and derive their own system.

See also the following definitions: Machine learning, model, and predictive model

BLEU score

It stands for bilingual evaluation understudy. It is an evaluation metric used to evaluate the quality of a translated text from a machine learning model. The score is between 0 and 1 where 1 is for perfect match and 0 is for completely missed translation. The score is computed by comparing with multiple reference translations as it counts the matchings between the reference text and the translated text.

See also the following definitions: Machine translation and evaluation metrics

Boosting

Boosting is a meta-algorithm in the family of ensemble models for supervising machine learning. It is a technic that combines weak learning (regressions, decision trees) and weak learner which means models with low performance (just better than randomness). Each model is trained sequentially based on a sample of dataset that are weighted based on the performance of the previous weak learner. So, each weak learner learns from the previous weak learner's mistakes. The most popular boosting technics are XGboost, LightGBM, and AdaBoost. Another popular type of ensemble model is bagging which is similar to boosting.

Hint: What is the difference between bagging and boosting? Bagging all input data has the same weight before sampling with replacement while in boosting, the input data is weighted based on the performance of the previous learner. Also, bagging builds weak learners in parallel while boosting builds models sequentially (one after the other). At the end, for bagging, the output is computed by average responses or by voting while in boosting, each weak learner is weighted based on its performance.

When to use bagging and when to use boosting? Applying bagging will help make the variance low while boosting will help make the bias low. This means that if we have a case where we have overfitting (high variance), it is better to use bagging, and if we have a performance issue (high bias), it is better to use boosting.

See also the following definitions: Bagging, ensemble model, and base learner

Bootstrapping

It is a statistical sampling technic in the family of resampling methods that helps estimate a characteristic of a population. In bootstrapping, we sample an original dataset with replacement until the sample has the same size as the original dataset. It is a useful technic when the data distribution is non-normal or has unknown statistical properties.

Bootstrapping in machine learning refers to the bagging ensemble technic. It is used to enhance the model performance by reducing the variance. For more details, see the definition of bagging.

See also the following definitions: Bagging and sampling

Bottleneck layer

A bottleneck layer in neural network is a layer with less neurons than the previous layer and the layer after that. This technic compresses the information from the previous layer which is called dimension reduction. The bottleneck layer is very popular within autoencoders. For more details, see the definition of autoencoder.

See also the following definitions: Hidden layer and deep learning

Bounding box

Bounding Boxes or anchor boxes are manually created boxes that are used in object detection in computer vision. For more details, see the definition of anchor box.

See also the following definitions: Deep learning and image recognition

Box plot

A box and whisker plot displays six summary statistics about a category of a dataset. The statistics are minimum, first quartile, median, third quartile, maximum, and outliers. A box plot can be drawn vertically or horizontally. A box plot is as follows:

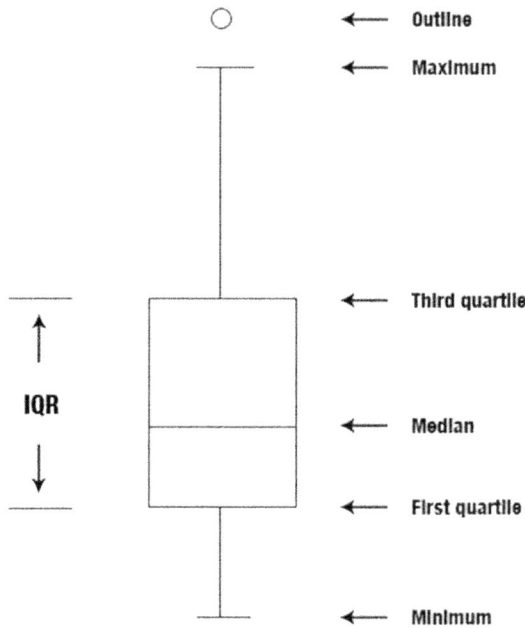

Figure 3.7: A box plot
(Source image: https://en.wikipedia.org/wiki/File:Box_plot_description.jpg)

This visualization is very useful to observe the dispersion and skewness in data.

See also the following definitions: Line chart, pie chart, and bar chart

Bucketing

Bucketing is regrouping a continuous or discrete variable into categories to create a new categorical variable. It can also be called binning. For more details, see the definition of binning.

See also the following definitions: Categorical variable, continuous variable, and discrete variable

Business analytics

Business analytics is the process where all decision-making inside an organization is driven by data. The tools used to explore and analyze the data are statistical and mathematical. The organizations that have business analytics in their processes are called data-driven. The result of business analytics is solutions or reports that bring value to the organization with a clear ROI (return on investment). The type of result can be a report including KPIs to view sales performance, a solution that can predict customer churn, analyze system logs, and send alerts to stakeholders. There are five types of business analytics levels:

- **Descriptive analytics**: It describes the situation based on historical data (sales reporting, marketing expenses, and so on).
- **Diagnostic analytics**: It tries to understand why a situation happened. (All KPIs and metrics that put that in perspective.)
- **Predictive analytics**: It can explain and predict the future. (Predicting sales for the next six months, predicting customer churn, predict system failure, and so on.)
- **Prescriptive analytics**: It can optimize a situation. (It tries to find the best driving path for a fleet of vehicles, optimize all employee schedules based on competencies and availabilities, and so on.)
- **Cognitive analytics**: It can enhance machine capabilities. (It adds visual recognition to a system to detect a hazardous situation, a system that can fetch text documents, summarize them, and so on.)

Hint: What is the difference between business analytics and data science? Business analytics and data science are two different terms as data science contributes to build some business analytics levels. Data science contributes in building three levels of business analytics: predictive analytics, prescriptive analytics, and cognitive analytics.

What is the difference between business analytics and business intelligence? Both terms are sometimes used interchangeably but they are two different terms as business intelligence contributes in building some business analytics levels. Business intelligence contributes in building two levels of business analytics: descriptive analytics and diagnostic analytics.

See also the following definitions: Business intelligence, data science, and big data

Business intelligence

Business intelligence is a sub-field that contributes to the business analytics process of a company by helping building descriptive and diagnostic analytics solutions. Business intelligence includes all the data extraction and storage that helps in accessing information more easily, since business intelligence is not just about reporting but also about structuring data by building data warehouses. The main purpose of business intelligence is to inform the stakeholders of the organization and enhance the decision-making. This is done by extracting, structuring, and reporting the data.

Hint: What is the difference between business intelligence and data science? Business intelligence focuses on creating two types of business analytics solutions: descriptive and diagnostic analytics. Data science focuses on creating three types of business analytics solutions: predictive, prescriptive and cognitive analytics.

Is business intelligence just about reporting? No, business intelligence includes extracting and structuring the data in data warehouses or data marts.

Is business intelligence performed by data scientists? Data scientists usually don't focus on business intelligence. It is performed by business intelligence analysts and data engineers.

See also the following definitions: Business analytics, data science, and big data

CHAPTER 4
C

Caffe

Caffe stands for 'Convolutional Architecture for Fast Feature Embedding' and it is an open-source deep learning framework. It supports languages like C, C++, and Python. Caffe first edge is speedy as it can support over sixty million images with a just one Nvidia K40 GPU on a daily basis.

See also the following definitions: Tensorflow, Pytorch, and Torch

Calibration

Calibration is a technic applied to a classification modeling problem that helps in increasing the accuracy and performance of a model. Calibration is based on probability distribution where instead of predicting labels in classification, we predict probabilities and then compare the predicted probabilities to the distribution of probability for each class. When the predicted probabilities match the distribution of the classes, we say that the class is calibrated. To use calibration, we first check if the predicted probabilities are calibrated and then, we adjust the calibration of the predicted probabilities with the distribution of the classes.

To diagnose the calibration, we usually use the calibration curve or reliability diagram where we plot the relative observed frequency of a class function of the predicted probabilities.

Some algorithms are natively calibrated such as logistic regression and others require calibration like neural network or support vector machine and all non-linear machine learning algorithms. To calibrate probabilities, there are two popular models: isolation regression and Platt scaling.

Note that to implement calibration, it is possible to use the function `CalibratedClassifierCV()` in scikit-learn. The reliability diagram is also accessible in `scikit-learn` with the function `calibration_curve()`.

See also the following definitions: Classification

Candidate generation

It means the number of actual recommendations that will be used to build a recommender system. Let's suppose we want to build a recommender system for movies. We have a set of 500,000 movies. Instead of using all the movies for recommending movies to the users, we will use a subset of 200 movies that will be selected on either the basis of popularity or any other criteria.

See also the following definitions: Recommendation engine and association rules

Candidate sampling

It is a technic to optimize training time for multi-label classification problems. It will compute the probabilities for all positive labels but only compute the probabilities for a subset of randomly selected negative labels. A positive label refers to a label that is tagged on an image as an actual label and a negative label refers to a label is not present on a specific image but is present in the overall dataset.

See also the following definitions: Sampling and deep learning

Categorical cross-entropy

Categorical cross-entropy is a loss function used in a deep neural network for multi-label classification where each sample corresponds to one label only. The categorical cross-entropy relies on a softmax activation function at the end of the neural network. It will compare the predictions' probabilities with the true values. Its formula is as follows:

$$L(y, \hat{y}) = - \sum_{j=0}^{M} \sum_{i=0}^{N} (y_{ij} * \log(\hat{y}_{ij}))$$

Another case of categorical cross-entropy is binary cross-entropy where the predicted output is one binary class. For more details, see binary cross-entropy.

See also the following definitions: Loss function, deep learning, and multi-class classification

Categorical variable

It is also known as nominal variable. These are variables that have discrete categories as values such as the category of fruits (apple, orange, banana, and so on). Note that in machine learning, some algorithms cannot process categorical variables as they are and require a transformation called one hot encoding or dummying categorical variables. When applied to a machine learning algorithm, categorical variables are called categorical features.

See also the following definitions: Variable, binary variable, continuous variable, discrete variable, dummy variable, nominal variable, and ordinal variable

Centroid

Centroid refers to the center of each cluster in unsupervised machine learning models. The parameter k refers to the number of k centroids that the algorithm finds and then each observation is allocated to the nearest cluster while keeping the centroids as small as possible.

See also the following definitions: Clustering and unsupervised learning

Centroid-based algorithm

It refers to a type of clustering method (unsupervised machine learning) where data is organized around a center of a cluster. It is opposed to a hierarchical cluster or density-based cluster. A representation of a centroid-based algorithm is as follows:

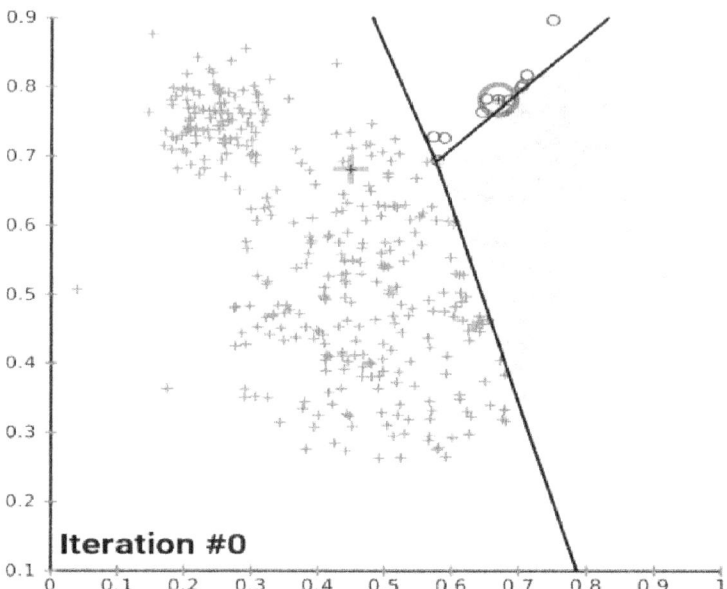

Figure 4.1: Centroid-based representation
(Source image: https://en.wikipedia.org/wiki/K-means_clustering)

Centroid-based algorithms are sensitive to outliers and to the parameter k or the number of centroids.

See also the following definitions: Hierarchical clustering, agglomerative clustering, and divisive clustering

Chain rule

Chain rule is a formula that helps in computing the derivative based on a composite function. It is one of the key concepts in neural network to perform backpropagation. An example of chain rule is as follows:

$$\frac{dz}{dx} = \frac{dz}{dy}\frac{dy}{dx}$$

See also the following definitions: Backpropagation and deep learning

Chainer

Chainer is an open-source deep learning framework developed by the company Preferred Networks. It is available on Python and it supports CUDA/cuDNN using CuPy. It is based on the define-by-run approach or dynamic computational graph as it defines the network while performing the training.

See also the following definitions: Caffe, Tensorflow, Pytorch, and Torch

Channel

Commonly used in deep neural network with convolutional neural network, it refers to the color channels or the number of distinct colors in an image. The common value of this parameter is 1 or 3 (1 is for a grayscale picture and 3 is for those colored with red, green, blue). The parameter channel is defined at the beginning with the input and the representation of the input is as follows (width, height, number of channels).

See also the following definitions: Convolutional neural network and deep learning

Checkpoints

Checkpoints is a very popular technic with deep neural network. It is a mechanism where the models (weights) are saved periodically during the training. This avoids losing all the results in case of system failure. So, when a system fails, the training restarts at the checkpoint. Checkpoints can be manually implemented or may already be implemented within the framework.

See also the following definitions: Deep learning and weights

Chi-square test

It is a statistical test that is used for hypothesis testing. The chi-square test is used to find any statistically significant difference between the expected frequencies and the observed frequencies. So, the test will try to explain if a difference between the two groups is significant or if it is due to luck and randomness.

See also the following definitions: T-test, z-test

Chi-squared distribution

The chi-squared distribution with k degrees of freedom is the distribution of the sum of squares of k independent reduced normal centered distribution. The probability density with various degrees of freedom for chi-squared distribution is as follows:

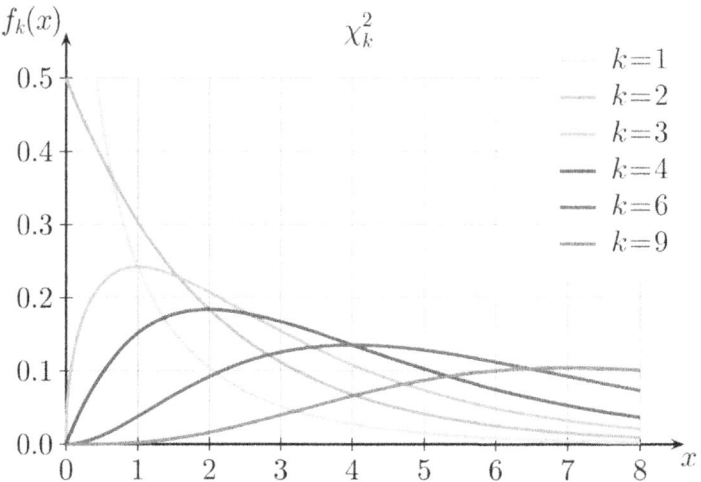

Figure 4.2: Chi-squared distribution
(Source image: https://commons.wikimedia.org/wiki/File:Chi-square_pdf.svg)

Note that the chi-squared is considered as a subcase of the gamma distribution and gamma is a part of the continuous probability distributions family.

See also the following definitions: Binomial distribution, Gaussian distribution, t-distribution, exponential family distribution, normal Distribution, Poisson distribution, and Bernoulli distribution

CIFAR:

CIFAR-10 is an open source dataset that contains 60,000 images with 10 classes. Images are of size 32x32. The train/test ratio is 5/1. It contains day-to-day images like dogs, ships, airplanes, automobiles, and so on.

To download CIFAR dataset, please refer to the following link:

https://www.cs.toronto.edu/~kriz/cifar.html

See also the following definitions: Dataset and COCO

Classification

Classification in machine learning refers to a supervised machine learning problem where the target value is a categorical variable. Classification is usually opposed to the regression problem where the target value is continuous. A case where a model identifies animals on images is a classification problem. A case where it detects spam emails is a binary classification problem. A binary classification is where there are only two classes (yes/no, spam/not spam, good/bad, and so on). There are several applications of classification in marketing, IoT, health, and so on. The algorithms used in classification problems are logistic regression, Naïve Bayes classifier, neural network, decision trees, random forest, support vector machine, and so on. To evaluate the performance of a classification problem, there are several metrics such as Precision/Recall, ROC curve, confusion matrix, and so on.

See also the following definitions: Binary classification, multi-class classification, and accuracy

Classification threshold

A classification threshold or decision threshold is a limit used to convert the probability output of a machine learning classification model to a binary output. Logistic regression or neural network can output probabilities and a threshold has to be fixed to convert the values to binary. Let's suppose that you have a neural network model that predicts spam. If the probability output is 0.05, the binary will probably be 0, and so, no spam. If the probability is 0.99, the binary will be 1. However, if the probability is 0.505, it is more difficult to say if it is 0 or 1. The most common threshold is 0.5 but in some cases, this threshold is changed depending on the context of the problem. Let's suppose that you are building a model to detect fraud. The cases where the model output is a false negative can be very costly for the company and the business are fine with a false positive. In this case, the threshold will be higher than 0.5 to have less false negatives.

See also the following definitions: Classification, binary classification, multi-class classification, and accuracy

Classifier

A classifier is a machine learning model that can assign classes to specific data points. So, it will map the input data to a specific category. A classifier is derived from a classification machine learning algorithm since a classifier is the resulted model of classification training. For more details, see the definition of classification.

See also the following definitions: Classification, binary classification, multi-class classification, and accuracy

Clipping

Clipping is a technic that helps in handling outliers. Clipping an outlier will result in replacing the value by the maximum or by the minimum. If a value of an outlier is around 100 and the maximum is 80, the outlier will be reduced to 80.

Clipping is also used in deep neural network where the gradient can be clipped. It is useful in cases where the gradient is exploding in a model. This brings the gradient value under a threshold in case it becomes too large.

See also the following definitions: Outlier

Cloud

Cloud or cloud computing is the access on demand of computer and server resources without having to manage and own the machines. It can be used for storage, computing power, application hosting, and so on. A cloud is actually a remote data center that can be accessed via the internet. The cloud resources are usually shared between different users which reduces the costs for the users. Cloud is a revolution for organizations as it helps in reducing the cost of IT operations and maintenance. It is also very practical for scaling infrastructure or applications; it allows usage based on consumption and access to additional resources if needed.

See also the following definitions: Big data

Clustering

Clustering is an unsupervised machine learning technic. Clustering regroups data points into a predefined number of groups based on the similarity between the observations in the same group and the dissimilarity with observations from other groups. The groups are called clusters. A simple representation of a clustering technic is as follows:

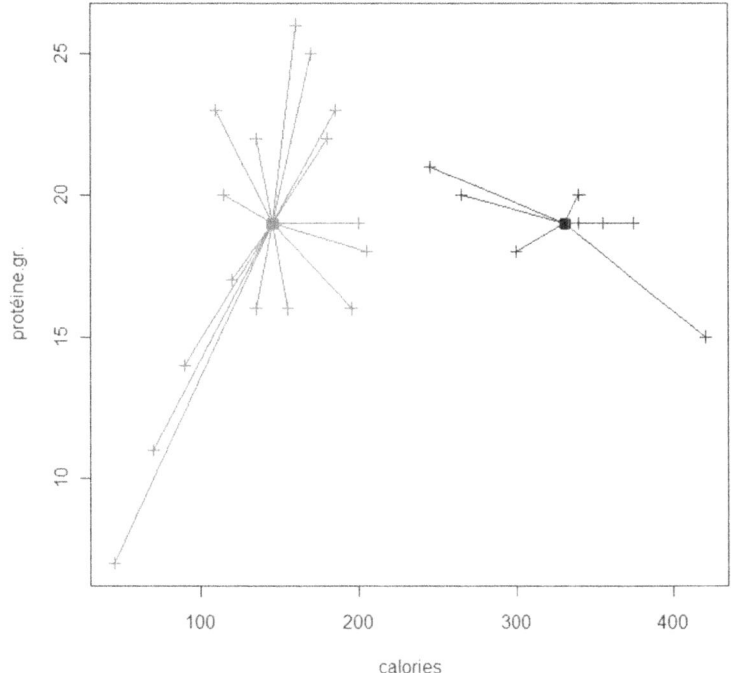

Figure 4.3: *Clustering representation*
(*Source image:https://www.geeksforgeeks.org/clustering-in-machine-learning/*)

There are different clustering technics such as: density-based, hierarchical based, partitioning and grid-based.

See also the following definitions: Hierarchical clustering, agglomerative clustering, divisive clustering, and unsupervised learning

CNN

It is one of the most popular deep neural network algorithms. It is mainly used in visual recognition tasks. The convolutional neural network or CNN takes an image as an input and learns the features from the different parts of the image. It doesn't perform any classification as it only learns the features from different parts of the image. CNN is usually combined with a fully connected layer and softmax activation to be able to convert the learned feature into probability classes. CNN is more performant than a multi-layer perceptron as it can learn more complex features from images. The way CNN works is that every portion of the image is multiplied by a filter or a kernel and then all the results are summed up with a bias to give a convoluted feature output. This operation objective is to extract high level features like shapes and edges from the image. The architecture of CNN is as follows:

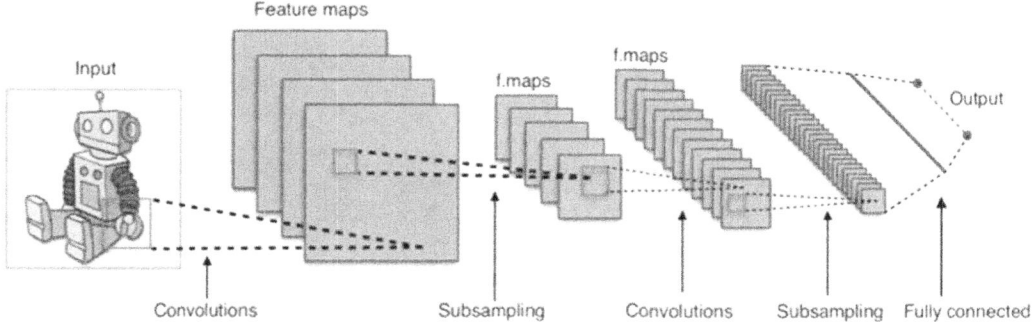

Figure 4.4: A representation of a convolutional neural network
(Source image: https://fr.wikipedia.org/wiki/Fichier:Typical_cnn.png)

Usually, a convolutional layer is combined with a max pooling function and ReLU activation to respectively reduce the computational costs of the neural network and learn non-linear patterns. When combined, they represent a convolutional block. In average, a convolutional neural network has more than five convolutional blocks.

See also the following definitions: Recurrent neural network and deep learning

CNTK

CNTK or Microsoft Cognitive Toolkit is a deep learning open-source framework developed by Microsoft Research. CNTK describes a neural network on a directed graph representation. This framework can be combined with Keras. CNTK can be implemented using C++, Python, C#, and Java. The CNTK library has both low-level and high-level developments.

See also the following definitions: Caffe, Tensorflow, PyTorch, and Torch

Co-adaptation

Co-adaptation is a neural network phenomenon where the neurons of one layer are too dependent on the output of a specific group of previous layer's neurons. This means that the neurons count on their outputs specifically instead of using the whole neural network behavior. One of the main consequences of co-adaptation is overfitting. To avoid this, we usually add a dropout to each layer.

See also the following definitions: Deep learning and overfitting

COCO

COCO or common objects in context is a large image dataset that is open-source with more than 330 thousand images with their corresponding label. It is usually used in projects for image classification as it has more than 80 classes for each image.

To download COCO dataset, please refer to the following link:

https://cocodataset.org/#home

See also the following definitions: CIFAR and dataset

Coefficient of determination

Also known as R squared, it is an output in regression models that gives the amount of variance in the dependent variable that is explainable by the independent variables. It is used to evaluate the model's performance. It varies between 0 and 1. Mathematically, it's the square of the correlation between the predicted values and actual values. It has the following formula:

$$R^2 = (\frac{1}{N}\sum(\frac{(x_i - \bar{x})*(y_i - \bar{y})}{\sigma_x * \sigma_y}))^2$$

N is the number of observations, x_i is the value of x at the observation, i, y_i is the value of y at the observation i, $\bar{x}$ and $\bar{y}$ are the means, and σ_x, σ_y are the standard deviations for x and y.

See also the following definitions: Regression and evaluation metrics

Cohen's kappa

It is a statistic that measures the inter-rater reliability. This means that it measures the true agreement between two raters (or two categorical variables) which correspond to the effective agreement minus the agreement by chance. It varies from 0 to 1 where 0 is completely disagreeing and 1 is completely agreeing. The formula is as follows:

$$kappa = 1 - \frac{1-p_o}{1-p_e}$$

Here, p_o is the relative observed agreement or the accuracy and p_e is the probability of the chance agreement.

In machine learning, Cohen's kappa is used as an evaluation metric for classification problems. It can be more effective than classification accuracy, especially with imbalanced datasets.

See also the following definitions: Evaluation metrics and classification

Collaborative filtering

Collaborative filtering is the most popular technic that is used to build recommender systems. It predicts the user's preference for items or goods based on the previous user's experience. It is usually opposed to content-based. Collaborative filtering means using the user's historical preferences for different items, and the rating associated to each item. The rating can be explicit (like star rating) or implicit rating (like purchase history). If the goal is to find similar users based on the rating, it is called user-based collaborative filtering. If the idea is to find similar items based on the rating, it is called item-based collaborative filtering. The way in which users and items interact is represented as follows:

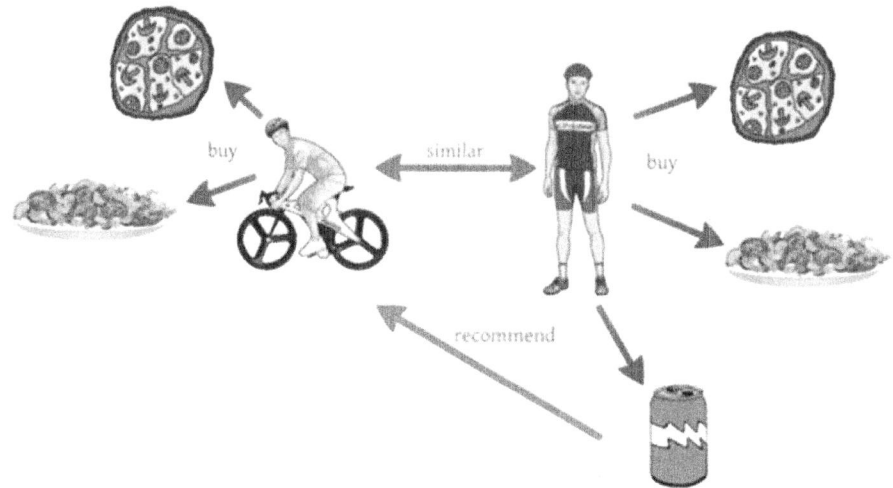

Figure 4.5: *A representation of user-based collaborative filtering*
(Source image: https://towardsdatascience.com/various-implementations-of-collaborative-filtering-100385c6dfe0)

The technic, in general, is based on finding similarities among users or items and ranking items based on associated ratings. The most popular algorithms are K-nearest neighbor or the truncated singular value decomposition.

See also the following definitions: Association rules and recommendation system

Complexity

Complexity represents a way of analyzing the execution of an algorithm. Time complexity analyzes the amount of time necessary for executing an algorithm. Space complexity analyzes the amount of space or memory necessary in executing an algorithm. Complexity is classified based on the type of function that appears in the Big O notation. For more details, see the definition of Big O notation.

See also the following definitions: Big O notation

Computer vision

Computer vision is a field in artificial intelligence where a machine is capable of analyzing and understanding an image or video. It seeks to automate tasks performed by the human vision such as categorizing an image, understanding the context in an image, and so on. Computer vision detection on an image is represented as follows:

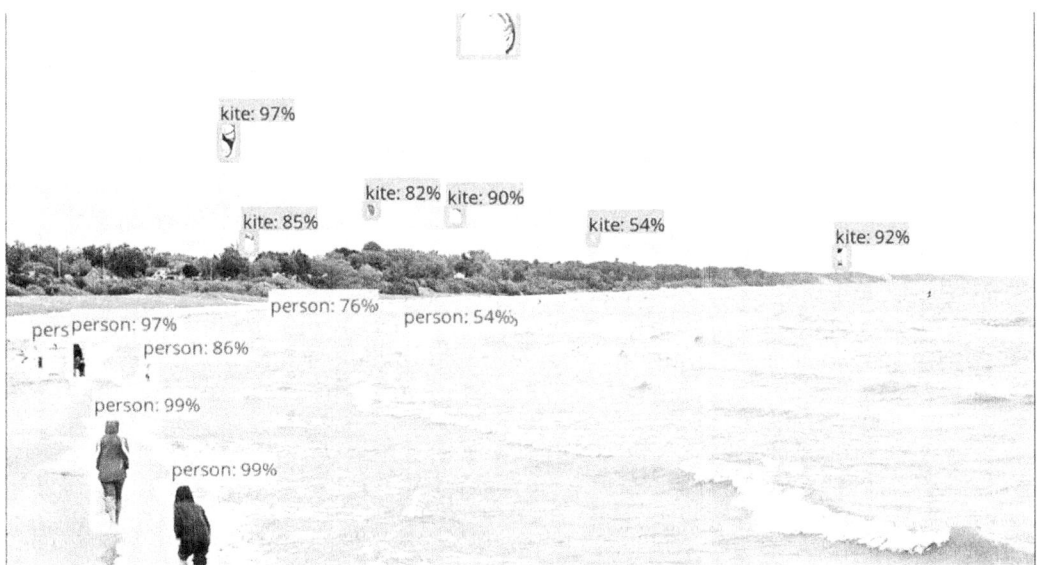

Figure 4.6: Computer vision
(Source image: https://www.flickr.com/photos/35899785@N00/35477618781)

Computer vision has seen significant growth in the last eight years, thanks to deep neural network and GPU enablement for deep learning. Nowadays, computer vision is democratized and available on several devices such as smartphones and cameras with object recognition or facial recognition. It is also used in several industries like healthcare, surveillance, traffic control, and so on.

See also the following definitions: Deep learning, Tensorflow, convolutional neural network, and deep dream

Concordant-discordant ratio

Concordant or discordant ratio is derived from concordant or discordant pairs which refer to the comparison of two pairs of data points and seeing whether their ranking is similar, in the same direction, or in opposite direction.

Let's suppose that you have a list of seven restaurants with two clients. The clients have to rank all the restaurants from good to bad ones. Client 1 and 2 ranked restaurant **A** as 1 which means that the pairs are tied for restaurant **A** as client 1 and 2 were in agreement. For restaurants, **D** and **G** the pairs are concordant. Even if the ranking is different, the direction is the same. Restaurant **D** is better than **G** for both clients. For restaurant **D** and **F**, the pairs are discordant as the ranking is in the opposite direction. For client 1, **D** is better than **F** and for client 2, **F** is better than **D**.

Restaurant	Client 1	Client 2
A	1	1
B	2	2
C	3	3
D	4	5
E	5	7
F	6	4
G	7	6

The concordant or discordant ratio is the number of concordant or discordant pairs divided by the total pairs evaluated.

Confidence interval

Confidence interval is a statistical technic used to derive an estimated range for a population characteristic based on the results from a sample. The formula is as follows:

$$\bar{x} + z * \frac{\sigma}{\sqrt{n}}$$

Here, $\bar{x}$ is the sample mean, z is the critical value for the standard normal distribution, σ is the population standard deviation, and n is the sample size.

Example: A group of students measure the population size of six postal codes in the city area (10000, 12000, 5000, 6000, 2000, 20000) with an average of 9166. All city postal codes have a standard deviation of 900. With this information, it is possible to measure the confidence interval for the mean of all the postal codes at any confidence level (usually its 95% of the confidence level).

See also the following definitions: Sampling

Confusion matrix

Confusion matrix is a table that is used as an evaluation method for the classification of machine learning models. The confusion matrix table is represented as follows:

		Predicted class	
		Positive	Negative
Actual class	Positive	TP	FN
	Negative	FP	TN

Figure 4.7: *A representation of a confusion matrix and the relevant information in the table (Source image: https://en.m.wikipedia.org/wiki/File:Binary_confusion_matrix.jpg)*

Confusion matrix represents the predicted values by the actual values and provides several insights to detect the accuracy, type I error, type II error, precision, recall, and so on.

It is composed of 4 types of crossed values: TP for true positive, TN for true negative, FN for false negative and FP for false positive.

See also the following definitions: Accuracy, machine learning, Area Under the ROC Curve (AUC), evaluation metrics, false negative, and false positive

Connectivity-based algorithm

It is also known as hierarchical clustering. It is a machine learning technic that is used for unsupervised machine learning tasks where similar observations are grouped together in clusters. This clustering technic can be represented by a dendrogram diagram. The dendrogram is as follows:

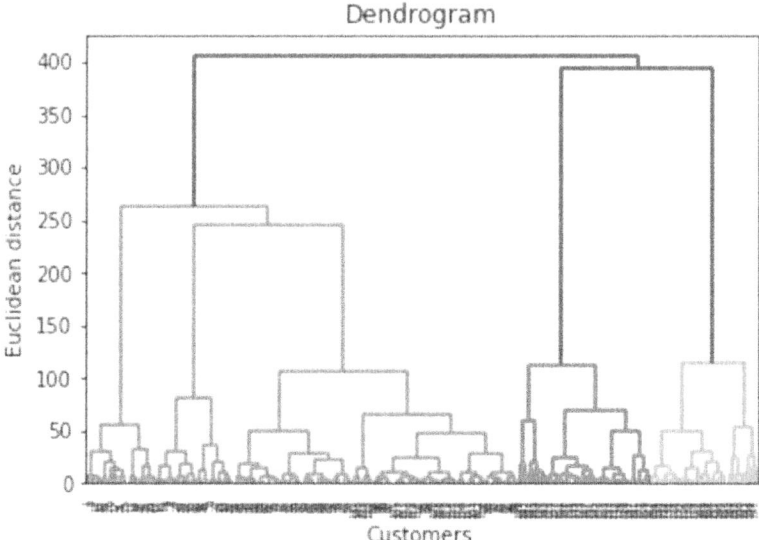

Figure 4.8: A dendrogram representation for connectivity-based clustering (Source image: https://www.kdnuggets.com/2019/09/hierarchical-clustering.html)

Hierarchical clustering creates one cluster for each observation at the beginning and then merges the clusters that are close to each other together. This process continues until no additional merging is possible.

See also the following definitions: Agglomerative clustering, clustering, and divisive clustering

Continuous learning

Continuous learning is the ability of a machine learning model to learn in the production environment with a stream of live data being used to train the model. This type of procedure can be useful in increasing the performance over time. It is also very practical as the model doesn't require to be retrained but continuously learns from the upcoming new data. Continuous learning can also refer to incremental learning or online learning. Some experts distinguish these concepts from each other but it is possible to use them interchangeably. Continuous learning is very useful in cases where data behaviors and patterns change very quickly over time.

See also the following definitions: Active learning, zero shot learning, machine learning, and deep learning

Continuous variable

It is a floating value with an infinite range of possible values. It is opposed to discrete values. For example, the revenue of a population is a continuous variable.

See also the following definitions: Categorical Variable, variable, binary variable, discrete variable, dummy variable, nominal variable, and ordinal variable

Contrastive divergence

Contrastive divergence is a way of training graphical models. It is very popular with a restricted Boltzmann machine. It approximates the gradient of the log-likelihood based on a short Markov chain starting at the last seen example.

See also the following definitions: Restricted Boltzmann machine, Markov chain, and gradient descent

Convenience sampling

Convenience sampling means selecting training data for machine learning using a non-scientific approach. For example, it can be selecting the first hundred thousand observations from the database. Usually, convenience sampling is used for quick experimentation, but is followed by scientific sampling.

See also the following definitions: Bias, sampling, and bootstrapping

Convergence

Convergence is when a model that has been trained doesn't see its error reduced anymore or even by little if we add additional data for training. Convergence is the state that is desirable to be reached in machine learning training. The convergence is not always synonymous to a good model fit because sometimes, the gradient can converge to a local minimum meaning that it has a solution but the solution is not the best one (the global minimum).

See also the following definitions: Overfitting and gradient descent

Convex function

It is a real value function which has a shape close to a U. It is similar to this shape as follows:

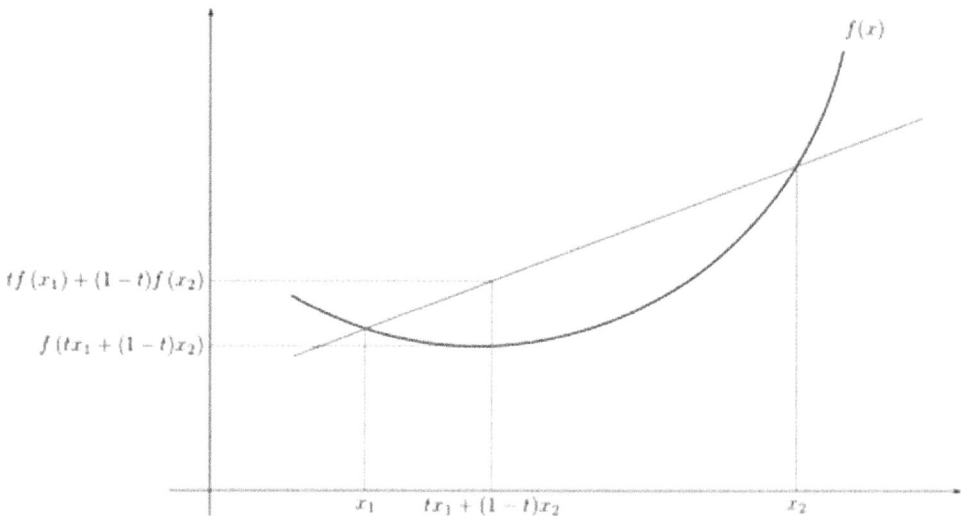

Figure 4.9: *A representation of a convex function*
(Source image: https://commons.wikimedia.org/wiki/File:ConvexFunction.svg)

In the optimization of the gradient in machine learning, some loss functions are convex functions like squared loss and log loss.

See also the following definitions: Sigmoid function

Convolution

Convolution is the dot product between a block of the input image and a convolutional filter and then summing up all the values of the output matrix. The convolutional filter is usually smaller than the block of pixels from the input image. The block of pixels is obtained by a sliding window on the input image. The convolution process is a key element in the convolutional neural network.

See also the following definitions: Convolutional neural network and deep learning

Convolutional layer

It is a deep neural network layer that contains a convolutional filter. This filter is multiplied by a block of pixels from the input image and the result matrix is summed up. For more details, see the definition of convolution.

See also the following definitions: Convolutional neural network and deep learning

Convolutional neural network

For more details, see the definition of CNN.

Correlation

Correlation is a statistical indicator that helps in discovering a causal relationship between two variables. This causal relationship can only be linear. The most popular correlation is the Pearson correlation. Mathematically, it represents the ratio of the covariance to a product of the variance of two variables. Its formula is as follows:

$$r = \frac{\sum_i (x_i - \bar{x})(y_i - \bar{y})}{\sqrt{\sum_i (x_i - \bar{x})^2} \sqrt{\sum_i (y_i - \bar{y})^2}}$$

See also the following definitions: Autocorrelation

Cosine similarity

Cosine similarity is a metric used in text mining to measure the similarities between documents. It has the following formula:

$$similarity = \cos(\theta) = \frac{A \cdot B}{\|A\| \, \|B\|}$$

The geometric representation of cosine similarity is as follows:

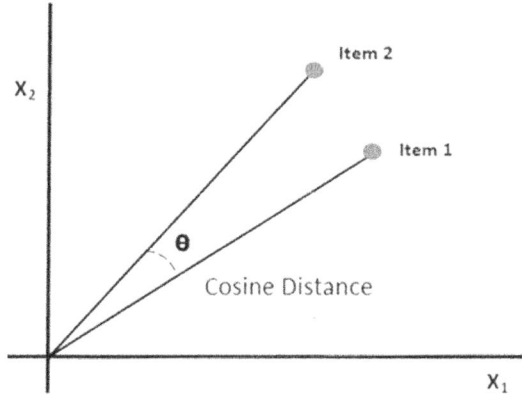

Figure 4.10: *A representation of cosine similarity*

Mathematically, it measures the cosine of the angle between two vectors. The smaller the angle, the higher is the similarity.

See also the following definitions: Natural language processing

Cost function

A cost function is also called loss function or objective function. It measures the errors of a machine learning model. It corresponds to the distance between the actual values vector and the predicted values vector. This cost function is then minimized in order to obtain a better model. There are different types of cost functions that behave differently such as mean square error, cross-entropy, exponential cost, Hellinger cost, KL divergence, and so on.

Hint:

How do we choose a cost function? Some cost functions are adapted to regression or classification problems. Also, based on their behavior, some cost functions amplify large errors such as mean square error compared to the mean absolute error.

See also the following definitions: Machine learning

Covariance

It is the measure of the join variability of two variables. This means that covariance captures the variation of two variables at the same time. It is similar to the variance except that the variance captures the variations of one variable. A positive covariance means that the variables move together in the same direction while a negative covariance means that the variables move inversely. Its formula is as follows:

$$cov(x, y) = \frac{\sum_i^n (x_i - \bar{x})(y_i - \bar{y})}{n - 1}$$

See also the following definitions: Variance, correlation, and autocorrelation

Coverage bias

Coverage bias means that a portion of the population is not represented in a sample. This bias is usually due to the way the sampling is performed. In machine learning, coverage bias relates to the fact that the sample that the model has been trained on doesn't match with the test dataset. Due to coverage bias, a machine learning model doesn't generalize very well.

See also the following definitions: Automation bias, bias, bias-variance trade-off, implicit bias, and sampling bias

CPU

It stands for central processing unit. It is an electronic component that executes all computer programs. In machine learning, CPU is a core component needed for the speed in training a model. Training a machine learning model can be time-consuming. Therefore, parallelized computing over the cores of the CPUs is necessary sometimes in order to speed up the training.

See also the following definitions: GPU

Cross-entropy

Cross-entropy is used in machine learning models to define the loss function of a classification problem. It is commonly used to quantify the difference between two probability distributions.

$$Crossentropy(p, q) = -\sum_{x} p(x)\log(q(x))$$

p is the true probability and q is the actual probability.

See also the following definitions: Classification and evaluation metrics

Cross validation

Cross validation is a sampling technic that is used to evaluate a machine learning model's performance. The training dataset is split in multiple subsets and during training; the model is evaluated against the subset. This technic is good for avoiding overfitting and to see if the model generalizes well. There are different types of cross validations such as k fold cross validation, stratified k fold cross validation, leave one out cross validation, and adversarial cross validation.

See also the following definitions: Sampling and bootstrapping

CUDA

It is a computing platform that allows developing and computing on a **GPU** (**graphical processing unit**). The computing is performed in parallel which makes the computing faster. CUDA is used as a layer for TensorFlow, PyTorch, and other deep learning frameworks.

See also the following definitions: GPU and NVIDIA

Chapter 5
D

Dashboard

A dashboard is a visual user interface that regroups the key KPI related to a business process. Sometimes, a dashboard is used interchangeably with the report. However, a dashboard is more focused on the global performance and the key metrics. An example of a dashboard is as follows:

Figure 5.1: *A representation of a financial dashboard*
(Source image: https://commons.wikimedia.org/wiki/File:Screenshot_Dashboard.png)

A dashboard is not static as it is updated continuously based on new information stored in the databases. A dashboard provides several benefits to a business as it helps in capturing trends, getting a better view of the business, defining objectives and goals, and so on.

See also the following definitions: Business intelligence and business analytics

Data analysis

Data analysis is the ability to transform, visualize, and model data in order to gather insights and conclusions. It can be used in several domains like science, business, or social science. In business, data analysis supports decision-making and explaining various phenomenon. In data science, data analysis is divided into descriptive statistics and exploratory data analysis.

See also the following definitions: Data science, big data, and data mining

Data augmentation

Data augmentation is the process of creating artificially new data from an original dataset. This process is useful in case when the training data is not enough for obtaining a good model performance. Data augmentation is very popular in training data with images. The process of data augmentation can be done using a deep neural network like the generative adversarial neural network. It can be used in increasing the size of the training set and also in increasing the diversity by modifying the original images (rotation, color channels, positions, and so on). This helps the model to generalize better.

See also the following definitions: Dataset

Data engineering

Data engineering in data science refers to the focus on data collection and data access. Data engineering allows data scientists to have access to consistent information continuously. It requires expertise such as system architecture, programming, database design, and so on and the knowledge of tools like Hadoop, Spark, NoSQL, SQL, and so on. Hence, data engineering not only focuses on relational data but also on big data and the ability to access this information.

See also the following definitions: Data science, big data, and ETL

Data mining

Data mining's goal is to discover patterns, correlations, anomalies, and knowledge in data using domains and tools such as machine learning, statistics, visualization, and mathematics applied to structured and unstructured data. Data mining is sometimes used interchangeably with data science or business intelligence. However, the term business intelligence refers to the visualization and reporting part only of data mining whereas data science refers to a larger domain that includes artificial intelligence.

See also the following definitions: Data analysis and data science

Data parallelism

Data parallelism is the parallelization of computing across multiple processors. Parallel computing can make the computing faster by using multiple processors at once. This technique is very popular in data science especially with large datasets that cannot be processed at once by a single processor.

See also the following definitions: GPU and CPU

Data preparation

Data preparation or data pre-processing is the part of a data science project where raw data is manipulated and transformed to obtain cleaner and more usable data for the next steps like data exploration or modeling. It includes steps like data aggregation, data cleansing, data transformation, deriving new variables, merging different data sources, and so on. This step is crucial in a data science project as raw data cannot be explored easily and modeling on data that is not prepared will result in a lower performance.

See also the following definitions: Data science, data transformation, and data wrangling

Data science

Data science is an inter-disciplinary field that helps in optimizing business processes based on a solution that exploits data. The outcome of data science is business analytics solutions such as predictive analytics, prescriptive analytics, or cognitive analytics. Data science is performed by data scientist with a background in computer science, mathematics, or statistics. The field of data science has popular sub-domains such as machine learning and artificial intelligence. Data science projects are managed by using the data science life cycle schema which helps in defining a routine in a data science project and increasing the chances of a project to become live.

Hint: What is the difference between business intelligence and data science? Business intelligence focuses on creating two types of business analytics solutions: descriptive and diagnostic analytics. Data science focuses on creating three types of business analytics solutions: predictive, prescriptive, and cognitive analytics.

What is the difference between business analytics and data science? Business analytics and data science are two different terms as data science contributes in building some business analytics levels. It also contributes in building three levels of business analytics: predictive analytics, prescriptive analytics, and cognitive analytics.

See also the following definitions: Data mining, data analysis, and business intelligence

Data transformation

Data transformation is a process that is performed by data scientists during the data preparation step. Data can be transformed in various ways depending on the format, the type, and the purpose. The most popular data transformation is natural logarithm for a continuous target variable to erase a skew in data. The one hot encoding transformation is used to transform categorical variables into dummies; binning transformation is used to create categories for continuous variables, and more.

See also the following definitions: Data preparation and data wrangling

Data wrangling

Data wrangling can also refer to data preparation except that data wrangling stores data for further analysis whereas data preparation is followed directly by another step which is data exploration. In data wrangling, raw data is manipulated, transformed, and enriched, and then stored for further analysis.

See also the following definitions: Data preparation and data transformation

Database

A database is a structured collection of data. The data is easily accessible using a programming language such as SQL. Relational databases are organized in tables with keys to link the tables. In data science, relational databases and databases in general are the main sources of data for data scientists.

See also the following definitions: Data engineering and ETL

Databricks

Databricks is a unified data science platform. It runs with Spark and allows access to notebooks in different programming languages. It is supported by different vendors such as Microsoft.

See also the following definitions: Watson Studio, Anaconda, and Jupyter notebook

DataFrame

It is a 2-dimensional data structure with columns and rows. This structure is created by pandas, a library in Python. A dataframe is the most-used pandas object in Python. While creating a dataframe, you can pass an argument like an index or column to specify each of them. A dataframe accepts many types of inputs such as 2-D numpy, ndarray, a series, another dataframe, lists, and so on.

See also the following definitions: Dataset and Python

Dataset

A dataset is a group or a collection of data. Each value in a dataset is associated with a variable and an observation (a row and a column). A variable regroups values that have the same attributes and an observation regroups values that describe the attributes of a unique unit. A dataset can be stored in a different format such as CSV, Excel, JSON, XML, and so on. A dataset can also consist of a collection of unstructured data such as a dataset of documents or images.

See also the following definitions: Data transformation, data preparation, and training set

Davies-Bouldin index

Davies-Bouldin index is an evaluation metric for a clustering algorithm. The index measures the similarity between the clusters using the distances between the center of the cluster. A cluster that is a part and less dispersed has a better index. The lower that the value of the index is, the better is the clustering.

See also the following definitions: Evaluation metrics and clustering

DBSCAN

It stands for "Density-Based Spatial Clustering of Applications with Noise." It is a density-based clustering algorithm for unsupervised machine learning tasks. This technic groups together points that are close to each other to create clusters. This clustering algorithm has two hyperparameters: distance between points and the minimum number of points to form a dense region. The way that this algorithm works is easy to understand: First, it will randomly select a point. Then, it will find all the points around it using the distance parameter. If there are enough points around, it will create a cluster. Then, a new point is selected and a new cluster is created. A density-based algorithm's visualization is as follows:

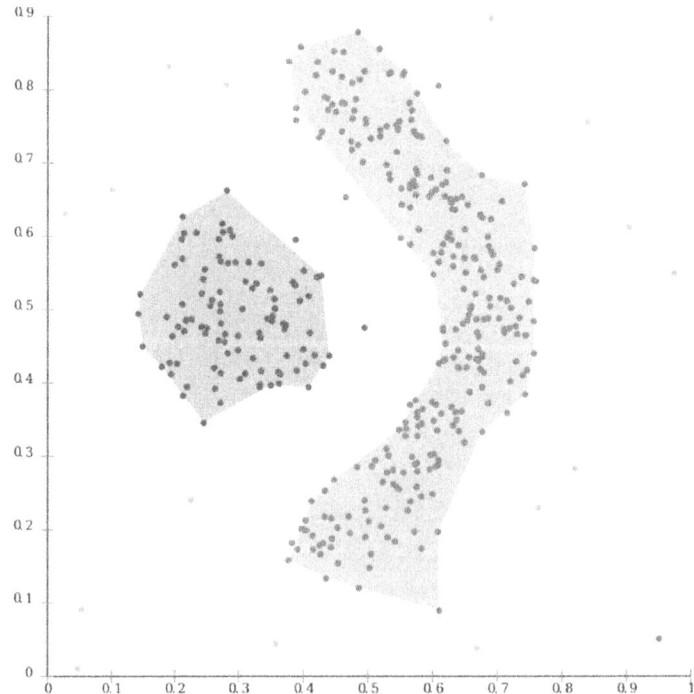

Figure 5.2: Density-based algorithm DBSCAN
(Source image: https://commons.wikimedia.org/wiki/File:DBSCAN-density-data.svg)

Note that for the points that have low density neighbors, they will be marked as outliers.

See also the following definitions: Agglomerative clustering, hierarchical clustering, clustering, and divisive clustering

Decile

Decile is a descriptive statistic that represents nine values that separate the data into ten equal parts. Each part represents 1/10th of the data. A decile table is as follows:

Decile	Number of Customers	Number of Responses	Response Rate (%)	Cumulative Responses	Cumulative Response Rate (%)	Cumulative Response Lift
top	2500	2179	87.2	2179	87.2	447
2	2500	1753	70.1	3932	78.6	403
3	2500	396	15.8	4328	57.7	296
4	2500	111	4.4	4439	44.4	228
5	2500	110	4.4	4549	36.4	187
6	2500	85	3.4	4634	30.9	158
7	2500	67	2.7	4701	26.9	138
8	2500	69	2.8	4770	23.9	122
9	2500	49	2.0	4819	21.4	110
bottom	2500	55	2.2	4874	19.5	100
Total	25,000	4874	19.5			

Figure 5.3: A table with data separated in decile
(Source image: Evolutionary Algorithms in Data Mining: Multi-Objective Performance Modeling for Direct Marketing - Scientific Figure on ResearchGate. Available from: https://www.researchgate.net/figure/Sample-Decile-Analysis_tbl1_2472517)

Note: A decile is similar to a quartile as it splits the data into equal parts.

See also the following definitions: Descriptive statistics

Decision boundary

Decision boundary is a method that is used in a classification problem to separate the vector space into regions where each class belongs to one region. Decision boundaries are represented in black as follows:

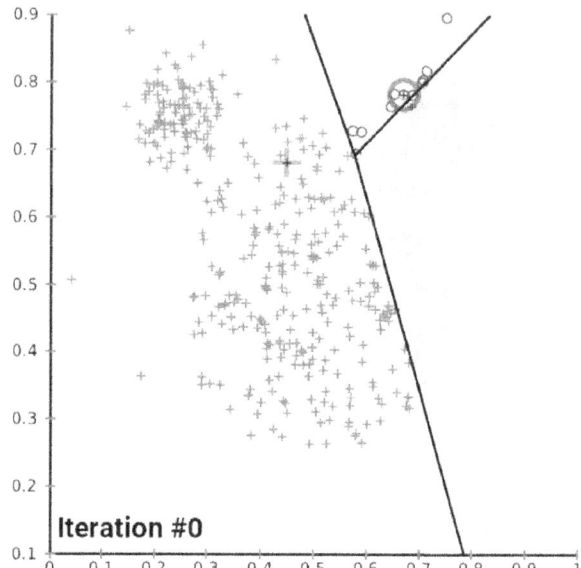

Figure 5.4: *A representation of decision boundaries for three classes (Source image: https://en.wikipedia.org/wiki/K-means_clustering)*

Decision boundary is a technique that is used to analyze a classifier's performance.

See also the following definitions: Classifier and classification

Decision tree

A decision tree is a tree graph-based algorithm that is used for supervised machine learning tasks, either regression or classification. It is one of the most popular algorithms for supervised machine learning, as it can map non-linear relationships. Methods like random forest or XGboost are based on decision trees. The way the decision tree works is that the sample is split into homogeneous subsets based on the most significant splitter in the input data. The following image illustrates how the decision tree split works:

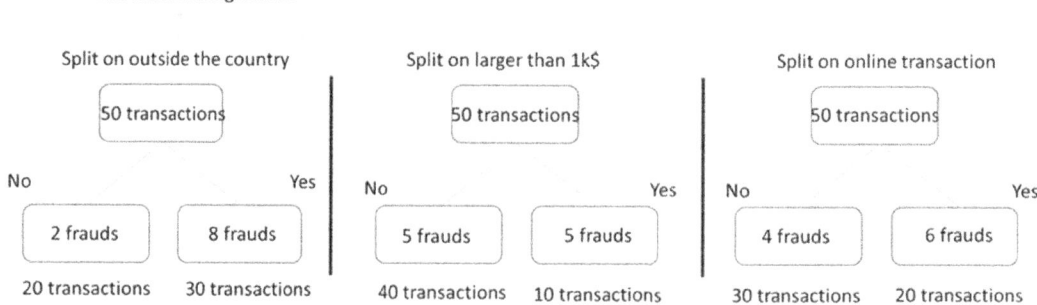

Figure 5.5: *A representation of how decision tree split is performed*

Let's take an example to explain the phenomenon: Let's say we have 50 bank transactions and the variables are: is the transaction outside the country, is the transaction larger than 1k$, is the transaction online. We know that 10 out of the 50 bank transactions are fraudulent. Now we would like to predict if a transaction is fraudulent or not. Among all three variables, we have to segregate transactions that are fraudulent based on highly significant variables. The decision tree will segregate the transaction by identifying the variable that creates the best homogeneous sets of transaction. Homogeneous means that the value of the variable is providing the same output for each group.

See also the following definitions: XGBoost and Random Forest

Deduction

Deduction or deductive reasoning is a basic reasoning type, where it goes from the general to the specific. It starts with a general statement and examines the possibilities to reach a specific conclusion.

See also the following definitions: Induction

Deep belief network

Deep belief network or DBN is a type of deep neural network composed of multiple restricted Boltzmann machines where each layer communicates with another but the nodes within a single layer don't communicate with each other and at the end, we have a feed-forward neural network. DBN works in two steps, first the pre-training and then the classification. The architecture of a DBN is as follow:

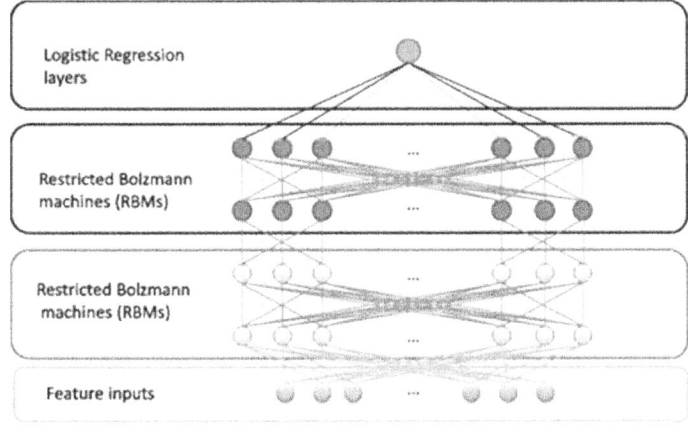

Figure 5.6: *An example of the architecture of a deep belief network*
(Source image: https://medium.com/analytics-army/deep-belief-networks-an-introduction-1d52bb867a25)

Deep belief network has several applications such as image recognition where an image is the input and the category is the output, video recognition, motion-capture data, and so on. Thanks to DBN it is possible to achieve faster training and better performance.

See also the following definitions: Deep learning and restricted Boltzmann machine

Deep dream

The deep dream is a technique in computer vision created by Google. This technique uses a deep convolutional neural network to generate images or transform images into a dream-like vision. An example of deep dream output is as follow:

Figure 5.7: *A representation of deep dream technique*
(Source image: https://commons.wikimedia.org/wiki/File:Deep-dream-white-noise-0046.jpg)

The initial idea of the program was to succeed in better understanding the functioning of convolutional neural networks, in particular, what happens at each layer.

See also the following definitions: Computer vision and AlexNet

Deep learning

Deep learning is a sub-field in machine learning based on an artificial neural network. It applies to supervised, semi-supervised, and unsupervised learning. Deep learning has several types of architecture, such as recurrent neural network, convolutional neural network, deep neural network, deep belief networks, and so on. A simple architecture of deep learning is as follow:

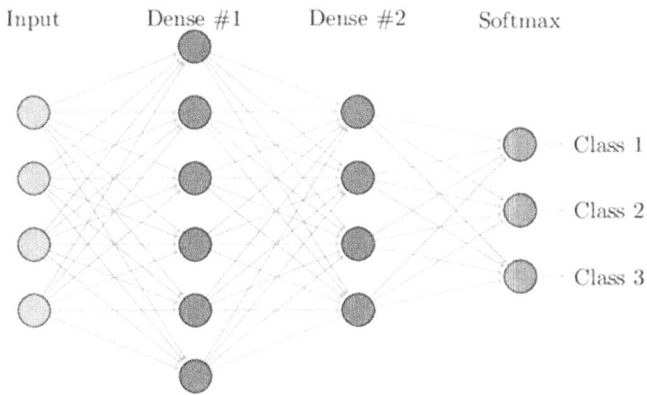

Figure 5.8: *A deep learning representation*
(Source image: Temporal Convolutional Neural Network for the Classification of Satellite Image Time Series - Scientific Figure on ResearchGate. Available from: https://www.researchgate.net/figure/Example-of-fully-connected-neural-network_fig2_331525817)

Its applications are numerous like image recognition, image generation, video recognition, audio generation, machine translation, speech recognition, natural language processing, autonomous cars, and so on. At the origin, in the '80s deep learning was costly in computing power and costly in data. Thanks to the democratization of GPUs and the access to a large amount of data, deep learning is now a technique used at large by scientists and professional data scientist. The difference between deep learning and a simple neural network is the add-on of multiple hidden layers. Compared to other traditional machine learning techniques, deep learning doesn't require feature extraction prior to training as it will extract its own abstract features from the data. This process is called representation learning. One of the most interesting parts about deep learning is the way parameters are updated; this process is called backpropagation. From the error, function weight updates are backpropagated until the first layer's parameters. Deep learning offers a lot more flexibility than traditional machine learning models. It is capable of saving parameters and then initiates a new deep learning model with the saved parameters and reuses the knowledge learned from a task to another one; this is called transfer learning.

See also the following definitions: Convolutional neural network, and recurrent neural network

Deep Q-network

In deep Q-learning, deep Q-network is a deep neural network that approximates the Q-value function. It takes the state as input and the Q-value of all possible actions as output.

See also the following definitions: Deep learning and Q function

Deeplearning4j

Deeplearning4j is an open-source deep learning library written for Java and Scala. The library includes several deep learning algorithms and has a distributed parallel version that integrates with Hadoop and Spark.

See also the following definitions: Caffe, Tensorflow, Pytorch, and Torch

Degree of freedom

Degree of freedom is a parameter used in hypothesis testing such as the Chi-squared test. It represents the number of values in a sample that have the freedom to vary independently. Usually, the formula of the degree of freedom is the sample size minus one. As an example, let's suppose you have five positive integers. The 5 integers are completely random and can be any value and each of them is independent of the others. Let's suppose now that 4 of them are {1, 4, 9, 10} and the mean of the 5 positive integers is 7. The fifth value has no choice to be 11. So, the degree of freedom is 4 which is 5 the sample size minus one.

See also the following definitions: Chi-squared test

Dense feature

Dense feature is an array or a tensor containing mostly non-zero values.

See also the following definitions: Tensor and deep learning

Dense layer

A dense layer is a layer in the deep neural network where all inputs of a previous layer are fully connected to the nodes in the next layer. The dense layer is also known as the fully connected layer or affine layer. For more details see affine layer definition.

See also the following definitions: Deep learning, convolutional neural network, and recurrent neural network

Density-based algorithm

It is an unsupervised machine learning technique that regroups data in a different cluster. As the name suggests, this clustering technique is based on creating a cluster around high-density points. One of the most popular density-based clustering algorithms is DBScan. For more details see the DBScan definition.

See also the following definitions: Clustering, hierarchical clustering, agglomerative clustering, divisive clustering, and unsupervised learning

Dependent variable

A dependent variable is a variable that changes based on other factors. For example, the study of the correlation between variable A and variable B to understand how A changes upon B, makes variable A dependent variable.

In machine learning, a dependent variable represents the target variable or the variable we would like to predict (output variable), based on independent variables or predictors (input variable).

See also the following definitions: Target variable

Deployment as API

After building a machine learning model, the idea is to deploy this model. Deploy means put it in production to be able to use it as a solution to optimize a business process. There are several deployment types depending on the business case. The most common deployment is as an API or REST API. To deploy in API means to wrap the model with the ability to predict or score and then deploy it on a server as a REST API. The API will be integrated with other software and the backend. It will then receive requests from the software to provide a prediction for a particular case. An API is a black box containing codes that allow communication with different software and programs. An API deployment is useful for a company when there is a need to consume prediction lives and to be integrated within the software.

See also the following definitions: Watson studio, Databricks, and deployment in batch

Deployment in batch

Batch deployment is a deployment against a database or within a program (ETL). The batch deployment in machine learning will score or predict multiple examples at once based on a schedule that runs periodically. Batch deployment is useful in case a company would like to have machine learning scores available on the database or dropped periodically in a repository (in CSV, JSON).

See also the following definitions: Watson studio, Databricks, and deployment as API

Depth

It represents the number of layers in the deep neural network algorithm. The layers included are hidden layers and the output layer.

See also the following definitions: Hidden layer, deep learning, and output layer

Depth-wise separable convolutional neural network

Depth-wise separable convolutional neural network or DSCNN is a type of convolutional neural network. This type of CNN is very popular as it reduces overfitting because it has less parameters and it's cheaper in computation because it supports less computation. Google has created several deep learning architectures that include DSCNN like MobileNet or Xception. The main difference between CNN and DSCNN is the way the convolution is computed. For DSCNN, the convolution is done using filters that are applied for every channel. With this approach, DSCNN computes 100 times fewer multiplications as compared to a normal convolutional neural network.

See also the following definitions: Convolutional neural network, recurrent neural network, and deep learning

Descriptive statistics

Descriptive statistics help describe, understand, and summarize features in a given dataset. Descriptive statistics can be mean, median, mode, minimum, maximum, standard deviation, variance, kurtosis, and skewness. Visualization in descriptive statistics can be distribution, frequency, bar char, and so on.

In machine learning projects, using descriptive statistics is very important as it helps to understand the data and potentially any bias in the data such as extreme values or outliers, skewed data, features that need to be normalized, and so on. Descriptive statistics is the first step in exploratory data analysis.

See also the following definitions: Decile, bar chart, variance, and mean

Device

It's a name used by some libraries or frameworks to identify the processor that can be either CPU or GPU.

See also the following definitions: CPU and GPU

Dimensionality reduction

Dimensionality reduction is a technique for reducing the number of variables in a dataset. The results obtained are the principal variables. Dimensionality reduction is possible by feature extraction or feature selection. In feature selection, dimensionality reduction consists of selecting the most relevant variables in the dataset using techniques like variance importance. In feature extraction, the dimensionality reduction consists of reducing data from high-dimension to lower dimension. The techniques used are principal component analysis, linear discriminant analysis, generalized discriminant analysis, and so on. The main advantages of dimensionality reduction are reducing space storage required for data, less memory usage when manipulating data, removing multicollinearity from data, improving machine learning model's performance by reducing the noise in data, and so on.

See also the following definitions: Principal component analysis (PCA), Factor Analysis

Discounted cumulative gain

It corresponds to a measure of ranking quality for information retrieval. It is used as an evaluation metric for search engines. It is based on the position of the document in the result listing and it has the following formula:

$$DCG_p = \sum_{i=1}^{p} \frac{rel_i}{\log_2(i+1)}$$

Where rel_i is the graded relevance of the result at position i.

See also the following definitions: Evaluation metrics

Discrete variable

A discrete variable is a variable with a finite amount of values, as opposed to a continuous variable. If the variable name is fruits, it is a finite amount of fruits so it is a discrete variable. If the variable name is time, it is an infinite amount of time so it is a continuous variable.

See also the following definitions: Binary Variable, variable, categorical variable, continuous variable, dummy variable, nominal variable, and ordinal variable

Discriminative model

A discriminative model models the decision boundary between classes for classification problems. It will distinguish between classes based on the different properties learned from data. A discriminative model is usually opposed to a generative model, which has different properties like explicitly models the distribution of each class instead of learning the different properties. Usually, discriminative models perform better than generative models if we have a large amount of data.

See also the following definitions: Classification, machine learning, and generative classification

Discriminator

It is one of the two models used in a generative adversarial neural network. The discriminator is in charge of distinguishing if the examples created by the generator are real or fake. So, the discriminator is a classifier and usually it is a recurrent neural network like LSTM.

See also the following definitions: Generative adversarial neural networks and generator

Divisive clustering

Divisive clustering is a specific type of hierarchical clustering. Divisive is a top-down approach where all observations start into an initial cluster and then are subdivided as we move down the hierarchy. The way divisive clustering works is as follow:

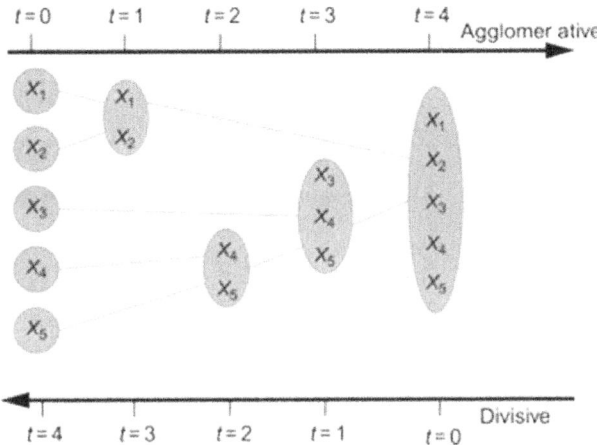

*Figure 5.9: Difference between agglomerative and divisive
(Source image: https://www.sciencedirect.com/topics/computer-science/divisive-clustering)*

Divisive clustering is opposed to the agglomerative approach, which consists of bottom-up when starting with one cluster per data point.

See also the following definitions: Clustering, hierarchical clustering, agglomerative clustering, and unsupervised learning

Downpour stochastic gradient descent

Downpour SGD is an asynchronous version of SGD created by Google. On a subset of training data, it runs copies of a model in parallel. Then the updates are sent to a parameter's server, which is split across multiple machines. A schema of downpour SDG is as follow:

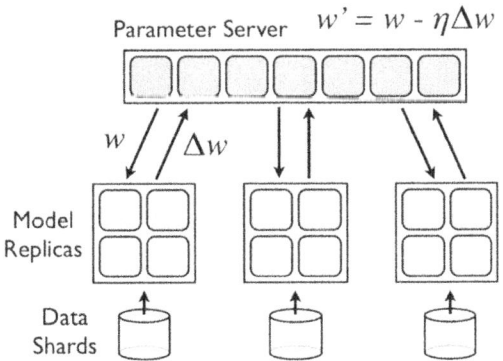

*Figure 5.10: A representation of downpour
(Source image: Dean, Jeffrey, Gregory S. Corrado, Rajat Monga, Kai Chen, Matthieu Devin, Quoc V. Le, Mark Z. Mao, Marc'AurelioRanzato, Andrew W. Senior, Paul A. Tucker, Ke Yang and Andrew Y. Ng. "Large Scale Distributed Deep Networks." NIPS (2012).)*

Each machine stores and updates a fraction of the model's parameters. However, models don't share updates and weights with each other; everything is centralized around the parameter's server. This approach puts the parameters of the replicas at risk of diverging. Still, the speed of training increases with this approach.

See also the following definitions: Gradient descent, AdaDelta, AdaGrad, Adam Optimization, and Optimizer

Downsampling

In the case where the dataset is imbalanced, with a class minority that is underrepresented and another class that is over represented (for example, 0.5% of group 1 and 99.5% of group 0), it is possible to use downsampling to resize the group that is overrepresented. This resizing means reducing the amount of observation in that group. With this technique, the classification model will better capture the underrepresented group and not consider it as noise. Downsampling helps balance between the majority class and minority class ratio.

Another type of downsampling in image recognition is reducing the image resolution from high-quality to low-quality or by reducing the image size.

See also the following definitions: Upsampling and sampling

Dplyr

Dplyr is a powerful package for data manipulation in R. It helps with data transformation, data cleaning, and data summarization very easily.

See also the following definitions: R and data transformation

DropConnect

Dropout works by randomly changing to zero a subset of activation functions output in a layer while DropConnect changes randomly to zero a subset of the weights in a layer. The difference between DropConnect and Dropout is illustrated below:

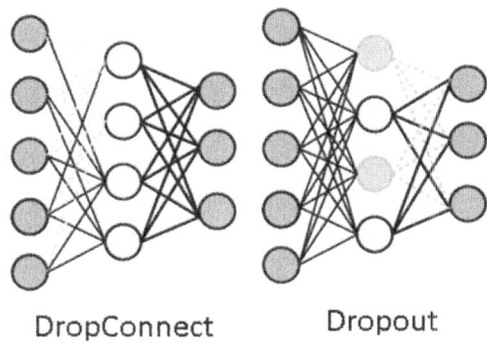

Figure 5.11: *A visual of how dropout and DropConnect works*

DropConnect is a generalization of Dropout applied to fully connected layers.

See also the following definitions: Activation function, weights, and layer

Dropout regularization

Dropout is a technique for the regularization of a neural network; it prevents overfitting. Dropout will randomly set to zero outputs of activation functions. This is helpful to avoid the neural network from relying on one pattern of weights which can cause overfitting.

See also the following definitions: Regularization, overfitting, neural network, and deep learning

Dummy variable

Also known as the Boolean variable, the dummy variable takes the values 0 or 1. For instance, is the email a spam True/1 or not a spam False/0.

See also the following definitions: Discrete variable, binary variable, variable, categorical variable, continuous variable, nominal variable, and ordinal variable

Dunn index

Dunn index is an evaluation metric for clustering algorithms. Dunn index tries to identify clusters that are compact with small variance, with clusters that are distinctively separated from each other. More Dunn index is high the better are the clusters.

See also the following definitions: Evaluation metrics and clustering

Dynamic model

A dynamic model is a machine learning model that is training online, meaning that each time a new data comes the model is trained on this new data. The dynamic model is opposed to the static model, which is trained offline. The trade-off between dynamic or static comes from the data, if the data doesn't change over time and has a constant pattern static model is preferred if the data changes over time very fast, a dynamic model is better.

See also the following definitions: Static model

Dynamic programming

Dynamic programming is in computer programming the ability to split complex problems into sub-problems that are simpler than all this in a recursive manner. So, the result of sub-problems will be stored to be reused later. This optimization reduces time complexity from exponential to polynomial.

See also the following definitions: Python and R

CHAPTER 6
E

Early stopping

Early stopping is a technique to avoid overfitting in machine learning algorithm training. Early stopping will stop the training before all iterations are completed, as it stops when the performance on the validation dataset stops increasing. Early stopping has two parameters – the number of iterations and the validation dataset. If the performance doesn't increase the algorithm will stop.

See also the following definitions: Overfitting and validation set

EDA

EDA stands for Exploratory Data Analysis; it is a step in a data science project life cycle where data scientists focus on understanding the data and gathering insights that will be useful to build machine learning models, through data visualization and statistical analysis. EDA is one of the most important steps in a data science project as it helps get key information on the data to be able to build the best and most performant machine learning model.

See also the following definitions: Data transformation and data preparation

ELU

Exponential Linear Unit (ELU) is an activation function used in a deep neural network and to add non-linearity to the neural network. ELU tends to make cost function converges to zero faster and it produces more accurate results. It has the following formula:

$$R(z) = \begin{cases} z & z > 0 \\ \alpha(e^z - 1) & z \leq 0 \end{cases}$$

The representation of the ELU function is as follows:

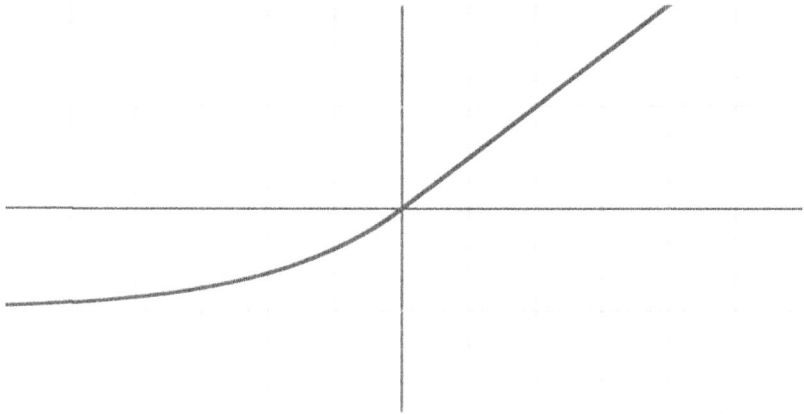

Figure 6.1: ELU activation function visual approximation (Source image: https://en.wikipedia.org/wiki/File:Activation_elu.svg)

ELU is a good alternative to the RELU activation function and it can produce negative values.

See also the following definitions: Activation function, ReLU and softmax

Embedding space

An embedding space is a low-dimensional space where we can map a higher-dimensional space. Embedding space or embedding is a useful technique in machine learning where we have a large input size and would like to reduce the size of the input, like in natural language processing with word embeddings. Embedding is a technique in the field of dimensionality reduction.

See also the following definitions: Natural language processing and embeddings

Embeddings

Embedding maps a high-dimensional vector with a low-dimensional vector. It is usually popular with natural language processing where a vector of words is represented first as a sparse vector where each value is either zero or one based on the words in a sentence. With embedding, this sparse vector can be converted to a dense vector with a smaller shape and where values are between zero and one.

See also the following definitions: Natural language processing and embedding space

Ensemble learning algorithm

Ensemble learning is a meta-algorithm that regroups predictions from multiple models into one result. The goal of the ensemble is either to reduce the bias or reduce the variance. The most popular ensemble techniques are bagging and boosting. The ensemble is usually based on multiple models called **weak learner** as they are individually weak but together they form a strong learner.

See also the following definitions: Boosting and bagging

Ensemble models:

For more details see the ensemble learning algorithm.

Entropy

Entropy is the measure of purity in the data or in the groups. It varies between 0 and 1. Suppose you have two groups A and B. Group A has 10 persons and group B has 0 persons in it. So, the entropy for group A and B is equal to 0, meaning that the purity or the way the data is ordered is perfect. Entropy can be used in machine learning as a statistical metric or in decision trees to help build trees:

$$E(S) = \sum_{i=1}^{c} -p_i \log_2(p_i)$$

See also the following definitions: Decision tree

Episode

An episode represents in reinforcement learning a complete sequence of states, actions, and rewards where the agent tried to learn the environment. Applied to gaming an episode can represent a completed game session or a group of game sessions. An episode is close to an epoch in meaning as they both represent a group of data presented to an algorithm.

See also the following definitions: Reinforcement learning, action, and agent

Epoch

An epoch is when a machine learning model has seen a full training dataset once. The epoch can be defined as a hyperparameter and its change can affect the model's performance as too many epochs can conduct to overfitting situation and fewer epochs can conduct to underfitting situation.

See also the following definitions: Training set, hyperparameter, and overfitting

Epsilon greedy policy

Epsilon greedy policy is a policy used in reinforcement learning that defines a decreasing factor that can cause either a random policy or a greedy policy. It means epsilon defines the factor randomly if the agent will state a random action (exploration) or will state a predicted action (exploitation). And the interaction of the epsilon greedy policy is as illustrated:

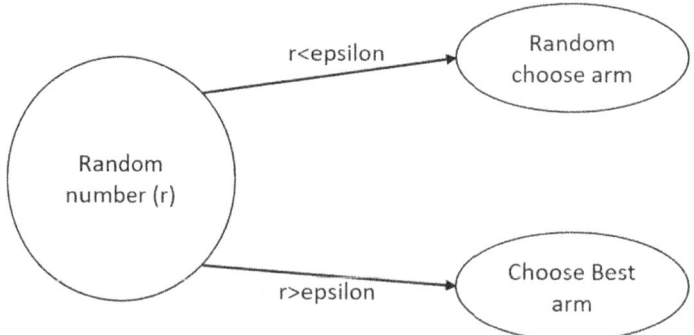

Figure 6.2: *The way epsilon defines random or not action*

Note that the epsilon greedy policy is useful for the agent to explore new paths.

See also the following definitions: Reinforcement learning, episode, action, and agent

ETL

Extract Transform and Load (ETL) is a process used to structure data from various sources. ETL will extract data from different sources, enhance data quality and cleansing, standardize format, and deliver data ready for exploitation. ETL is usually used to help build applications for business intelligence and data-driven solutions.

See also the following definitions: Data engineering, data preparation, and data science

Euclidean distance

The Euclidean distance is the distance that connects two points in ordinary Euclidean space. The Euclidean distance is the most common way to compute distances between two points. The formula of the Euclidean distance is based on the Pythagorean theorem as follow:

$$Euclidean_{Distance} = \sqrt{\sum_{i=1}^{n}(p_i - q_i)^2}$$

Another way to compute the distance is by using Manhattan distance. For more details see Manhattan distance.

See also the following definitions: Manhattan distance

Evaluation metric

An evaluation metric is a way of measuring a machine learning model performance. Each type of machine learning algorithm (classification, regression, unsupervised, binary classification, and so on) has its own evaluation metric. Some evaluation metrics are formulas, while others are visuals. For the classification metric, we have cross-entropy, confusion matrix, AUC ROC, accuracy, and F1 Score and for regression, we have mean square error, mean absolute error, and coefficient of determination. For the unsupervised metric, we have machine learning silhouette coefficient, Dunn index, Davies-Bouldin index, and so on.

See also the following definitions: Accuracy, Dunn index, area under the ROC curve (AUC), and coefficient of determination

Example

An example corresponds to one observation within a dataset. This observation contains one or more features and a label (target variable). If the label is not provided, we talk about the unlabeled example.

See also the following definitions: Dataset and training set

Experimentation

Usually in machine learning, and especially in deep learning, finding the optimal model with the right hyperparameters requires multiple trials and errors. These trials and errors are called experimentation. Experimentations are done in a way that all the hyperparameters and parameters are saved for further analysis and we keep a track record of the work done.

See also the following definitions: Hyperparameter and machine learning

Expert system

The expert system was the first form of artificial intelligence built by human. They are designed to solve complex problems by reasoning based on a set of knowledge and by using a rule-based algorithm (if-then algorithms). The expert system doesn't necessarily rely on machine learning as its inference engine can be based on the rules fixed by engineers.

See also the following definitions: Artificial intelligence

Exploding gradient problem

Exploding gradient problem is opposed to vanishing gradient problem. In exploding the gradient problem in a deep neural network, the gradient updates become very high (explode) during backpropagation. This makes the model almost impossible to train; the weights updates are very large at each batch and the model cannot converge. A way to avoid the exploding gradient problem is gradient clipping. For more details see clipping definition.

See also the following definitions: Vanishing gradient problem and backpropagation

Exploration vs. exploitation

Exploration or exploitation is usually a trade-off. In machine learning, exploration vs exploitation can be used in production to compare the model's performance, where the best model is being used 80% of the time and the remaining 20% we test other models in order to discover the new potential best models. This trade-off is called exploration vs. exploitation as the idea is to find the right balance between acquiring new knowledge (exploration) and maximizing revenues/performance (exploitation).

Exploration and exploitation are also used in reinforcement learning with the epsilon greedy policy where we set an epsilon value and compare it to a random value to know if we explore new paths or we exploit the best model, as epsilon decreases over time, the exploitation is more frequent.

See also the following definitions: Deployment as API and reinforcement learning

Exponential family distribution

Exponential family regroups the following distribution: normal, exponential, gamma, chi-square, beta, Bernoulli, categorical, Poisson, geometric, and so on. And they correspond to a single-parameter for a discrete or continuous probability distribution.

See also the following definitions: Bernoulli distribution, binomial distribution, chi-squared distribution, Gaussian distribution, t-distribution, normal distribution, and Poisson distribution

Exponential loss

It represents all loss functions that contain an exponential function such as AdaBoost. The exponential loss is convex and grows exponentially for negative values so it is more sensitive to outliers as it will return a high error for outliers.

See also the following definitions: Loss function, hinge loss, focal loss, log loss, magnet loss, Huber loss, L1 loss, L2 loss, and squared loss

Exponential smoothing

Exponential smoothing is a forecasting technique in time series forecasting. Exponential smoothing is simple techniques where the actual observation is summed up with the forecasted observation and both are weighted with an exponentially decreasing weight, forecasted observation are given more weight than the actual observation. It has the following formula:

$$F_{t+1} = \alpha A_t + (1 - \alpha)F_t$$

F_{t+1} is the forecasted value at t+1, α is the parameter for exponential smoothing, A_t is the actual value at t, F_t is the forecasted value at t.

Note that exponential smoothing is a good technique for short-term forecasting since long-term forecasting with exponential smoothing is less reliable.

See also the following definitions: ARIMA and time series

Extrapolation

In mathematics, extrapolation is the calculation of a point on a curve for which there is no equation outside the interval (or zone) for which it has experimental data. The extrapolation is opposed to the interpolation, where estimation is related to a point inside the experimental zone.

In machine learning, it corresponds to the ability of a model to predict values based on an unseen situation. A visual representation of extrapolated and interpolated is illustrated as follows:

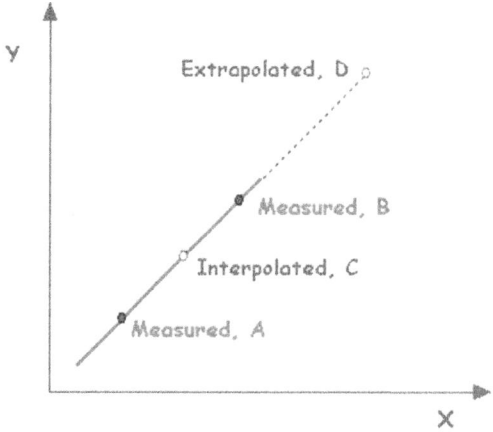

Figure 6.3: *Interpolation vs. extrapolation*
(Source image: https://commons.wikimedia.org/wiki/File:NM19_103.gif)

Extrapolation is a close concept to generalization.

See also the following definitions: Deduction and induction

Extreme values

Extreme value or extremum corresponds to a minimum or maximum value in data. Sometimes extremum falls outside the distribution of the data, in this case, it is common to apply a transformation on the extreme values. Especially in machine learning, we try to discard the extreme values that are at the extreme of the data distribution, a technique to discard the extreme values is by replacing them with mean or median, or delete the observation containing the extreme value. A specific type of extreme values is outliers that are values outside the general trend of the data.

See also the following definitions: Outlier and clipping

CHAPTER 7
F

F1 Score

F1 score or F-measure is an evaluation metric for classification problems and it combines both precision and recall to create a balance between both of them. F1 score is a good alternative to classification accuracy as it can handle better a large imbalanced number of true negative vs. true positive. It has the following formula:

$$F1 = 2 * \frac{Precision * Recall}{Precision + Recall}$$

See also the following definitions: Evaluation metrics, classification, precision, and recall

Face recognition

Face recognition is a technology capable of detecting and identifying a person on an image using the face's unique characteristics from images or videos. Face recognition is used in security as an alternative to biometrics technique like fingerprints or iris recognition. A visual representation of face recognition is as follows:

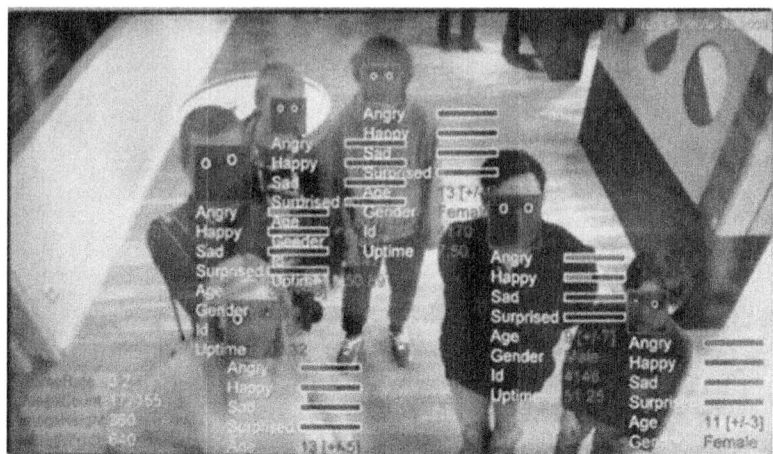

Figure 7.1: *A representation of face recognition in action*
(Source image: https://www.flickr.com/photos/sk8geek/17086044837)

Face recognition became more popular and accurate thanks to deep learning techniques, such as DeepFace.

See also the following definitions: Computer vision, image recognition, and deep learning

Facet

A facet is a type of plot where data is split into subsets and plotted in a row. The facets can be placed in a row or a grid. An example of facet plotting is as follows:

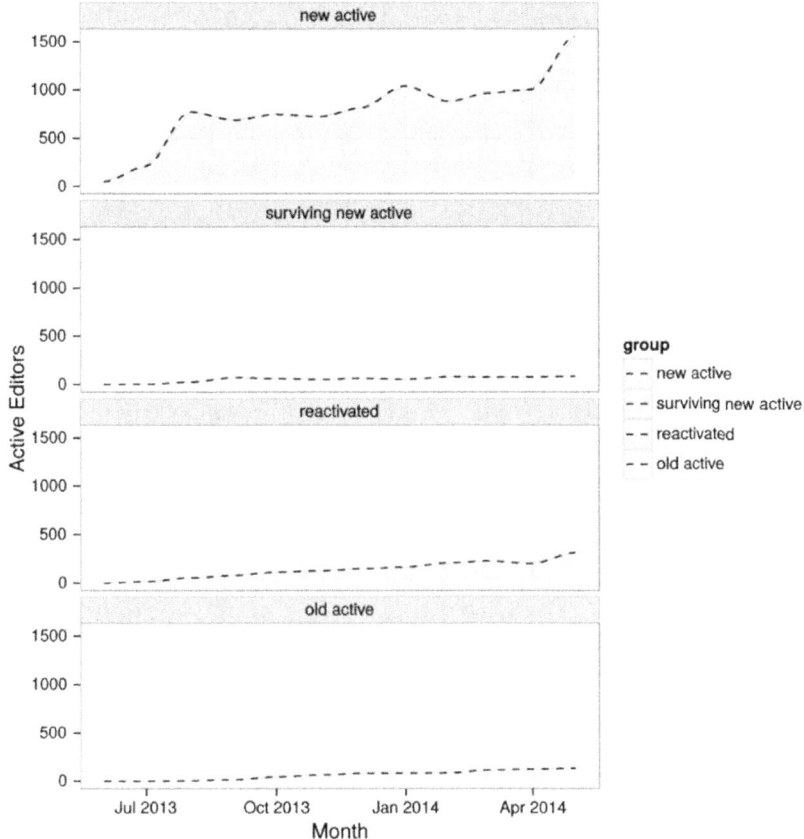

Figure 7.2: A representation of a faceting plot
(Source image: https://commons.wikimedia.org/wiki/File:Monthly_active_editors.
facet_group.en_mobile.svg)

The splitting of data is performed based on a categorical variable or variables. It visually represents the variation of two continuous variables based on a third categorical variable or more.

See also the following definitions: Bar chart, box plot, line chart, and pie chart

Factor analysis

Factor analysis is a technique to reduce the number of variables into fewer factors. In other words, it is a technique that estimates a model which explains variance and covariance between a set of observed variables by a set of unobserved factors. Factor analysis is a type of dimensionality reduction. With factor analysis, we assume several assumptions: there is a linear relationship between variables and unobserved factors, there is no multicollinearity, only relevant variables are included, there is a true correlation between factors and variables. Also, factor analysis comes up with multiple assumptions about the data, such as there is no outlier, the sample size is optimal, etc. The most common factor analysis techniques are principal component analysis, common factor analysis, image factoring, and the maximum likelihood method.

See also the following definitions: Dimensionality reduction and **Principal component analysis (PCA)**

False negative

A false negative is a case in classification where the model predicted that the output is false while the actual value is true. For example, in email spam, a model predicted that the observation is not spam while the actual value says that the email is spam.

For some cases, a false negative can be very costly for a company as for fraud detection, where a case of fraud not detected can cost a lot to a bank or the insurance company. That's why we can try to weight the model or higher the detection threshold to avoid a false negative.

See also the following definitions: Classification, confusion matrix, and false positive

False positive

A false positive is a case in classification where the model predicted that the output is true while the actual value is false. For example, in anomaly detection, a model predicted that the signal is an anomaly while the actual value says that it is not an anomaly.

See also the following definitions: Classification, confusion matrix, and false negative

Feature

A feature is an attribute or a characteristic of an example in a dataset. Features are inputs of machine learning models. A feature can be numerical or categorical. For example, for a dataset of bank transactions features can be the amount of transaction, country of the transaction, hour of the transaction, and so on.

See also the following definitions: Dataset and machine learning

Feature cross

The feature cross is a generated feature obtained by multiplying two or more features between them. The obtained feature can become a better predictor than individual features. The feature cross can help a model learn non-linearity from data.

See also the following definitions: Feature, machine learning, dataset, and data transformation

Feature engineering

Feature engineering is the process of selecting the most relevant feature in a dataset for training a model. Feature engineering is a mandatory step for traditional machine learning training (not for deep learning). This helps improve model performance as raw data without feature engineering can perform badly. To select features, feature engineering includes using statistical techniques, visualization, and domain knowledge.

See also the following definitions: Dataset, machine learning, and data transformation

Feature hashing

Feature hashing is the ability to transform a feature into a vector of indices. It works by applying a hash function to the feature. Hashing feature looks like the following:

$$\begin{pmatrix} \text{John} & \text{likes} & \text{to} & \text{watch} & \text{movies} & \text{Mary} & \text{too} & \text{also} & \text{football} \\ 1 & 1 & 1 & 1 & 1 & 0 & 0 & 0 & 0 \\ 0 & 1 & 0 & 0 & 1 & 1 & 1 & 0 & 0 \\ 1 & 1 & 0 & 0 & 0 & 0 & 0 & 1 & 1 \end{pmatrix}$$

Figure 7.3: Words feature hashing
(Source image: https://en.wikipedia.org/wiki/Feature_hashing)

Feature hashing is useful to encode categorical variables or words into vectors.

See also the following definitions: Data transformation and natural language processing

Feature learning

Feature learning, also known as representation learning, is a learning technique where a machine learning model automatically extracts features from raw data. This means that manual feature engineering is not required in these kinds of tasks. A simple way to understand feature learning is by visuals like the following:

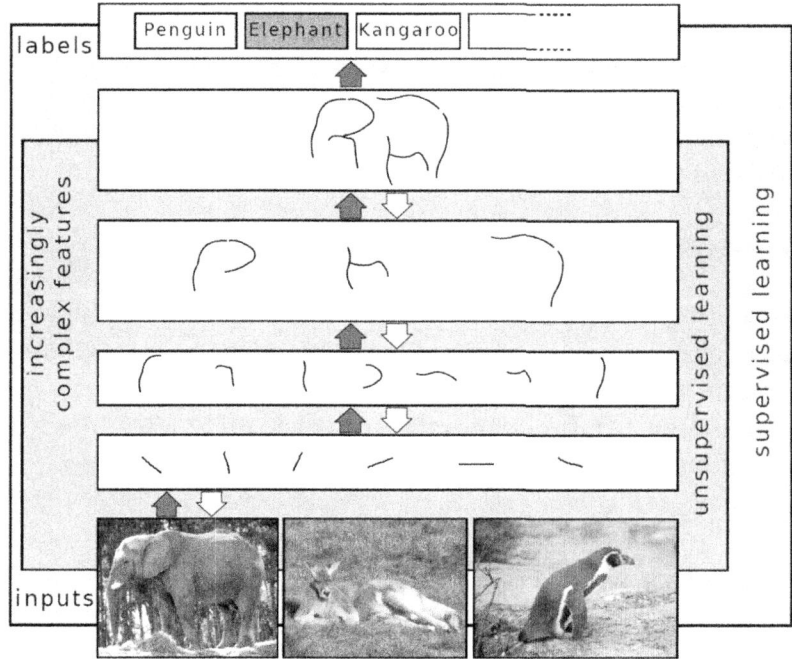

Figure 7.4: Feature learning in neural networks vs. feature extracting in traditional machine learning
(Source image: https://commons.wikimedia.org/wiki/File:Deep_Learning.jpg)

As opposed to feature engineering, feature learning doesn't extract meaningful or interpretable features. Features extracted are usually abstract and unique for each model and data. Feature learning is usually associated with a neural network where hidden layers extract features from raw data.

See also the following definitions: Deep learning and neural network

Feature reduction

Feature reduction, also known as dimensionality reduction, is a technique to reduce the number of features in a dataset by representing the data in a lower-dimension. One of the most common techniques for feature reduction is the PCA. PCA is represented as follows:

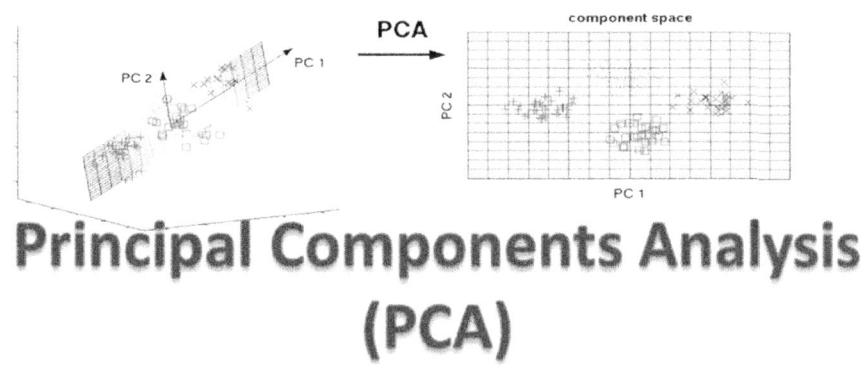

*Figure 7.5: Principal component analysis representation
(Source image: http://phdthesis-bioinformatics-maxplanckinstitute-molecularplantphys.
matthias-scholz.de/)*

Note that feature reduction doesn't induce loss of information as the lower-dimension space represents the higher-dimension space.

See also the following definitions: Dimensionality reduction, PCA, and factor analysis

Feature selection:

Feature selection is a process in a data science project where we select relevant features for modeling. Feature selection helps increase model performance. A feature selection can be done by filtering features (using variance importance for example) or by combining features (multiplication or substitution). Feature selection is not required for some types of machine learning algorithms, such as a deep neural network. Feature selection is an iterative process where we can use forward selection by keep adding the most relevant features until the performance stops increasing.

See also the following definitions: Feature engineering, machine learning, and data transformation

Federated learning:

Federated learning is a machine learning technique where training is distributed across multiple servers or devices. The training of each model in a device is using local sample data, the model updates are then shared with a central server to create a robust model. Federated learning is different from other machine learning distributed learning as the data used to train the distributed model is not the same from a machine to another. The steps for federated learning are as follow:

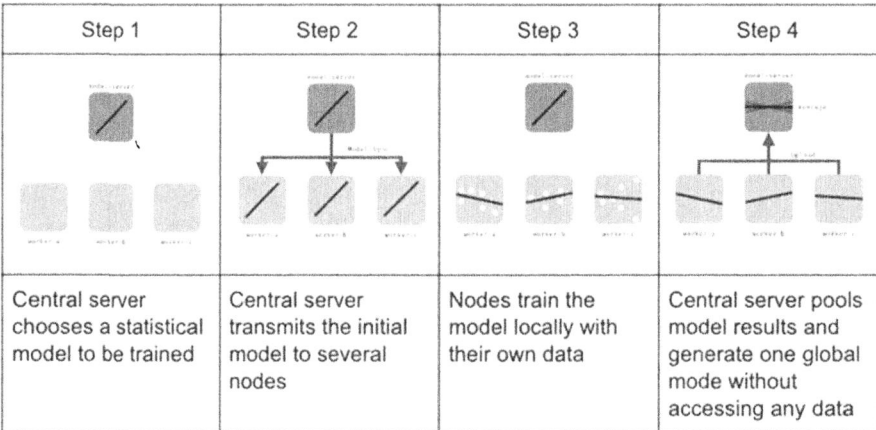

Figure 7.6: A step-by-step approach for federated learning (Source image: https://commons.wikimedia.org/wiki/File:Federated_learning_process_central_case.png)

Federated learning is useful for data privacy and data security. It is also very popular with use cases relying on mobile phones and applications on mobile phones.

See also the following definitions: Downpour Stochastic Gradient Descent

Feedback loop

A feedback loop is a situation when a model prediction in production will influence future training data for the same model. For example, a model in production that recommends items in e-commerce will produce a recommendation to users, this output will influence user selection and this data will later be used to update the model. So the model update is influenced by model prediction; this is a feedback loop.

A feedback loop also refers to situations where the model prediction is directly reused for training the same model; the output prediction can sometimes be slightly modified by a human annotator. It is commonly used in computer vision and image recognition when there are a few labeled data and numerous unlabeled data.

See also the following definitions: Machine learning and predictive model

Feedforward

Feedforward corresponds to the characteristic of a neural network where information moves only forward, it doesn't form a cycle at the node level. So, the information goes directly from input to output through hidden layers. A graphical representation of the feedforward neural network is as follows:

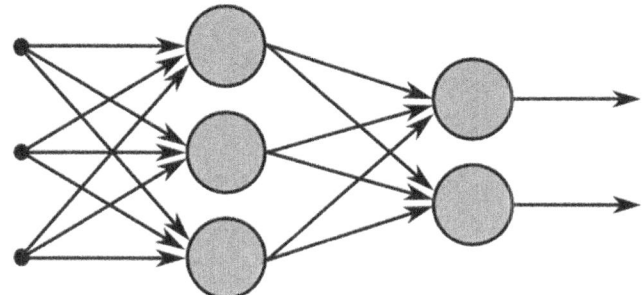

Figure 7.7: Feedforward neural network
(Source image: https://fr.wikipedia.org/wiki/Fichier:MultiLayerNeuralNetwork.png)

In contrast, the recurrent neural network is a neural network where information forms a cycle before moving forward.

See also the following definitions: Neural network and backpropagation

Few-shot learning

Few-shot learning is a technique used to build machine learning models with fewer data. Usually, a machine learning model requires a large amount of data. With this technique, it is possible to bypass this requirement and build a robust model using only a few observations. Few-shot learning is very popular in computer vision. If we have only one sample per category, the technique that can be used is called one-shot learning. The most popular few-shot learning algorithms are Siamese network, matching learning, and prototypical network.

See also the following definitions: Active learning, zero-shot learning, machine learning, deep learning, and continuous learning

Fine-tuning

Fine-tuning is an approach in transfer learning. In neural network, fine-tuning means training a model using other model parameters. This is done by initializing a neural network algorithm with a parameter from another neural network model in the same domain problem. Some ways of performing fine-tuning is by truncating the last layer with a new Softmax layer, defining a smaller training rate, and fixing the weights of the first layer.

Note that fine-tuning is also used to refer to the process of hyperparametrization, where we optimize the high-level parameters of a machine learning model to find the optimal model with the highest performance.

See also the following definitions: Transfer learning, neural network, and hyperparameter

Flume

The Apache flume is a log stream service in the Hadoop ecosystem that can collect, aggregate, and move a large amount of data. It is suitable for online analytics application and is fault-tolerant with several recovery mechanisms. It can collect data from various data sources.

See also the following definitions: Big data and Apache Spark

Focal loss

"The focal loss was proposed for dense object detection task […] It enables training highly accurate dense object detectors with an imbalance between foreground and background classes at 1:1000 scale […] The focal loss is designed to address class imbalance by down-weighting inliers (easy examples) such that their contribution to the total loss is small even if their number is large. It focuses on training a sparse set of hard examples."

From https://www.dlology.com/blog/multi-class-classification-with-focal-loss-for-imbalanced-datasets/

See also the following definitions: Object detection, computer vision, and neural network

Forget gate

Forget gate is a concept in LSTM in the recurrent neural network. Gates in LSTM are mechanisms to help avoid short memory issues and find in a data sequence which information should be kept. The forget gate decides which information to keep and which information to forget. In forget gate, information from the previous hidden state and information from the input is passed to a sigmoid function. If the value is close to 0 it means to forget the information if the value is close to 1 it means to remember.

See also the following definitions: LSTM and neural network

Frechet inception distance

Frechet Inception Distance (FID) is a score that evaluates the quality of image generation, especially for an adversarial neural network. It compares similarities between real images and generated images. A low score means a high similarity. The FID score estimates the quality of synthetic images based on how well inceptionv3 classifies the synthetic images as one of 1000 classes.

See also the following definitions: Generative adversarial neural networks and computer vision

Frequentist statistics

Frequentist statistics also called frequentist inference is a way of working with statistics and it is opposed to Bayesian statistics. Frequentist statistics is considered as the basics of statistics by using rigid formulas such as p-value, confidence interval, hypothesis testing, and so on. It draws a conclusion based on the sample data and using frequencies from the sample. For example, if you flip a coin 10 times, the probability of head is the number of heads in the sample divided by the sample size.

See also the following definitions: Bayesian Statistics

F-score

F-score is also known as F1-score. For more information see the F1-score definition.

Full softmax

Full softmax is an activation function in the neural network. It produces probabilities from 0 to 1. It is used as the activation function of the last layer to produce probabilities of classes in classification problem. For more details see the Softmax definition.

See also the following definitions: Activation function, Softmax, and classification

Fully connected layer

A fully connected layer is also known as an affine layer. For more details see the Affine layer definition.

Chapter 8
G

Gain and Lift Charts

Gain and lift charts are visual support to help evaluate predictive model performance. Lift and gain can be calculated using the following formulas:

$$Gain = \frac{Expected\ response\ using\ predictive\ model}{Expected\ response\ using\ randomness}$$

$$Lift = \frac{Expected\ response\ for\ X\ sample\ using\ prective\ model}{Expected\ response\ for\ X\ sample\ using\ randomness}$$

An example of the gain and lift charts is as follows:

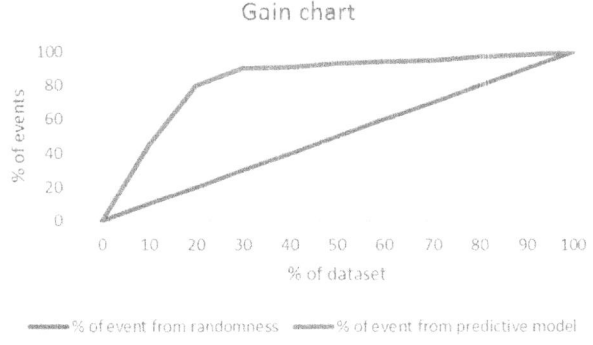

Figure 8.1: *A representation of the gain chart*

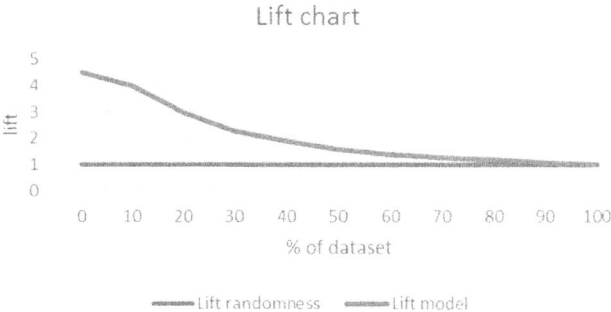

Figure 8.2: A representation of the lift chart

Note that the area between the baseline and the lift or gain curve represents the model performance compared to randomness.

See also the following definitions: Evaluation metrics and predictive model

Gated Recurrent Unit (GRU)

A gated recurrent unit is used in a recurrent neural network, similar to LSTM; it has simpler calculations that have fewer parameters and is faster to compute. It also helps the recurrent neural network reduce the vanishing gradient problem. A GRU unit looks like the following illustration:

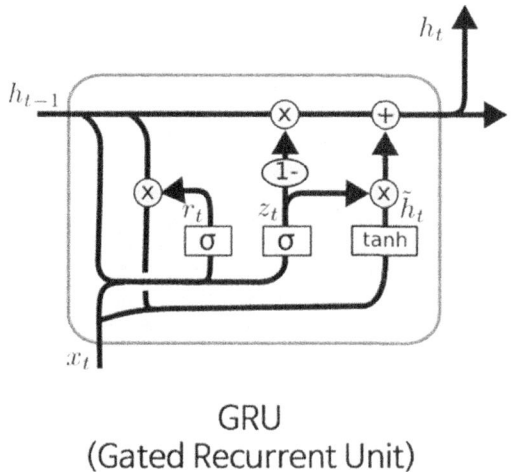

GRU
(Gated Recurrent Unit)

*Figure 8.3: A representation of Gated Recurrent Unit
(Source image: https://commons.wikimedia.org/wiki/File:GRU.png)*

GRU has 2 gates; update gate and reset gate that help define how much memory to keep and how to combine the new input with the older memory.

See also the following definitions: LSTM, neural network, and deep learning

Gaussian distribution

The Gaussian distribution also known as normal distribution is a bell-shaped curve that falls in the family of the continuous probability distribution. The normal distribution is symmetric around the mean. Normal distribution helps represent problems in physics, data science, and other fields. We usually use the normal distribution as a hypothesis based on a sample. If the mean is zero and the standard deviation is equal to one, then the normal distribution is a standard normal distribution. A normal distribution has the following shape:

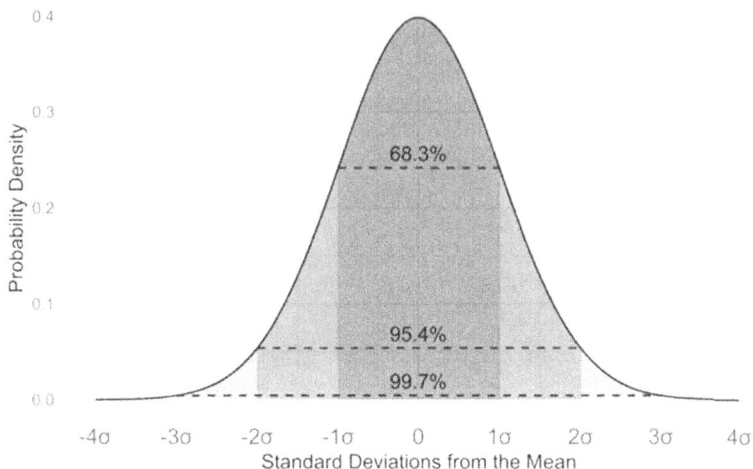

Figure 8.4: *A normal distribution*
(Source image: https://fr.wikipedia.org/wiki/Fichier:Standard_Normal_Distribution.png)

Note that to compute the distribution we use the probability density and for the normal distribution it has the following formula:

$$p(x) = \frac{1}{\sigma\sqrt{2\pi}} e^{-\frac{1}{2}\left(\frac{x-\mu}{\sigma}\right)^2}$$

See also the following definitions: Bernoulli distribution, binomial distribution, Chi-squared distribution, T-distribution, exponential family distribution, normal distribution, and Poisson distribution

General AI

It is an artificial intelligence that can perform the full range of human intelligence; it is also referred to as the strong AI. For more details see the Artificial General Intelligence definition.

See also the following definitions: Artificial intelligence and Artificial Narrow Intelligence (ANI)

Generalization

Generalization is a key concept in machine learning that refers to how well a model predicts unseen data, meaning data that was not used for training. Generalization is derived from the induction concept where we go from specific examples to generalizing a concept. There are two concepts related to generalization, overfitting and underfitting, both are situations where the model is not capable of generalizing and provides poor results.

See also the following definitions: Extrapolation, deduction, and induction

Generalization curve

It is a curve showing the loss or error for training and validation during multiple iterations. If the loss of validation is going higher than the training curve, then we might be facing a generalization problem. A representation of the generalization curve with issues is as follows:

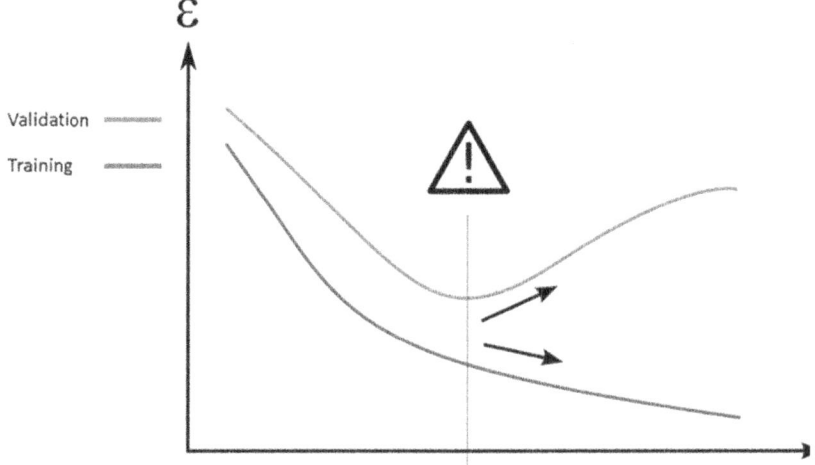

Figure 8.5: *Generalization issues with a generalization curve*

In the preceding chart, we can see that the validation curve, after some iteration, is getting higher error than training, which leads to the conclusion that we might have a generalization issue.

See also the following definitions: Generalization, extrapolation, and iteration

Generalized Linear Model (GLM)

A generalized linear model is a generalization of linear regression, where the response variable (target variable) has an error distribution in the exponential family (Poisson, Chi-square, and so on). The GLM generalizes linear regression with linear models linked to the target variable with a link function. A GLM is composed of three elements: a probability distribution of the response variable, a linear predictor, and a link function.

Hint: When to use a GLM?

When the target variable has a non-normal distribution or when the relationship between the dependent and independents variables is non-linear. A GLM can be used for regression and classification (multi-class and binary).

See also the following definitions: Linear regression and machine learning

Generative adversarial neural network (GAN)

GAN is a neural network system that can be used to generate data in a supervised or unsupervised machine learning task. The GAN is composed of two neural networks, a generator that generates data from a latent space in the input and a discriminator that detects if the data is fake or real. Both the generator and the discriminator are trained at the same time. The goal is to make the generator enough a performant to fool the discriminator with fake data. The generator is typically a recurrent neural network, while the discriminator is a convolutional neural network. GANs are very popular for image generation and anomaly detection.

See also the following definitions: Discriminator and generator

Generative classification

A generative classification or generative model is a statistical model based on the joint probability between the target variable and the predictor. The type of generative models is the Naïve Bayes classifier and the linear discriminant analysis.

See also the following definitions: Discriminative model and classification

Generator

A generator is a part of the generative adversarial neural network and it is responsible for generating fake data from randomness within a latent space. A generator incorporates the loss discriminator feedback based on how good the fake data were generated. A generator is usually a recurrent neural network.

See also the following definitions: Discriminator and generative adversarial neural networks

Genetic algorithm

A genetic algorithm is an algorithm for optimization problems in operational research in the family of evolutionary algorithms. It is inspired by the process of natural selection. As in natural selection, the most performant combination of attributes creates children based on a combination of attributes from the parents. It is considered as a heuristic approach, with the ability to find an optimal solution but not always the best solution (global optimum). The measure of performance for the genetic algorithm is called fitness and it measures how optimal is the solution. It has hyperparameters such as cross over and mutation. It is common to use a genetic algorithm in routing problems and gaming as well as in finance and more.

See also the following definitions: Algorithm, neural network, and random forest

Ggplot2

Ggplot2 is a popular data visualization package in R programming. An example of plot is described as follows:

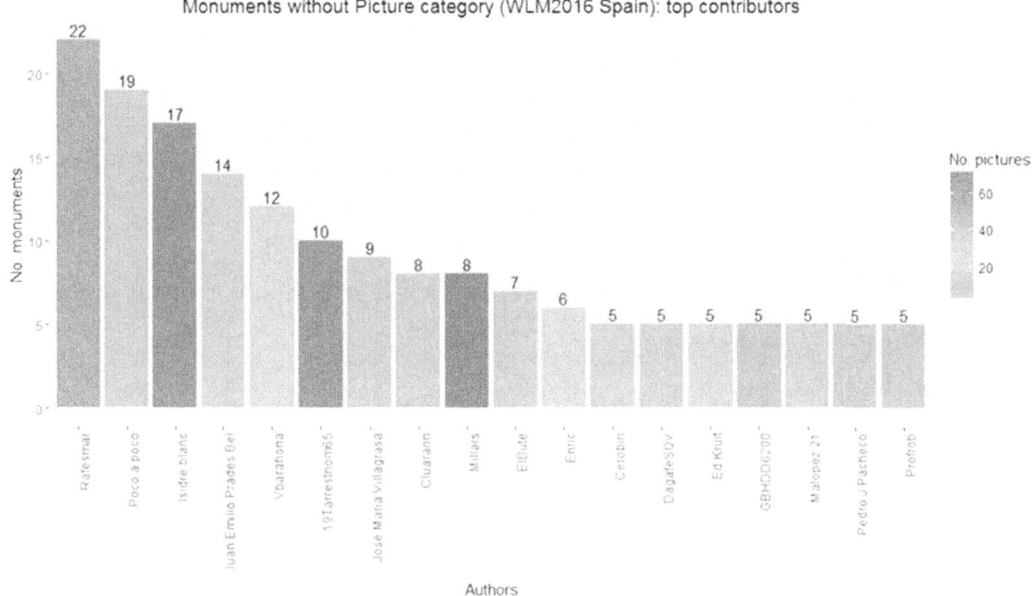

Figure 8.6: A graphic with ggplot2
(Source image: https://commons.wikimedia.org/wiki/File:Monuments_without_Picture_category_(WLM2016_Spain)_-_top_contributors.png)

Ggplot2 is known to be very user-friendly to create great visuals that are ready to be shared.

See also the following definitions: Dplyr, R, and bar chart

Gini coefficient

The Gini coefficient or the Gini index is a statistical measure for distribution; it measures the dispersion across a variable, for example, income. It is very popular in economics for measuring inequality across a population. An index of 0 means perfect equality across a variable and an index of 1 means perfect inequality.

In machine learning, the Gini index is used as an evaluation metric for classification problems. It is also used in decision trees' internal processes to measure the level of impurity and to split the leaf.

See also the following definitions: Evaluation metrics and classification

GloVe

GloVe stands for Global Vector and is an unsupervised machine learning model that outputs vector representation from words: word to vector. It is a very popular process in natural language processing. The algorithm maps the words into a space and measures the distances between words; close distances are usually synonyms. The GloVe is an open-source project at Stanford University.

See also the following definitions: Unsupervised learning and natural language processing

Go

Go is an open-source programming language. It helps build simple and reliable software. It has been developed by Google and has been inspired by C and Pascal. During the last year, Go has gained popularity in data science and software engineering.

See also the following definitions: Python and R

Goodness of fit

The goodness of fit measures how well a predictive model fits the data by measuring its predicting power. This kind of measure can also be used with hypothesis testing where we would like to know if two samples have identical distribution. Examples of the goodness of fit measures in hypothesis testing are the chi-squared test, Kuiper's test, Moran test, and in predictive model fits are the coefficient of determination, reduced chi-squared, and so on.

See also the following definitions: Predictive model and Chi-squared test

GoogleNet

GoogleNet is a deep learning architecture that won the contest ImageNet 2014 also called "LeNet" or inception v1. GoogleNet is based on the architecture of 22 layers and contains convolutional layers, fully connected layers, average pooling, and global average pooling. Note that it has 12 times fewer parameters than the AlexNet architecture so it is faster in computing.

See also the following definitions: AlexNet, VGG, deep learning, ILSVRC, and deep dream

GPU

A GPU or graphics processing unit is an electronic circuit designed for manipulating graphics and image processing. In data science, it has been hacked to perform heavy computing, especially in deep learning. The GPU is now a standard in deep learning and makes computing a lot faster.

See also the following definitions: CPU and device

Gradient accumulation

Gradient accumulation is a mechanism in a deep neural network where we split the batches into mini-batches and we compute the gradient for each mini-batch. Weights are then updated based on the accumulation of the gradient values for each mini-batch and performed per batch. This mechanism is useful to optimize memory and computing power usage, especially in the case we have a large input size.

See also the following definitions: Batch, Gradient descent, and deep learning

Gradient descent

In several machine learning algorithms, gradient descent is an optimization mechanism that minimizes the loss function or the error. The gradient descent will find updates to the weights or parameters of the algorithms based on the loss or the error generated by the algorithm. In neural network computing, gradients are based on the derivative of the loss with respect to each weight. We then use chain rules to compute the gradient for each weight. There are different types of gradient descent; the most popular are batch gradient descent and stochastic gradient descent.

See also the following definitions: Backpropagation, chain rule, and neural network

Greedy policy

A greedy policy in reinforcement learning is a policy that selects an action by trying to maximize the return or reward. For more details see the epsilon greedy policy definition.

See also the following definitions: Reinforcement learning, action, and agent

Grid search

Grid search is a technique to find the optimal hyperparameters of a machine learning model. Basically, the model runs on a set of possible combinations of hyperparameters and the combination with the highest performance on validation dataset is selected as optimal.

See also the following definitions: Hyperparameter and machine learning

Ground truth

The ground truth represents the correct answer provided by direct observation on the field. In machine learning, the term is used to qualify any reality or real values computed on the field.

See also the following definitions: Predictive model and machine learning

CHAPTER 9

H

Hadoop

Apache Hadoop is open-source software created for distributed computing. It enables distributed processing of very large datasets across clusters of computers. Hadoop keeps copies of data to ensure reliability. It is also a time-saving technology as it handles execution in parallel. Hadoop helps build archiving solutions, big data application in various sectors, analyze structured and unstructured data, and so on.

See also the following definitions: Big data, Apache Spark, and Flume

Hashing

Hashing is a mechanism to reduce the number of buckets in categorical data. If we have a data set with a large number of buckets for categorical data, we can use hashing to reduce the number of buckets in the categorical data. This can be processed by grouping categories together in the same bucket.

See also the following definitions: Binning, categorical variable, continuous variable, and discrete variable

Heuristic

The heuristic technique is a mechanism that doesn't focus on finding the optimal or best solution but finding a fast solution. The heuristic approach makes the computing to find a solution faster. An educated guess can be considered as a heuristic approach, as it finds a fast solution but nothing guarantees that it is optimal. Heuristic methods can be used as an alternative to a machine learning algorithm especially if there is not enough data to train a machine learning model.

See also the following definitions: Machine learning, deduction, and induction

Hidden layer

Hidden layers are layers between the input layer and the output layer in a neural network. Usually, a hidden layer is complemented with an activation function. A deep neural network contains more than one hidden layer:

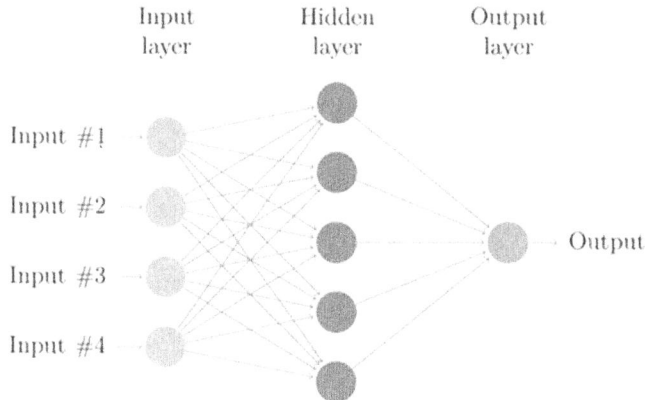

Figure 9.1: *Hidden layer in a neural network*
(Source image: http://www.texample.net/tikz/examples/neural-network/)

The role of hidden layers is to learn features from input data. This is called representation learning.

See also the following definitions: Deep learning, layer, and activation function

Hidden Markov model

The hidden Markov model is a type of Markov model that is based on an environment that we assume to be a Markov process. This Markov process contains hidden states. These states represent something we cannot observe directly; these hidden states are complemented with another process that depends on the hidden states. Based on the second process, we can compute the conditional probability of the hidden states. The hidden Markov model is very popular for reinforcement learning, speech recognition, robotics, bioinformatics, and so on.

So, we can represent the hidden Markov model as follows, using transition probabilities and emission probabilities:

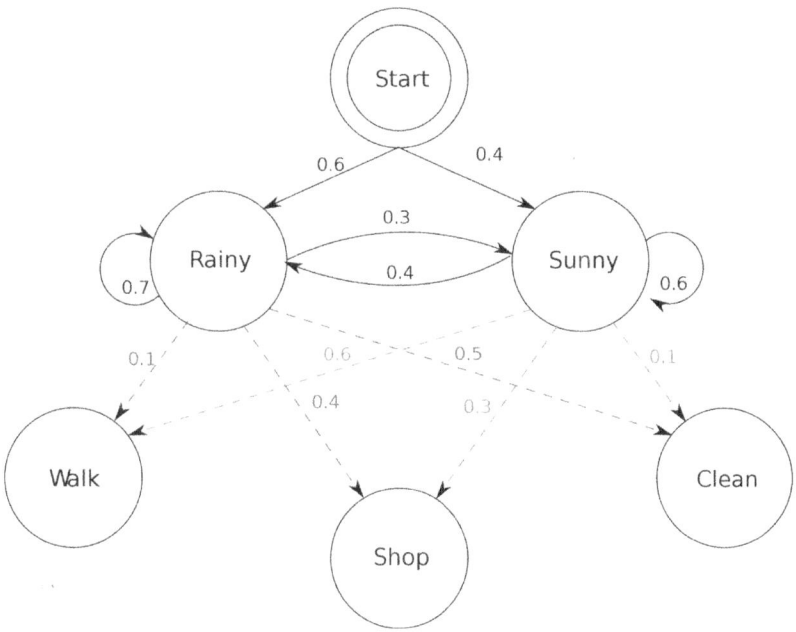

Figure 9.2: *Hidden Markov model*
(Source image: https://en.wikipedia.org/wiki/Hidden_Markov_model)

As an example, let's suppose that we would like to know if it is a sunny or rainy day based on a person's activity. We do not have any way to observe directly if it's sunny or rainy (hidden states) but we can observe a person's activity (walk, shop or clean) and this person's activities are based on the weather.

See also the following definitions: Markov chain and reinforcement learning

Hierarchical clustering

Hierarchical clustering is a type of clustering algorithm in unsupervised machine learning algorithms. For more details see the connectivity-based algorithm definition.

See also the following definitions: Agglomerative clustering, clustering, and divisive clustering

Highway layer

In cases where it is very hard for the gradient to go through a deep neural network, we add a highway layer which consists of a weighted sum of the input with the output result. And it has the following formula:

$$y = c(x) * f(x) + (1 - c) * x$$

Where $f(x)$ is the output of the neural network, x is the input and c is the assigned weight.

See also the following definitions: Hidden layer and deep learning

Highway network

A highway network is a neural network that helps train very deep neural networks. It contains gates (transformation and carry gates) that allow information to flow across the layers. It prevents the gradient from vanishing and shows an increase in performance for very deep neural networks (hundreds of layers and more). It is used for text sequence labeling and speech recognition.

See also the following definitions: Deep learning and speech recognition

Hinge loss

Hinge loss is a loss function used for classification problems. It is used mainly with support vector machines. And it has the following formula for binary classification:

Where y is the true label between -1 and 1 and y' is output from the classifier model.

$$loss = \max(0, 1 - (y * y'))$$

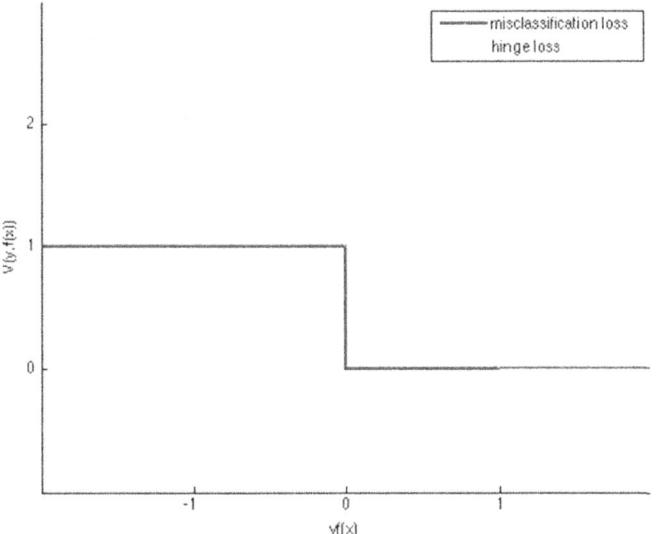

Figure 9.3: *Hinge loss graphical behavior*
(Source image: https://commons.wikimedia.org/wiki/File:Hinge_and_Misclassification_Loss.png)

Hinge loss has the following behavior, note that hinge loss penalize prediction with y<1 which corresponds to the margin in a support vector machine.

See also the following definitions: Exponential loss, loss function, focal loss, log loss, magnet loss, Huber loss, L1 loss, L2 loss, squared loss

Histogram

A histogram is a graphical representation of a continuous or categorical variable frequency with vertical bars.

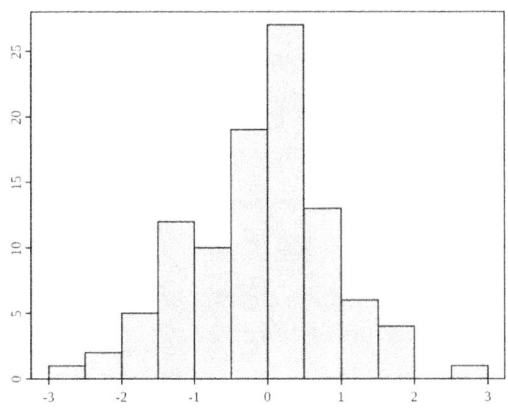

Figure 9.4: *A histogram*
(Source image: https://commons.wikimedia.org/wiki/File:Histogram_example.svg)

It helps study the variable distribution and verifies the quality of the data, if it contains any skew or has abnormal behavior.

See also the following definitions: Bar chart and normal distribution

Hive

Apache Hive is a data warehouse infrastructure integrated with Hadoop, that allows to analyze, summarize, and query data based on a language similar to SQL called HiveQL. Hive can operate on compressed data stored in the Hadoop ecosystem. It converts query into MapReduce jobs, which allows to query on very large data volumes. Hive has a faster response time than any other type of queries.

See also the following definitions: Hadoop, Big data, and database

Holdout sample

A holdout sample represents a part of the data that hasn't been used during the training. We can consider validation and test data as holdout samples. A holdout sample is useful to evaluate how a model is capable of generalization on data it never saw before. We can use a holdout sample to compare multiple model performances and have a better idea of their ability to generalize.

See also the following definitions: Test set and validation set

Holt-Winters forecasting

Holt-Winters forecasting is also known as exponential smoothing with trend and seasonality. The model has 8 different parameters: $\alpha, \beta, \gamma, \phi$, the length of a season, and the number of periods in a season, the trend type, dampen type. One of the approaches used to find optimal parameters is Nelder-Mead optimization. Holt-Winters are also known as triple exponential smoothing as it applies three times exponential smoothing. Single exponential smoothing is exponential smoothing applied to data only without trend or seasonality, double exponential smoothing is exponential smoothing applied to data with the trend and triple exponential smoothing is exponential smoothing applied to data with trend and seasonality.

See also the following definitions: Exponential smoothing, ARIMA, and time series

Huber loss

Huber loss is a loss function used in regression problems; it is convenient as it is less sensitive to outliers than the mean squared error loss function. Huber loss is also known as smooth absolute error loss. And it has the following formula:

$$L_\delta(y, f(x)) = \begin{cases} \frac{1}{2}(y - f(x))^2 & for \ |y - f(x)| \leq \delta \\ \delta |y - f(x)| - \frac{1}{2}\delta^2 & otherwise. \end{cases}$$

Where y is the actual value, $f(x)$ is the forecasted value, is the hyperparameter to be tuned.

See also the following definitions: Hinge loss, exponential loss, loss function, focal loss, log loss, magnet loss, Huber loss, L1 loss, L2 loss, and squared loss

Hyperparameter

Hyperparameters are parameters in machine learning algorithms that have to be optimized during the training experimentation. Learning rate, batch size, and the number of iterations are types of hyperparameters. Each machine learning algorithm has its own hyperparameters. Note that hyperparameter selection can have a high impact on model performance. Hyperparameters are not to be confused with model parameters as parameters are internal values generated by the model during training which support the construction of a machine learning model and are computed by the algorithm during the training.

See also the following definitions: Machine learning and algorithm

Hyperparameter tuning

Hyperparameters are not natively optimized in a machine learning algorithm. They need to be optimized or tuned during the training experimentation. This tuning helps increase the model performance. To tune hyperparameters there are several techniques, such as grid search, random search, Bayesian optimization, and so on.

See also the following definitions: Grid search, random search, and hyperparameter

Hyperplane

A hyperplane is a frontier that splits a space into two subspaces. So, a line in a two-dimensional space is a hyperplane or a plane in a three-dimensional space is a hyperplane. In machine learning, a hyperplane is a boundary that separates a high dimensional space representing features.

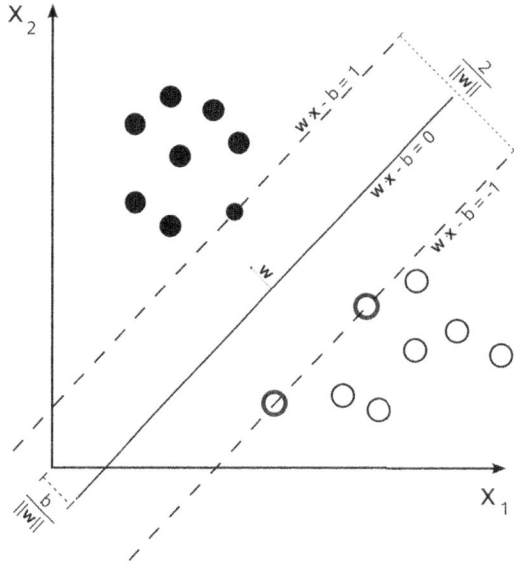

Figure 9.5: *A hyperplane in support vector machine*
(Source image: https://commons.wikimedia.org/wiki/File:Svm_max_sep_hyperplane_with_margin.png)

It is used in clustering techniques for unsupervised machine learning or in support vector machine where we separate values of each class by a hyperplane in a high dimensional space.

See also the following definitions: Linear regression and decision boundary

Hypothesis

A hypothesis is an assumption made about a situation or an environment. In statistics, hypothesis are being tested using hypothesis testing and null hypothesis. In machine learning, a hypothesis represents an assumption made about data or about the problem itself.

See also the following definitions: Generalization

CHAPTER 10

I

International Conference on Machine Learning (ICML)

International Conference on Machine Learning (ICML) is a yearly academic conference focused on machine learning. It is one of the most important conferences around the subject and has a high impact on machine learning and artificial intelligence research.

See also the following definitions: ILSVRC

Integrated Development Environment (IDE)

Integrated Development Environment (IDE) is a set of tools that enhance the productivity of programmers. It can contain program editing console, debugger, and other practical tools. The most popular IDE in data science are RStudio, Pycharm, Spyder.

See also the following definitions: Rstudio, R, and Python

ImageNet Large Scale Visual Recognition Challenge (ILSVRC)

ImageNet large scale visual recognition challenge is an annual software contest in artificial intelligence and computer vision based on the ImageNet project. It compares algorithms for object detection and image classification. ImageNet is a database of images that are annotated and used in research and development for image classification.

See also the following definitions: ICML and ImageNet

Image recognition

Image recognition or image classification is based usually on machine learning (especially deep learning) and the goal is to classify objects or shapes within an image. An example is the following image where the algorithm classifies people emotions:

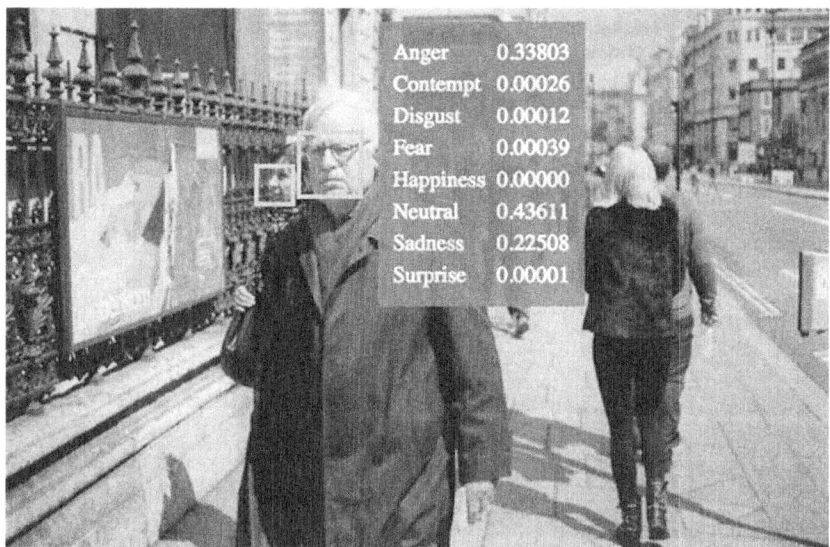

Figure 10.1: Image recognition for emotion classification (Source image: https://www.flickr.com/photos/fotologic/23768573841)

Image recognition is considered as one of the main branches in artificial intelligence.

See also the following definitions: Deep learning and computer vision

ImageNet

ImageNet is a database of images that has annotation, classes, and bounding boxes. This database is useful for image classification problems. It contains more than 14 million images with annotation and 20 thousand categories. ImageNet is also the source of a contest called ImageNet Large Scale Visual Recognition Challenge that runs annually.

See also the following definitions: ILSVRC, dataset, and bounding box

Imbalanced dataset

An imbalanced dataset in a binary classification problem is when the ratio between the two classes is too high, meaning that one class is over-represented and another class is less represented. For example, a dataset of 10 thousand observations where the negative label has 9950 observations and the positive label has only 50 observations. There are different techniques to rebalance the dataset such as SMOTE or downsampling.

See also the following definitions: Dataset, dependent variable, and majority class

Implicit bias

Implicit bias is making an assumption prior to a machine learning project that is actually wrong or partially true. This kind of bias can impact the collection of data and the machine learning model itself. An example of implicit bias is a case where a data scientist wants to create a model that recognizes people on an image; however, in the data collection process he collected images with only white people. This is an implicit bias because his machine learning model will only recognize white people and not people from other ethnicities.

See also the following definitions: Automation bias, bias, bias-variance trade-off, coverage bias, and sampling bias

Imputation

Imputation is a technique used in a dataset when it contains missing values. Missing values can be NA, NaN, Null or blank. An example of imputation by mean will be as follows:

Group	Age
Blue	20
Yellow	NA
Green	15
Purple	20
Black	NA
White	18

Group	Age
Blue	20
Yellow	18.25
Green	15
Purple	20
Black	18.25
White	18

Figure 10.2: Imputation with mean

To deal with missing values, imputation can be done by replacing with the mean or the median or the complete observation can be deleted. Another technique is replacing the missing values using regression approximation, such as a regression with the target value in the missing value column.

See also the following definitions: Dataset and NaN

Inception

Inception is the architecture in deep learning especially CNN (convolutional neural network) for image classification. This architecture is one of the most innovative architectures of the last five years. It has several versions such as Inception v1/v2/v3/v4, Inception-ResNet.

See also the following definitions: Alexnet, VGG, Deep learning, ILSVRC, and deep dream

Inception module

The inception module is incorporated into a convolutional neural network to reduce computation costs. The inception module is an engineering process where instead of making a neural network deeper, the neural network is wider as some convolutional layers can be performed at the same level and not sequentially and then the output is concatenated together and sent to the next layer.

See also the following definitions: Convolutional neural network, deep learning, and hidden layer

Independent and identically distributed (i.i.d.)

A collection of variables is independent and identically distributed if the variables have the same distribution and are independent of one another. An i.i.d. is used to qualify random variables. In machine learning, i.i.d. is used as an assumption on training data.

See also the following definitions: Machine learning and hypothesis

Independent Component Analysis (ICA)

Independent component analysis is a dimensionality reduction technic that creates independent variables that represent hidden factors from an original large dataset. Some variations of ICA are either linear or non-linear. The distribution of the generated variables is non-Gaussian and independent. ICA is close to the principal component analysis technique but ICA is considered to be more powerful and relevant.

See also the following definitions: Dimensionality Reduction, Principal component analysis (PCA), and Factor Analysis

Induction

Induction is a reasoning type to discover a general rule from specific facts. We go from the specific to the general. Induction is the process in machine learning in which a model is capable to generalize based on the training data.

See also the following definitions: Deduction and generalization

Inferential statistics

Inferential statistics is one of the main branches in statistics where we use a set of techniques to infer a set of characteristics of a population from a sample with a degree of certainty or error. For example, we want to measure the average age of the Canadian population. To do so we measure the average age of a representative sample and then based on the sample we generalize the characteristic of the population. Machine learning is considered as an inferential statistic as we generalize based on the training data (a sample).

See also the following definitions: Sampling and generalization

Input gate

Input gate is one of the three gates that compose an LSTM cell or Long Short-Term Memory cell that is a type of layer in a deep neural network. In an input gate, the previous hidden state and the actual state are processed to a sigmoid function. Then it returns values between 0 and 1, to decide which information will be kept (0 is not important, 1 is important). In parallel the hidden state and current state are passed to a tanh function, which output values from -1 and 1, this operation helps regulate the network. Then the output of sigmoid and tanh are multiplied. The sigmoid output decides which information form tanh output will be kept. The visual representation of an input gate in an LSTM cell is as follows:

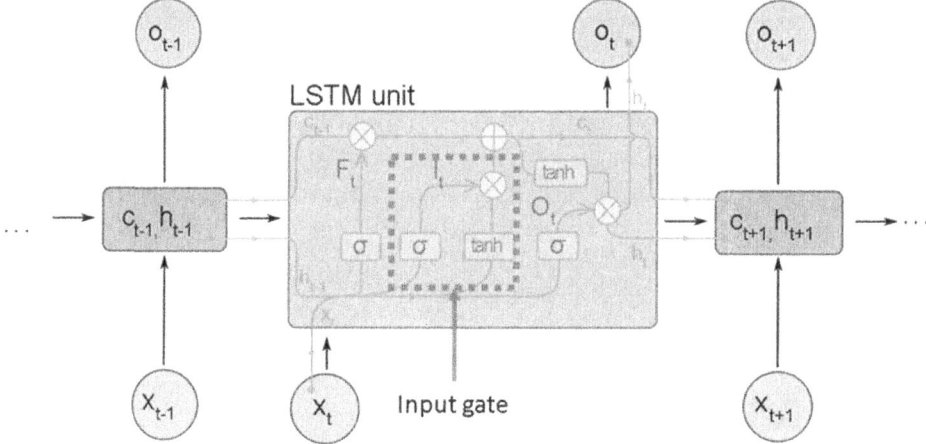

Figure 10.3: Input gate in an LSTM cell
(Source image:https://fr.wikipedia.org/wiki/Fichier:Long_Short-Term_Memory.svg)

LSTM is a recurrent neural network architecture used in a deep neural network or deep learning.

See also the following definitions: Output gate and LSTM

Input layer

The input layer is the first layer in a neural network algorithm. This first layer processes information from input data. A typical neural network is composed of input, hidden, and output layers. The visual representation is as follow:

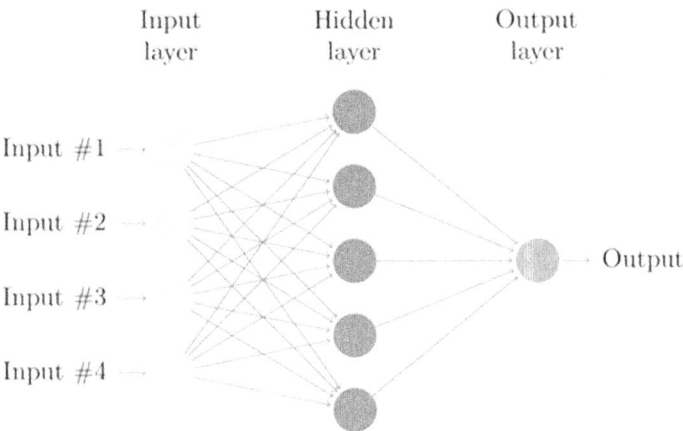

Figure 10.4: Input layer in a neural network

The input layer is considered passive because it doesn't receive information from previous layers but the input neurons in the input layers can be weighted based on the case.

See also the following definitions: Hidden layer and neural network

Instance

An instance is also known as an example and it is an observation within a dataset. For more details see the example definition.

Instance-based learning

Instance-based learning or memory-based learning is a type of machine learning algorithm that, instead of generalizing based on training data keeps the training data in memory and compares new coming data to data stored in memory. The most popular memory-based algorithm is k nearest neighbors.

See also the following definitions: kNN

Interpretability

Machine learning model interpretability is the ability to explain model behavior and results. This means that a model with high interpretability provides details about each feature weight and why we reach such a result. The models with the most interpretability are linear regressions and the models with less interpretability are deep learning models.

See also the following definitions: Machine learning and generalization

Intersection over Union (IoU)

Intersection over Union (IoU) is a metric used to evaluate the performance of the image detection machine learning model. It compares the intersection of the predicted bounding box and the ground-truth bounding box by computing the ratio between the overlapping area and the total area. A visual representation of the IoU is as follows:

Figure 10.5: Two bounding boxes to compute the Intersection over Union (Source image: https://en.wikipedia.org/wiki/Jaccard_index)

The value is between 0 and 1, 0 means no overlapping and 1 means perfectly overlapping.

See also the following definitions: Bounding box and image recognition

Intersection over Union (IoU)

IoU or Intersection over Union is an evaluation metric for image detection tasks. For more details see the Intersection over Union definition.

Interquartile Range (IQR)

IQR or interquartile range is the measure of dispersion in a dataset, which is the difference between the first quartile and third quartile.

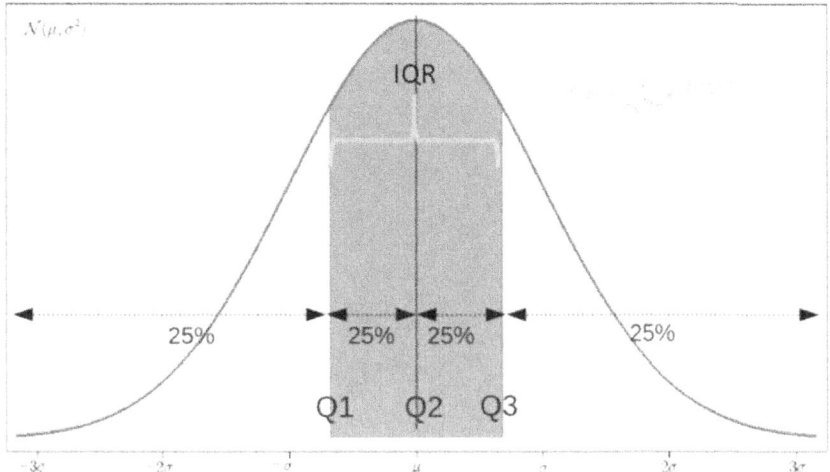

Figure 10.6: *Representation of IQR*
(Source image: https://commons.wikimedia.org/wiki/File:Iqr_with_quantile.png)

It is used to build box plot charts. It is also used as a statistic to describe the dispersion of a dataset.

See also the following definitions: Normal distribution and decile

Item matrix

In recommendation systems, an item matrix is the result of matrix factorization and represents the latent factors about each item in the dataset. The user matrix is also a result of matrix factorization and represents the latent factors about each user. The item matrix has the same number of columns as the original matrix. For example, if the original matrix contains 100 columns representing 100 shopping items, the item matrix will have 100 columns.

See also the following definitions: Recommendation engine and matrix factorization

Iteration

Iteration represents the number of times a machine learning model will update its parameters. The number of iterations within one epoch will be the number of observations in the dataset divided by the batch size. In a neural network, the iteration will occur at the end of a batch data and the update of parameters will be performed based on the average of gradient descent of each observation in each batch.

See also the following definitions: Batch and Epoch

CHAPTER 11
J

Jacobian

Jacobian is a matrix that contains all the first-order partial derivatives for vector-valued function. In a neural network, a Jacobian can be used to calculate the gradient, but this technic is very inefficient when there is a large dataset size.

See also the following definitions: Gradient descent, neural network, and chain rule

Julia

Julia a high-level programming language. Performant and dynamic, it has been created for scientific computation. It is a programming language that gained traction in the data science community and being more and more used. Compared to Python or R, Julia is lightweight and efficient which means it takes less computing power and it can match the speed of C programming. Julia can also call Python, R, C, and Fortran packages and libraries.

See also the following definitions: Python, R, and Java

Jupyter notebook

Jupyter notebook is an open-source web-based dynamic computational environment that helps create notebooks document. A notebook is a document that is composed of input and output cells and can contain code, text or markdown, plots and media. Jupyter notebook is the most used support for coding in data science. It is appreciated by data scientist as it helps create reports containing codes and notes around a project. Jupyter notebook can support several languages such as Python or R.

See also the following definitions: Watson Studio, Databricks, and Rstudio

CHAPTER 12
K

Keras

Keras is a high-level open-source neural network library written in Python. It can learn on top of another deep learning framework Tensorflow. Keras is appreciated in data science as it helps develop deep neural network models faster and is user friendly. Keras supports convolutional and recurrent neural network and also other popular neural network features.

See also the following definitions: Caffe, Tensorflow, Torch, and Pytorch

Kernel

In computer science, a kernel refers to the core component of an operating system, it is the main interface between computer hardware and all the processes.

In statistics and machine learning, a kernel is the measure of resemblance where a kernel function defines the distribution of similarity of points around a given point.

See also the following definitions: Kernel support vector machine

Kernel support vector machine

Kernel support vector machine or KSVM is a classification algorithm that map input data vectors in a higher-dimensional space in order to solve the problem as if it was a non-linear one. There are different types of kernel SVM, such as linear, non-linear, polynomial, radial basis function, and sigmoid.

See also the following definitions: Classification and machine learning

KL divergence

KL divergence is a metric to compare the difference between two probability distributions. It can be used to measure the divergence between discrete and continuous probability distribution.

See also the following definitions: Normal distribution

K-means

K-means is a clustering algorithm in the unsupervised machine learning. It clusters data in exactly k clusters. An example is illustrated with three clusters as follows:

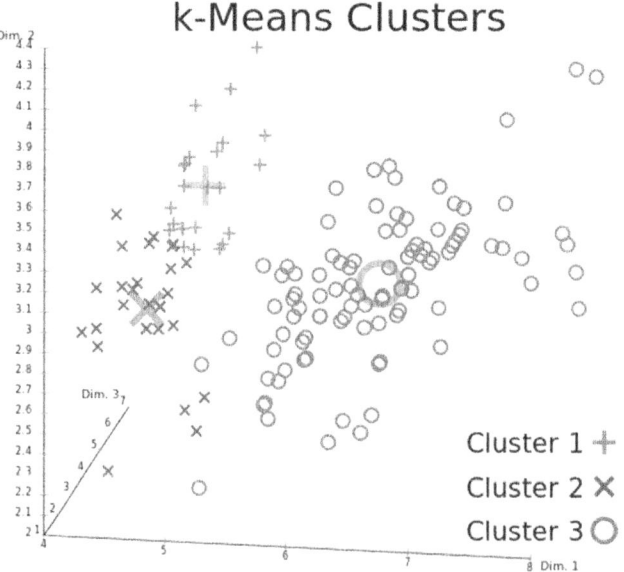

Figure 12.1: k-means cluster representation

First it defines the initial clusters centroid, and then it assigns each observation to the closest cluster after it recomputes the centroids based on the cumulative squared distance between each example and the closest centroid.

See also the following definitions: Agglomerative clustering, hierarchical clustering, clustering, and divisive clustering

K-median

K-median is a clustering-based algorithm in unsupervised machine learning. It is close to k-means algorithm except that centroids in k-median are determined based on the sum of the distance between the centroid and each observation, whereas in k-means it is determined based on the sum of squared distance. Also, in k-median the distances computed are Manhattan distances instead of Euclidian distances.

See also the following definitions: Agglomerative clustering, hierarchical clustering, clustering, and divisive clustering

K-nearest neighbors (kNN)

K-nearest neighbors (kNN) is a memory-based machine learning algorithm used for both regression and classification. For classifying or scoring a new unknown label observation, the k-nearest neighbors' algorithm computes the distances between the unknown label observation and the training data, and then it finds the k closest observations. If it is a classification problem, a vote is performed to define the class of the observation, if it a regression an average is performed to find the value.

See also the following definitions: Instance based learning

Kolmogorov Smirnov chart

Kolmogorov Smirnov chart (KS) chart measures the performance of classification models. Moreover, it measures the degree of separation between positive and negative distributions. It measures the distance between the plotted cumulative distribution of two classes. The values of KS chart are between 0 and 100, the higher the value the better the model can separate between positive and negative cases.

See also the following definitions: Evaluation metrics and classification

Kurtosis:

Kurtosis is a direct measure of sharpness and an indirect measure of the flattening of the distribution of a real random variable. If normalized, the Kurtosis value equal to zero means that it's a perfect normal distribution. If it's negative, it means that the distribution is flat and if it's positive it means that the distribution is peaked. Kurtosis a complementary concept to skew as skew measures the asymmetry of a distribution.

See also the following definitions: Skew and descriptive statistics

CHAPTER 13
L

L1 Loss

L1 loss stands for least absolute deviations. It is a loss function in machine learning algorithms to minimize the error. It corresponds to the sum of the absolute difference between actual values and predicted values. L1 loss is less sensitive to outliers and is preferred in cases where the data contains outliers. It has the following formula:

$$L1\ loss = \sum_{i=1}^{n} |y_{true} - y_{predicted}|$$

Where y_{true} is the actual value and $y_{predicted}$ is the predicted value.

See also the following definitions: Exponential loss, loss function, hinge loss, focal loss, log loss, magnet loss, Huber loss, L2 loss, and squared loss

L1 regularization

Regularization is a technique used in machine learning to avoid overfitting. L1 regularization works by adding a term to the loss function. This term corresponds to the sum of the absolute value of the parameters multiplied by a constant. If

L1 regularization is applied to a linear regression it is called lasso regression. L1 regularization has the following formula:

$$Loss = Error(y, \hat{y}) + \gamma \sum_{i=1}^{N} |w_i|$$

Where $Error(y, \hat{y})$ corresponds to the error between actual values and predicted values, γ is a regularization parameter and is defined manually and >0, w_i is the model parameters.

See also the following definitions: Regularization, overfitting, and L2 regularization

L2 loss

L2 loss stands for least square errors and is a loss function in machine learning algorithms to minimize errors. It corresponds to the sum of all squared difference between actual values and predicted values. L2 loss is sensitive to outliers and is preferred in the majority of cases except for the cases where the data contains outliers. It has the following formula:

$$L2\ loss = \sum_{i=1}^{n} (y_{true} - y_{predicted})^2$$

Where y_{true} is the actual value and $y_{predicted}$ is the predicted value.

See also the following definitions: Exponential Loss, loss function, hinge loss, focal loss, log loss, magnet loss, Huber loss, L1 loss, and squared loss

L2 regularization

Regularization is a technique used in machine learning to avoid overfitting. L2 regularization works by adding a term to the loss function. This term corresponds to the sum of the square value of the parameters multiplied by a constant. If L2 regularization is applied to a linear regression it is called ridge regression. L2 regularization has the following formula:

$$Loss = Error(y, \hat{y}) + \gamma \sum_{i=1}^{N} (w_i)^2$$

Where $Error(y, \hat{y})$ corresponds to the error between actual values and predicted values, γ is a regularization parameter and is defined manually and >0, w_i is the model parameters.

See also the following definitions: Regularization, overfitting, and L1 regularization

Labeled data

Labeled data describes a dataset that has for each observation a corresponding tag or label. For example, a set of images has as the labels dog or cat. Labeled data is mandatory to perform supervised machine learning. The process of labeling data is performed by a data annotator and can be time consuming and expensive.

See also the following definitions: Training set and dependent variable

Lasso regression

Lasso regression is a linear regression that implements L1 regularization. This helps avoid overfitting and it implements variable selection to enhance model performance. Lasso regression is used when data contains multicollinearity or when it is convenient to automate the variable selection or when a linear regression model shows overfitting. The equation for the loss function of lasso regression is as follows:

$$Loss = Error(y, \hat{y}) + \gamma \sum_{i=1}^{N} |w_i|$$

See also the following definitions: Linear regression and L1 regularization

Latent variable

Latent variables are variables that cannot be directly observed but are derived from observable variables. Latent variables are usually inferred using a model such as principal component analysis based on observable variables. Latent variables can mean less to a human reader but are full of statistical information.

See also the following definitions: Principal Component Analysis (PCA)

Layer

A layer is a group of neurons in a neural network model. There three types of layers: input, hidden, and output layer. A layer will process the coming data from a previous layer and then forward it to the next layer and in between it will concatenate multiple mathematical computations and transform the input.

See also the following definitions: Hidden layer and neural network

Leaky ReLU

Leaky ReLU is an activation function in a neural network. It is one of the most popular and widely used activation functions with ReLU. As advantages compared to other activation function, Leaky ReLU solves the dying ReLU problem as it is not equal to zero when the values are negative and it speeds up the training. It has the following equation:

$$f(x) = \begin{cases} 0.01x & x < 0 \\ x & x \geq 0 \end{cases}$$

See also the following definitions: Activation function and ReLU

Learning rate

It corresponds to one of the most important hyperparameters in a machine learning model. The learning rate defines how much rate the parameters of a model will be updated based on the gradient. So, a small learning rate means that the updates will be small and a large learning rate means that the updates will be important. With too large learning the algorithm might miss the optimal.

See also the following definitions: Hyperparameter and neural network

Least squares regression

Least squares regression is a linear regression that minimizes the least squares error or L2 loss. Which behaves as follows:

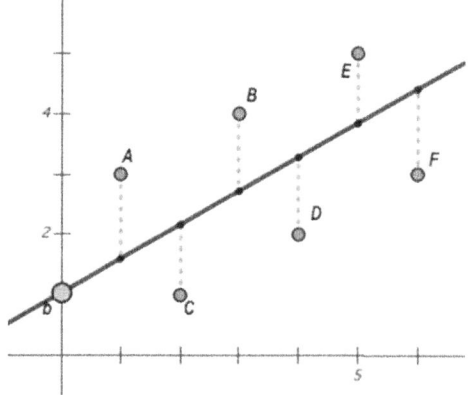

Figure 13.1: Least squares regression

The method of least squares makes it possible to compare experimental data that comes with measurement errors and with a mathematical model supposed to describe this data.

See also the following definitions: Linear regression and L2 loss

Line chart

A line chart is a basic chart type that displays points over time that is connected to each other by a line. The following chart shows a line chart for speed evolution over time:

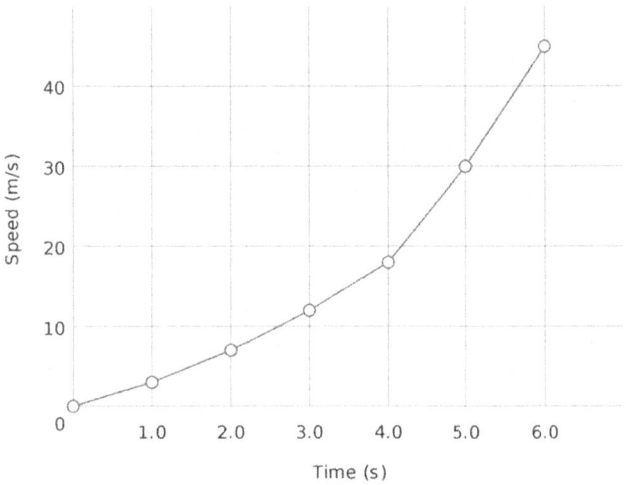

Figure 13.2: A line chart

A line chart can reveal information about a series such as trend, seasonality, and so on.

See also the following definitions: Bar chart, line chart, pie chart, and box plot

Linear activation function

Linear is an activation function for neural networks. It takes an input of a layer and transforms it using a linear function that has the following formula:

$$f(x) = Ax$$

Note that a neural network composed only with linear activation functions is just a linear regression as linear activation cannot help discover complex non-linear patterns in the data.

See also the following definitions: Activation function and neural network

Linear discriminant analysis

Linear Discriminant Analysis or LDA is a dimensionality reduction technique; LDA can also be used for classification problems. LDA modeling is based on assumptions such as is the data Gaussian and is the variance the same for each feature. To make the prediction, LDA is based on the Bayes theorem and returns probabilities for each class output.

See also the following definitions: Dimensionality reduction, principal component analysis, and factor analysis

Linear model

A linear model is a model in machine learning that gives one weight to each feature in the data. A linear model is capable of mapping only linear patterns; it has the following general equation:

$$y' = b + w_1 x_1 + w_2 x_2 + \cdots + w_n x_n$$

The most popular linear models are linear regression and logistic regression. Note that we can consider any model as a linear model if a part of its equation contains the preceding equation.

See also the following definitions: Linear regression and logistic regression

Linear regression

The goal of linear regression is to find the linear relationship between X the independent variable(s) and Y the dependent variable. When there is more than one independent variable, we call it a multiple linear regression. It has the following formula:

$$y = Ax + b$$

Where y is the dependent variable, x is the independent variable, A is a parameter, and b is a constant.

Linear regression can be represented on a chart as follows:

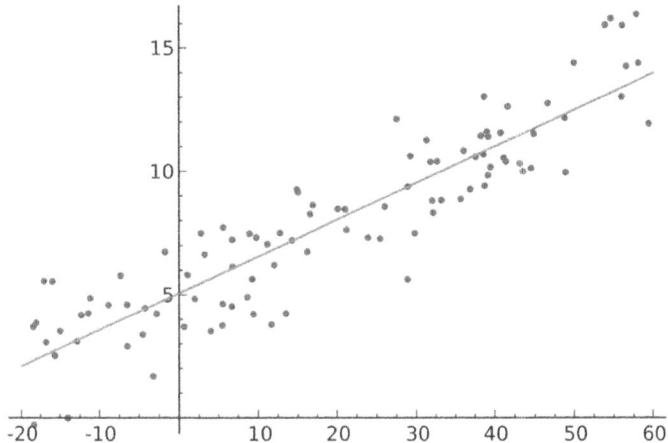

Figure 13.3: *A linear regression*
(Source image: https://fr.wikipedia.org/wiki/Fichier:Linear_regression.svg)

Linear regression is one of the most basic machine learning models.

See also the following definitions: Linear model and machine learning

Log loss

Log loss or cross-entropy loss is the loss function used for logistic regression. The lower the log loss the better is the performance. Log loss has the following formula:

$$Logloss(y) = -(y log(p) + (1-y) \log(1-p))$$

Note that log loss penalizes a lot of confident error, where the value is at the complete opposite of the truth.

See also the following definitions: Exponential loss, loss function, hinge loss, focal loss, magnet loss, Huber loss, L1 Loss, L2 loss, and squared loss

Log-Cosh loss

Log-Cosh is a loss function used for regression problems. It is the logarithm of the hyperbolic cosine of the prediction error. It has a similar behavior to mean squared error except that it is less sensitive to high mistakes. It has the following formula:

$$L(y, \hat{y}) = \sum_{i=1}^{n} \log(\cosh(\hat{y} - y))$$

Where y is the actual value and $\hat{y}$ is the predicted value.

See also the following definitions: Exponential loss, loss function, hinge loss, focal loss, magnet loss, Huber loss, L1 Loss, L2 loss, squared loss, and log loss

Logistic regression

Logistic regression is a binary classification algorithm that applies a sigmoid function to a linear model to convert into probabilistic values between 0 and 1. Compared to linear regression, logistic regression will fit an S-shaped curve called a logistic function instead of a linear function. Instead of calculating the squared error like linear regression to fit the curve, logistic regression computes the product of all maximum likelihood. It has the following equation:

$$p = \frac{1}{1 + e^{-(b_0 + b_1 x_1 + \cdots + b_n x_n)}}$$

Where is the predicted probability, b is the parameters, and x is the independent variables.

See also the following definitions: Linear model and linear regression

Logits

In a neural network, logits correspond to the raw non-normalized output in a classification problem. Logits is usually passed to a Softmax function to become a normalized value that corresponds to the probability for each class. In mathematics, logits refer to a function that maps probabilities to a real value.

See also the following definitions: Classification and output layer

Log-odds

Log-odds, also known as logit, is the logarithm of the odds of an event. For more details see the mathematical definition of logits.

Long Short-Term Memory (LSTM)

LSTM are units for layers in recurrent neural networks. LSTM is good for addressing the vanishing gradient descent problem and is internally composed of three gates: input, output and forget gate. This gate process helps an LSMT unit to remember previous information from another unit and forget other information. LSTM is popular for time series forecasting, speech recognition, handwriting recognition, and so on.

See also the following definitions: Input gate, forget gate, and GRU

Loss curve

A loss curve is a curve that shows the evolution of the general error or loss over iterations. It looks like the following:

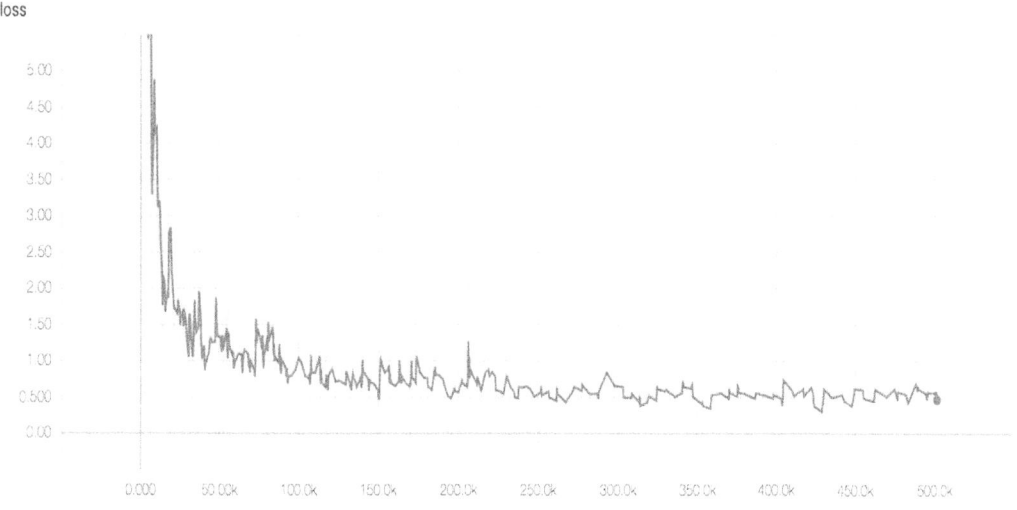

Figure 13.4: Loss curve

The loss curve can help see if a model is converging or if it is diverging or if there is overfitting.

See also the following definitions: Loss function

Loss function

The loss function is the function that computes the difference between the actual label and the predicted label by a model. There are many types of loss functions based on the problem type, like for linear regression the most popular is mean squared error or mean absolute error while for logistic regression we use log loss.

See also the following definitions: Loss curve, exponential loss, hinge loss, focal loss, magnet loss, Huber loss, L1 loss, L2 loss, squared loss, and log loss

Loss surface

A loss surface is the visualization of loss and weights. The idea is to find the best weights for which the loss surface is at an optimal minimum.

See also the following definitions: Loss function

Chapter 14
M

Machine Learning

Machine learning is a technique that allows a computer to learn from data instead of being explicitly programmed. Machine learning is a complex field based on computer science, mathematics, and statistics. Machine learning is composed of different phases, the first phase consists of training the algorithm on data, then comes the validation step, then the test phase where we test the machine learning model on unseen data to evaluate its performance.

See also the following definitions: Linear regression, random forest, and deep learning

Machine translation

It is a machine specialized in translating a text from one language to another. Machine translation is increasingly being based on machine learning, and more precisely deep learning, which shows good results in language translation.

See also the following definitions: Natural language processing

Magnet loss

It is a type of loss function used in machine learning problems that are focused on distance metric learning. It is considered to be an improvement to other losses such as triplet loss and other loss functions designed for distance metric learning.

See also the following definitions: Loss function, loss curve, exponential loss, hinge loss, focal loss, Huber loss, L1 loss, L2 loss, squared loss, and log loss

Mahout

Mahout is an open-source framework from Apache that is dedicated to the creation of machine learning models. It implements various types of machine learning such as recommendation systems, classification problems, clustering algorithms. Mahout is convenient in case we have a large volume of data and would like to apply machine learning.

See also the following definitions: Hadoop, big data, and Apache spark

Majority class

Majority class corresponds to the class that is dominant in an imbalanced dataset. For example, if in a dataset the group from class 0 has 99% of observations and group from class 1 has 1%, the class 0 is the majority class.

See also the following definitions: Imbalanced dataset

Manhattan distance

Manhattan distance represents the distance between two points. It is an alternative to the Euclidian distance. Manhattan distance has the following equation:

$$d(A, B) = |X_B - X_A| + |Y_B - Y_A|$$

See also the following definitions: Euclidian distance

MapReduce

MapReduce is a program created by Google, that allows to process big data using a parallel and distributed cluster. The term MapReduce refers to two separate tasks that are completed, the map process and the reduce process.

See also the following definitions: Hadoop and Big data

Market basket analysis

Market basket analysis is a tool in marketing that analyses what customers purchase as potential combinatory of products or services. This potential combinatory is performed using association rules (apriori algorithm). Then the rules are used by the marketing department to create sales strategy and to define cross selling.

See also the following definitions: Association rules

Market mix modeling

It is a method that is based on historical data from sales data to measure the component of sales. The sales component is usually focused on marketing spends and the idea is to see what is the true ROI of marketing spends on sales. Market mix modeling is usually done using linear regression to model sales with marketing spends.

See also the following definitions: Market basket analysis and linear regression

Markov chain

Markov chain is a system that defines a stochastic process where variables transition from one state to another according to probabilistic rules. With continuous time, it is called Markov process. In machine learning, Markov chain is used in reinforcement learning, it can also be used as a classifier for text recognition.

See also the following definitions: Hidden Markov Model

Markov decision process

Markov decision process is a stochastic model where an agent takes actions and the result of the actions are random. Markov decision processes are used to explore optimization problems with help of dynamic programming or reinforcement learning. At each step, the process is at state s and the agent takes action a. The probability that that the process reaches the states' is based on the selected action.

See also the following definitions: Dynamic programming, Markov chain, and Hidden Markov Model

Markov property

A stochastic process is validating the Markov property if and only if conditional probability distribution of future states, knowing past and present states, depends only on present states and not on past states. The process that respects this condition is called Markov process.

See also the following definitions: Markov decision process

Matplotlib

Matplotlib is an open-source framework in Python that makes it easy to create interactive and animated data visualization. Matplotlib can also be combined with others Python libraries such as NumPy and SciPy.

See also the following definitions: Python and bar chart

Matrix factorization

Matrix factorization is a procedure in collaborative filtering used in recommendation systems, where the matrix factorization will decompose the user item interaction matrix into two matrices of lower dimension. One matrix for user matrix composed by the number of users with the number of embedding dimensions. And one matrix for item matrix composed by the number of embedding with dimensions the number of items.

See also the following definitions: Association rules, recommendation engine, and item matrix

Max pooling

Max pooling is a pooling technique used in convolutional neural network, as it compresses the input matrix in a lower dimension. The manipulation performed by max pooling is represented follows:

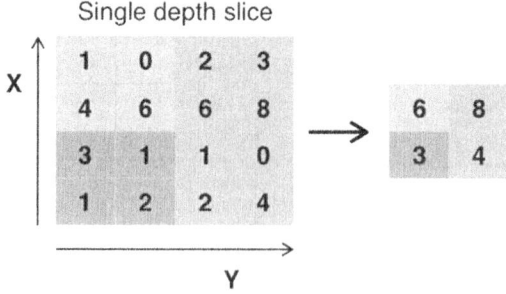

Figure 14.1: *Max pooling*
(Source image: https://en.wikipedia.org/wiki/File:Max_pooling.png)

In contrary to average pooling, max pooling takes the maximum of the values in the rolling window instead of taking the average.

See also the following definitions: Convolutional neural network and average pooling

Maximum likelihood estimation

Maximum likelihood estimation is a technique involved in finding the probability density estimation for a sample. In statistics, the maximum likelihood estimation is a statistical estimator used to infer the parameters of the probability distribution of a given sample by searching for the values of the parameters maximizing the likelihood function.

Mean

The mean corresponds to the average of all values in a dataset. The mean is a number that is usually used as a representation of the whole dataset. It is computed by adding all the values divided by the number of items in the dataset.

See also the following definitions: Median and descriptive statistics

Mean absolute error

The mean absolute error is a metric that computes the error by taking the average of all absolute errors. The mean absolute error can be used to evaluate model performance so it is in this case the difference between the predicted value and actual value in absolute value. It has the following formula:

$$MAE = \frac{1}{n}\sum_{i=0}^{n}|y_i - \hat{y}_i|$$

See also the following definitions: Evaluation metrics and regression

Mean reciprocal rank

Mean reciprocal rank is a statistical measure that helps evaluate the return of a ranked list of answers to queries. For a single rank the value corresponds to $\frac{1}{rank_i}$, where rank is the position of ranked answers, it has the following formula:

$$MRR = \frac{1}{Q} \sum_{i=1}^{Q} \frac{1}{rank_i}$$

See also the following definitions: Evaluation metrics and association rules

Mean squared error

Mean squared error is an error metric calculated by taking an average of squared error. In the context of evaluating a model's accuracy, mean squared error is the average squared between the expected and predicted values, and it has the following formula:

$$MSE = \frac{1}{n} \sum_{i=0}^{n} (y_i - \hat{y}_i)^2$$

See also the following definitions: Evaluation metrics and regression

Median

The median represents the middle value of a set of numbers. If the set of numbers is even, the median is the average of the two middle values. Median is considered as a good alternative to the mean, and is more accurate when it comes to describe the central tendency of a set of numbers.

See also the following definitions: Mean and descriptive statistics

Memory-based learning

For more details about memory-based learning, see the instance-based learning definition.

Mini-batch

It represents a small set that is randomly selected from all the potential examples and presented in a single iteration to the machine learning model for training. The mini-batch has a size between 1 to 1000 depending on the case. It is frequent to talk about mini-batch in a neural network.

See also the following definitions: Batch, iteration, deep learning, and mini-batch gradient descent

Mini-batch gradient descent

It is a neural network algorithm with gradient descent optimizer that uses mini-batches. Mini-batch estimates the gradient based on a small training data subset. If the mini-batch size is equal to 1, we talk about vanilla gradient descent. The models based on mini-batch gradient descent show a robust convergence and it is computationally more efficient.

See also the following definitions: Batch, mini-batch, gradient descent, and vanilla gradient descent

Minimax loss

Minimax loss is a loss function used for generative adversarial networks as it simultaneously the discriminator and generator simultaneously. The minimax algorithm is an algorithm that applies to game theory for two-player zero-sum games of minimizing maximum loss.

See also the following definitions: Generative adversarial neural networks and loss function

Minority class

The label in an imbalanced dataset where one of the two classes are underrepresented. For example, a dataset with spam and not spam, where 99% are not spam and only 1% are spam, spam class here is a minority class.

See also the following definitions: Majority class and Imbalanced dataset

Management Information System (MIS)

Management Information System (MIS) is an information system that supports decision making in an organization. It helps management and operation save time and takes efficient decisions by providing them with relevant information about the business.

See also the following definitions: Database

Machine learning (ML)

ML is an abbreviation for machine learning. For more details see the machine learning definition.

ML-as-a-service (MLaaS)

Machine learning as a service is a range of tools provided as a service in the cloud as part of cloud computing services. It includes tools like text mining, natural language processing, visual recognition, speech to text, predictive analytics, and so on. Some ML-as-a-service providers are: Google machine learning engine, IBM Watson machine learning, AWS machine learning, and so on.

See also the following definitions: Natural language processing, machine learning, and deployment as API

MLOps

MLOps or machine learning operations are a practice where data scientists and IT operation professionals collaborate together to put machine learning models in production. MLOps goal is to get more automation and increase the quality of machine learning production.

See also the following definitions: Deployment as API, deployment in batch, Watson studio, and databricks

MNIST

MNIST is an open-source dataset containing 60 thousand images. The images are 28x28 pixels, and represent hand written digits from 0 to 9. The color channel is one with grayscale.

To download the dataset please use the following link:

http://yann.lecun.com/exdb/mnist/

See also the following definitions: Dataset and ImageNet

Mode

The mode represents the most frequent value in a dataset. It measures the central tendency. One distribution might have multiple modes.

See also the following definitions: Median, mean, and descriptive statistics

Model capacity

A model capacity represents the complexity of problems that a model can learn. The higher the model capacity, the more complex the problem that the model can learn. A model capacity varies based on the model number of parameters.

See also the following definitions: Complexity and predictive model

Model parallelism

Model parallelism is a situation where a deep neural network model is split into multiple sub layers and then each part runs on a device where the data shown by all the parts is the same. Model parallelism is usually opposed to data parallelism where data is split across devices on the same model.

See also the following definitions: Data parallelism

Model selection

Model selection is the ability during the training phase, to select the most performing models to become the primary models. Usually model selection is performed on models that have not been tuned or their hyperparameters optimized.

See also the following definitions: Feature engineering and training set

Model

When a machine learning algorithm is trained on data, the result is called a model. A model is considered as a mathematical equation with parameters, where each parameter is learned by training the machine learning algorithm.

See also the following definitions: Machine learning and predictive model

Momentum

Momentum is a gradient descent algorithm that prevents the loss function from being stuck in local minima as it accelerates gradient vectors in the right direction, leading to a faster convergence. Gradient descent with momentum computes an exponentially weighted average of the gradients, and then uses that gradient to update the weights. It has the following equation:

$$V_t = \beta V_{t-1} + (1 - \beta)\nabla_w L(W, X, y)$$

See also the following definitions: Gradient descent, AdaDelta, AdaGrad, Adam Optimization, and optimizer

Monte Carlo simulation

Monte Carlo simulation uses a random sample of inputs to explore the behavior of a process. Monte Carlo simulation produces several potential outcomes, from a sample of probability distribution of each variable.

Moving average

Moving average is an effective technique to smooth out time series by retrieving the noise from random fluctuations. The simple moving average takes the mean of a given set over the past number of periods, so it could be the simple moving average over the previous 15 days, and so on.

See also the following definitions: Time series analysis and ARIMA

Multi-agent reinforcement learning

Multi-agent reinforcement learning is when we have multiple agents interacting in the same environment. There are three main categories for multi-agents. First, cooperative where agents in the same environment cooperate with each other to get the reward. Second, competitive where agents compete against each other to get the reward, so it's a zero-sum game. Third, cooperative and competitive at the same time, where it has in the same environment agents that cooperate with each other and agents that compete with each other. For example, a hockey game is an environment with cooperative and competitive multi-agents, as it has teammates and the competition team.

See also the following definitions: Reinforcement learning, agent, and action

Multi-class classification

A multi-class classification problem is a problem where the target variable has more than two classes. For example, we would like to classify images into classes each image can be from the following class: cat, dog, flower, car, and balloon. The problem is a 5-class classification problem.

See also the following definitions: Classification

Multilayer perceptron

A multilayer perceptron is a feedforward neural network that is one of the simplest forms of neural network as it is usually called a vanilla neural network. A multilayer perceptron has at least one hidden layer; it is also based on non-linear activation functions and uses backpropagation for training.

See also the following definitions: Neural network

Multinomial classification

For more details about multinomial classification, see the multi-class classification definition.

Multivariate analysis

Multivariate analysis helps analyze and compare the relationship between multiple variables. There are different techniques that help perform multivariate analysis such as additive trees, multidimensional scaling, cluster analysis, PCA, correspondence analysis, and so on.

See also the following definitions: Covariance and Principal Component Analysis (PCA)

Multivariate regression

A multivariate regression refers to a multiple dependent variables' regression. It is a model designed to deal with multiple outputs or targets. For example, we would like to be able to predict for a sample of a population what the age and revenue are. To do so, we have data that contains characteristics about the population, our independent variables, and we have our multiple dependent variables: the age and the revenue. This is multivariate regression.

See also the following definitions: Dependent variable and linear regression

MXNet:

MXNet is an open-source framework that supports training and deploying deep neural networks. It supports several programming languages and it is scalable and flexible.

See also the following definitions: Caffe, Tensorflow, Torch, and Pytorch

Chapter 15
N

Naïve Bayes

It is a classification probabilistic machine learning algorithm that is based on the Bayes theorem. A naïve Bayes classifier starts with the assumption that all predicators are independent. Naïve Bayes are mostly used for document classification, sentiment analysis, spam filtering, and so on. They train fast and are easy to implement, but their main disadvantage is the fact that predicators have to be independent.

See also the following definitions: Machine learning, random forest, and XGboost

NaN

NaN means 'not a number' and it represents a data that is missing. It is a numeric data type that is undefined.

See also the following definitions: Imputation and dataset

Nash equilibrium

Nash equilibrium is a group of strategies, one per player, such that no player has incentive to change his strategy knowing what the other players are doing.

Intuitively, Nash equilibrium is a law no one would like to break even in the absence of an effective control.

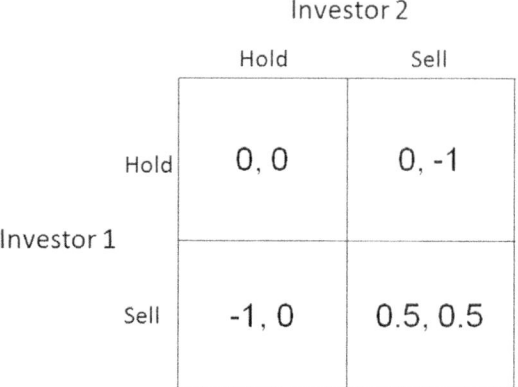

Figure 15.1: A representation of Nash equilibrium
(Source image: https://en.wikipedia.org/wiki/Self-fulfilling_crisis)

For example, following the stoplights in car traffic is Nash equilibrium. As if two players are in an intersection with one having a red light and the other one a green light, both players have no incentive not to follow the color of the light traffic.

Natural language generation

Natural Language Generation or NLG is the usage of machine learning to generate content from an original dataset. NLG is very effective for all time sensitive data analysis and reporting, such as news generation. NLG is slightly different from natural language processing or NLP, where NLP reads a text and extract key information while NLG writes a text from a specific dataset.

See also the following definitions: Natural language processing and natural language understanding

Natural language processing

Natural Language Processing (NLP) is a sub-field of artificial intelligence where a raw text data is processed, structured, and categorized. The most common applications are language translation, word processors that helps check the grammar of a text, interactive voice response used to answer the phone and speaks to human, personal assistant, and so on.

See also the following definitions: Natural language generation and natural language understanding

Natural Language Understanding (NLU)

Natural Language Understanding (NLU) is the ability of a machine to understand human language; it is considered as a branch of natural language processing. NLU doesn't just focus on recognition of speech it actually looks for user intent. NLU is powered by machine learning and is used to build virtual assistant.

See also the following definitions: Natural language generation and natural language processing

Negative class

In binary classification, there are two classes – one is qualified as positive and the other one as negative. For example, spam/not spam, where spam is the positive class and not spam is the negative class.

See also the following definitions: Positive class and classification

Negative log likelihood

Negative log likelihood is a loss function used for machine learning and deep learning algorithms. It is used for classification algorithms and can be used for binary classification.

$$Loss = -\log(y)$$

See also the following definitions: Classification and loss function

Nesterov accelerated gradient

Nesterov's gradient acceleration is a global approach that is used to improve the initial convergence by using a gradient descent-type method.

See also the following definitions: Gradient descent

Neural Machine Translation (NMT)

Neural Machine Translation (NMT) is a machine learning approach for automated translation that shows better results than traditional translation systems. NMT can be computationally expensive and can have difficulty with not common words.

See also the following definitions: Machine translation

Neural network

It is a machine learning algorithm composed of layers (at least one hidden layer with an input and output layer). Each layer is composed of neurons that are connected to each other and followed by a non-linear function called the **activation function**:

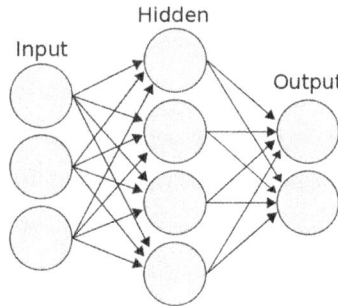

*Figure 15.2: Neural network representation
(Source image: https://commons.wikimedia.org/wiki/File:Artificial_neural_network.svg)*

If a neural network has more than one hidden layer it is called a deep neural network algorithm. A deep neural network has become very popular in the last year thanks to its capabilities in computer vision and speech recognition.

See also the following definitions: Deep learning, machine learning, and multilayer perceptron

Neural Turing machine (NTM)

A **Neural Turing Machine (NTM)** is a type of recurrent neural network that combines neural networks with programmable computers.

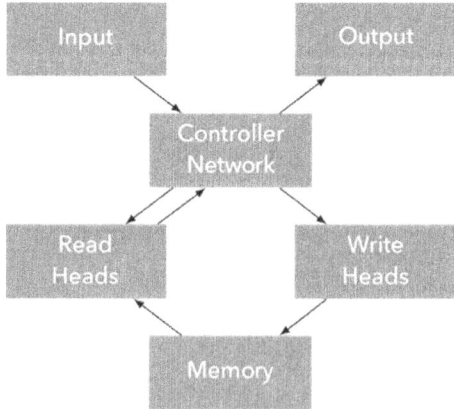

*Figure 15.3: A representation of a neural Turing machine
(Source image: https://en.wikipedia.org/wiki/Differentiable_neural_computer)*

An NTM has a controller that is a neural network merged with external memory resources that interacts through attentional mechanism.

See also the following definitions: Recurrent neural network

Neuron

A neuron represents a node in a neural network algorithm. A neuron takes multiple inputs and provides one output. Each neuron calculates the sum of weighted inputs plus bias then applies an activation function.

See also the following definitions: Neural network

N-gram

N-gram represents an ordered sequence of N words. For example, black t-shirt is a 2-gram as it is composed of 2 words. Several natural language understanding models rely on N-gram to predict the next word a user will say.

See also the following definitions: Natural language processing

No free lunch theorem

The no free lunch theorem means that there is a trade-off in machine learning as no good result is free. To find a good machine learning algorithm you need to get the right data and have the knowledge for the subject matter expertise. A universal machine learning model for all problems doesn't exist. Each algorithm cannot be preferred over the others as for each problem there is a model that performs well.

See also the following definitions: Machine learning, overfitting, and generalization

Node

Node means neuron. For more details see the neuron definition.

Noise

Noise represents anything that blocks the true signal from data. For example, an error coming from a human annotator where labels are misannotated represents a noise. Or a sensor that provides data containing sensor miscalibration is noise. Noise is usually something we would like to not model with machine learning. And we can erase noise from data either by doing some data transformation or data engineering or by using machine learning, as some algorithms can detect noise and not taking it in consideration during modeling.

See also the following definitions: Annotator, machine learning, and data transformation

Noise contrastive estimation

In word2vec with next word prediction, using a neural network can be costly with softmax function at the end of the network, as the output layer end up to be very large. We replace softmax to estimate the output probability, by a logistic regression. So, instead of predicting the next word, the classifier predicts if two words are good or bad.

See also the following definitions: Word2vec, softmax, and neural network

Nominal variable

A nominal variable represents a categorical variable with two or more categories that has no explicit order. For example, a variable named color that contains color names such as blue, green, yellow, red, and so on. This is a nominal variable as it contains categories but don't have any specific order.

See also the following definitions: Binary variable, variable, categorical variable, continuous variable, discrete variable, dummy variable, and ordinal variable

Nonlinear transform function

A nonlinear transform function is a function that modifies the linear relationship between variables, such as applying root square to a variable, the linear relationship between this variable and another will definitely change. For regression, when a residual plot shows a set of variables to be nonlinear, the data scientists apply nonlinear transformations to the independent or dependent variables. This transformation lets the data scientist use linear regression techniques appropriately with nonlinear data.

See also the following definitions: Linear regression and activation function

Normal distribution

Normal distribution or Gaussian distribution is the most common and most used statistical distribution. Normal distribution has the following shape:

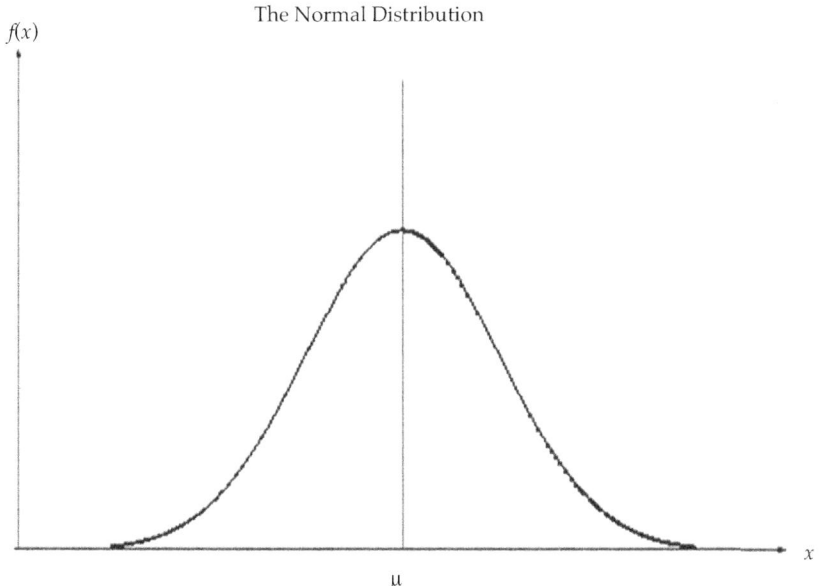

Figure 15.4: Normal distribution
(Source image: https://commons.wikimedia.org/wiki/File:Normal_Distribution_NIST.gif)

It is usually used as an assumption or hypothesis to represent real-valued random variables whose distribution are unknown.

See also the following definitions: Bernoulli distribution, binomial distribution, chi-squared distribution, Gaussian distribution, t-distribution, exponential family distribution, and Poisson distribution

Normalization

Normalization is the process of rescaling a variable so that all continuous variables are on the same scale. Being on the same scale means having values between 0 and 1 or -1 and 1. For example, suppose a continuous variable has a range of values from 100 to 1200, normalizing this variable will bring the values from 0 to 1 or from -1 to 1.

See also the following definitions: Data transformation

Normalized discounted cumulative gain

Normalized Discounted Cumulative Gain or NDCG is an evaluation metric for recommendation systems. It is derived from the discounted cumulative gain and has its value from 0 to 1. NDCG is more practical than the discounted cumulative gain as it is normalized so it's easier to sum all results for each user to get a unified final score.

See also the following definitions: Recommendation engine and evaluation metrics

NoSQL

NoSQL stands for not only SQL. It gives the ability to store and retrieve data in ways other than the relations available in relational databases. NoSQL is considered to be non-tabular and is very popular for big data applications and real time analytics. NoSQL comes in a variety of types such as document, key-value, wide-column, and graph.

See also the following definitions: Database and SQL

Notebook

A notebook is document that is composed of input and output cells and can contain code, text or markdown, plots and media. The notebook format is the most used support for coding in data science. It is appreciated by data scientists as it helps create reports containing codes and notes around a project. The most popular notebook is the Jupyter notebook.

See also the following definitions: Jupyter notebook, Watson Studio, and DataBricks

Null

Null is considered either as a constant or as a value. We can find it in several computing languages such as Python, C, C++, and so on. Null value means that the variable doesn't have any value or was not initialized. It has a close meaning to NaN or NA.

See also the following definitions: NaN and imputation

Null accuracy:

A baseline accuracy that is computed by only predicting the most frequent class.

See also the following definitions: Evaluation metrics and accuracy

Numerical data

Numerical data represents data that is measurable and it comes always in the number form. For example, the number of people that visited the hospital during the last month is a numerical data.

See also the following definitions: Dataset

Numpy

Numpy is an open-source mathematical library in Python. It is one of the most popular libraries in Python for data science. With Numpy, it is possible to perform an efficient array operations.

See also the following definitions: Python and Matplotlib

NVIDIA

NVIDIA is a GPU (graphics processing unit) designed for manipulating graphics and image processing. In data science, it has been hacked to perform heavy computing, especially in deep learning. NVIDIA is now a standard in deep learning and significantly increases the speed of the computing.

See also the following definitions: GPU

Chapter 16

O

Object Detection

Object detection is an artificial intelligence application related to computer vision. It detects classes (such as car, human, birds, and so on.) in images and videos and is capable to locate where exactly is an object in an image.

Figure 16.1: Object detection representation in an image
(Source image: https://commons.wikimedia.org/wiki/File:Detected-with-YOLO--Schreibtisch-mit-Objekten.jpg)

One of the most famous tools for object detection is called **You Only Look Once** (**YOLO**).

See also the following definitions: Image recognition and deep learning

Objective

An objective represents the metric that a machine learning algorithm is trying to optimize. It is mandatory to define an objective for each machine learning algorithm for each problem.

See also the following definitions: Loss function and machine learning

Objective function

An objective function is metric or an equation that a machine learning algorithm is trying to optimize. It usually represents the gap between predicted values and real values and the algorithm has to minimize the objective function. For example, squared loss or L2 loss is an objective function for a linear regression. In some cases, instead of minimizing the objective function the goal will be to maximize it.

See also the following definitions: Loss function and machine learning

One hot encoding

One hot encoding is a feature engineering technique that consists of encoding a categorical variable into a dummified variable, so each new variable will be a dummy representing one category from the categorical variable.

Color	Green	Blue	Red
Green	1	0	0
Blue	0	1	0
Red	0	0	1
Green	1	0	0
Blue	0	1	0
Red	0	0	0
Green	1	0	0

Figure 16.2: One hot encoding transformation

One hot encoding is useful in case where the machine learning algorithm doesn't support categorical variable such as neural network or linear regression.

See also the following definitions: Data transformation

One shot learning

One shot learning is a machine learning approach where it creates a classifier based only on one training example. It is often used for object classification. A way to obtain a model capable of one-shot learning is to use representation learning, to deduce representations that can be used to accurately classify one example.

See also the following definitions: Zero shot learning and continuous learning

One vs all

One vs all consists of converting a classification problem with multiple classes to a binary classification where one class represent one class from the classification problem and the other class represent all the rest of classes. For example, we have a classification problem where the target has the following output red, blue, and yellow. If we convert it to one vs all, we will get the following classes:

- Red vs Not red
- Blue vs Not blue
- Yellow vs Not yellow

See also the following definitions: Classification and multi label classification

Online inference

Online inference corresponds to a situation where a machine learning model generates prediction on demand. It is usually opposed to offline inference, where we score against a machine learning model in batch and then we store results waiting to get requests for predictions.

See also the following definitions: Deployment as API

Online learning

Online learning or incremental learning consumes data sequentially, meaning that a stream of data comes and data is consumed by the machine learning model one after the other, which opposed to batch learning where the model is created by learning on the entire dataset. It is common to use this technique in the case where it is not feasible to learn on the entire dataset or in case the data behaviors change very fast.

See also the following definitions: Active learning and continuous learning

Oozie

Apache Oozie is a workflow scheduling server-based system that supports Hadoop jobs. It is composed of two parts: workflow engine and coordinator engine.

See also the following definitions: Hadoop and Big data

OpenCV

OpenCV (Open Computer Vision) is a free graphics library, originally developed by Intel, specializing in image processing in real time.

Figure 16.3: Face detection using OpenCV
(Source image: https://fr.wikipedia.org/wiki/Fichier:Face_detection_example_openCV.jpg)

The OpenCV library provides many diversified functionalities allowing to create programs starting from raw data to go as far as the creation of basic graphical interfaces.

See also the following definitions: Image recognition and deep learning

Optimizer

An optimizer is the solver that implements the gradient descent algorithm. The most popular ones are AdaGrad, Adam, AdaBoost, Momentum, and so on. An optimizer is key in a deep neural network as it is what updates the parameters based on the cost function.

See also the following definitions: AdaGrad, AdaDelta, AdaBoost, Adam Optimization, and deep learning

Ordinal variable

An ordinal variable is a variable that has discrete values with a certain order in it. For example, a variable with values large or 3, medium or 2, small or 1 is an ordinal variable.

See also the following definitions: Binary variable, variable, categorical variable, continuous variable, discrete variable, dummy variable, and nominal variable

Outlier

An outlier is a value that is distant from other values in a dataset. So, an outlier is divergent from the pattern in a sample.

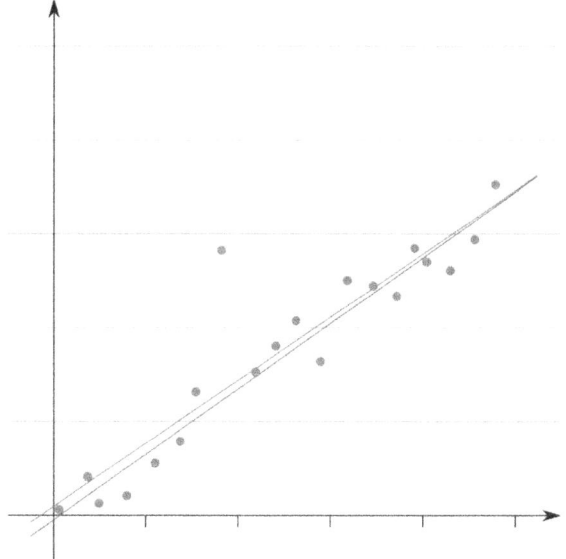

Figure 16.4: Outlier representation
(Source image: https://commons.wikimedia.org/wiki/File:Outlier_statistics.svg)

Usually, outliers can cause problems in machine learning models so one way to avoid using outliers is clipping.

See also the following definitions: Extreme value

Output gate

Output gate is one of the three gates that compose an LSTM cell or Long Short-Term Memory cell that is a type of layer in a deep neural network. The output gate has as an output in the next hidden state knowing that the hidden state has information on past inputs. At the beginning, the current input and the previous hidden state are passed into a sigmoid function. Then the new created cell state is passed to the tanh function, and then the tanh output is multiplied with the sigmoid output. This operation supports hidden state and what information it should include. The new cell state and the new hidden are then carried over to the next time step.

See also the following definitions: Input gate, forget gate, and LSTM

Output layer

The output layer is the last layer in a neural network. That is represented at the right of the following image:

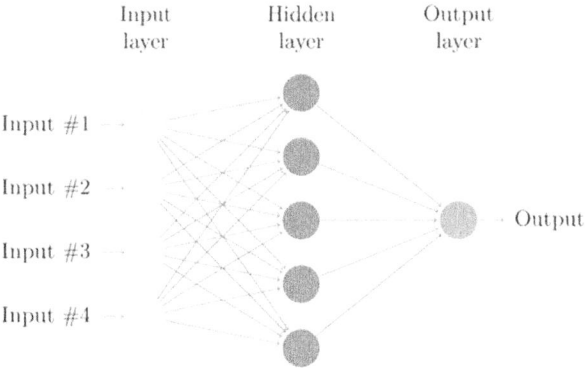

Figure 16.5: Output layer and neural network
(Source image: http://www.texample.net/tikz/examples/neural-network/)

The output layer produces the final result that is compared to the actual values and then the error is backpropagated to update the weights.

See also the following definitions: Input layer, hidden layer, and neural network

Overfitting

Overfitting is a machine learning situation where a model is well performing on training data but is poorly performing on test data or new data. This is due to the model learning too much from training data even random patterns and noises. To avoid overfitting, it is possible to use techniques such as regularization or early stopping.

See also the following definitions: Convergence and underfitting

CHAPTER 17
P

Pandas

Pandas is an open-source data manipulation and data analysis framework on Python. It is one of the most popular frameworks on Python as it is fast and efficient for reading data, for data manipulation, for reshaping data, for merging, and for joining data.

See also the following definitions: Numpy, Python, and Matplotlib

Parallel processing

Parallel processing is a technique in computer science of running two or more processors or CPUs to deal with separate parts of a task. Splitting up multiple parts of a task among multiple processors is good way to reduce the amount of time a program runs.

See also the following definitions: Data parallelism and model parallelism

Parameter update

During the training of a machine learning model, the parameters of a model are being updated based on an iteration of gradient descent. This parameter update is based on the error or loss computed.

See also the following definitions: Batch, iteration, hyperparameter, and machine learning

Parameters

Parameters represent in machine learning model internal variables that are updated based on data. Parameters evolve and change during the training based on loss or error. In neural networks, parameters are weights. Parameters are not to be confused with hyperparameters as hyperparameters are parameters that are defined at the beginning prior to training.

See also the following definitions: Machine learning and loss function

Part of speech tagging

Part of speech tagging or POS tagging is a technique of marking up a word in a text, based on its context and definition, as corresponding to a part of a speech tag. This task can be more complex, as a specific word can have a different part of speech depending on the context where the word is used.

See also the following definitions: Natural language processing

Partial derivative

A partial derivative is the derivative of a function of multiple variables as derivative with respect of only one variable and the other are constant. A partial derivative is used in a neural network as one of the key concepts for backpropagation.

See also the following definitions: Chain rule, neural network, and parameter update

Participation bias

Participation bias or non-response bias is a situation where the results of a survey, an election, and so on are non-representative as the sample characteristics are different from the population characteristics.

See also the following definitions: Automation bias, bias, bias-variance trade-off, coverage bias, implicit bias, and sampling bias

Partitioning

In machine learning, portioning data is an important step prior to model training. The data is split in three or two sets, one for training, one for validation and one for testing or one for training and one for testing. After what the training data are used for training and the rest of the data is used for validation or for testing. Partitioning is a powerful technique to avoid overfitting.

See also the following definitions: Training set, test set, and validation set

Pattern recognition

Pattern recognition is a domain in machine learning that focuses on finding patterns in images. It has applications in signal processing, image analysis, information retrieval, bioinformatics, and so on. Nowadays, pattern recognition is usually based on the deep neural network, especially for pattern recognition that involves classification.

See also the following definitions: Deep learning and image recognition

Peak signal-to-noise ratio:

Peak Signal-To-Noise Ratio or PSNR is a ratio used to compared the quality between a compressed or reconstructed image and its original. The higher the PSNR the better the quality. PSNR is commonly used to approximate the efficiency of compressors, filters, and so on.

See also the following definitions: Image recognition

Perceptron:

A perceptron in deep neural networks represents a node that takes values from one or multiples inputs and applies a linear or nonlinear function to the weighted sum of the input plus a bias. The function applied to the weighted sum can be ReLU, sigmoid, tanh, and it is represented as follows:

$$f(x_1, x_2) = \tanh(w_1 x_1 + w_2 x_2)$$

It can be visually represented as follows:

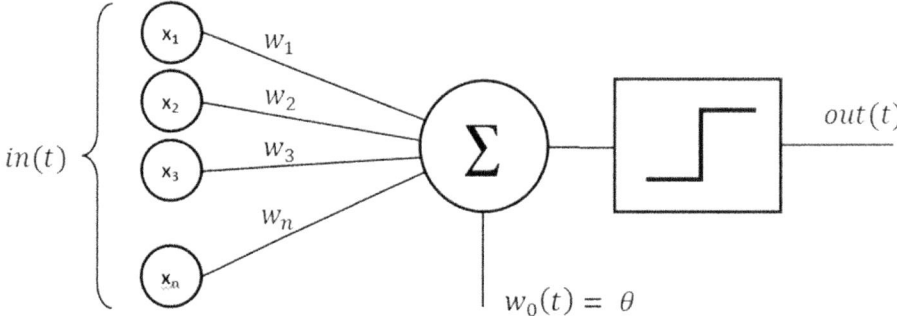

Figure 17.1: A representation of a perceptron
(Source image: https://commons.wikimedia.org/wiki/File:Perceptron_moj.png)

A perceptron is a component of a neural network and a multilayer perceptron is considered as a vanilla neural network.

See also the following definitions: Activation function, hidden layer, and deep learning

Performance

Performance is a term that is used to designate many things; the most common usage is to describe how well a model is either against training data or testing data. Performance in machine learning is usually associated to how good the evaluation metric of a machine is learning model.

See also the following definitions: Evaluation metrics and machine learning

Perplexity

Perplexity is a measure to show how well a task is performed by a machine learning model. It is used to compare the performance of probability model. A low value of perplexity indicates that the model is good at predicting for a sample.

See also the following definitions: Predictive model and machine learning

Pie chart

A pie chart is circular graphic representing statistics and it is divided into slices that represent the proportion of each category. It is represented as follows:

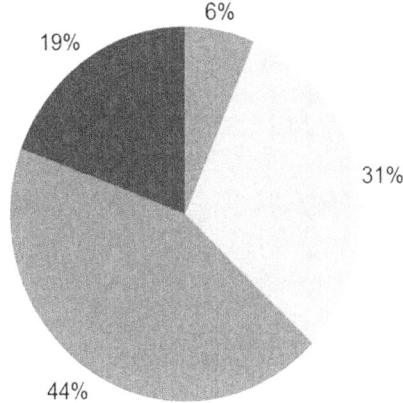

Figure 17.2: A representation of a pie chart
(Source image: https://commons.wikimedia.org/wiki/File:Pie-chart.jpg)

The arc of each slice represents proportionally the quantity of a category.

See also the following definitions: Bar chart, line chart, and box plot

Pig

Pig is a high-level scripting language that is used with Apache Hadoop. Pig enables data workers to write complex data transformations without knowing Java. Pig is complete, so one can do all the required data manipulations in Apache Hadoop with Pig. Through the User Defined Functions (UDF) facility in Pig, Pig can invoke code in many languages like Ruby, Python, and Java."

Source: https://www.analyticsvidhya.com/glossary-of-common-statistics-and-machine-learning-terms/#fourteen

See also the following definitions: Hadoop and Big data

Pipeline

A pipeline is all the necessary structure surrounding building a machine learning model, it includes data extraction, data transformation, data cleansing, training a model, deploying a model, retraining a model, and so on. A pipeline can be automated or manual.

See also the following definitions: Data transformation and data preparation

Poisson distribution

Poisson is discrete probability distribution that helps find the probability of an event to occur over a fixed interval of time. In this case, suppose that events are occurring independently and randomly.

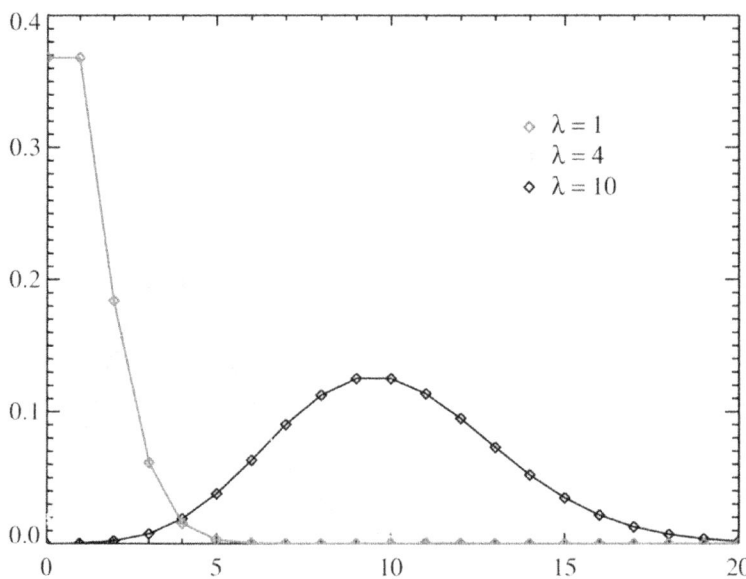

Figure 17.3: Poisson distribution
(Source image: https://commons.wikimedia.org/wiki/File:Poisson_distribution_PMF.png)

As in the given chart, Poisson can have multiple potential distribution based on the value of lambda. Lambda is usually equal to the mean and to the variance.

See also the following definitions: Bernoulli distribution, binomial distribution, chi-squared distribution, gaussian distribution, t-distribution, exponential family distribution, and normal distribution

Polynomial regression

A polynomial regression is similar to a linear regression except that one or more independent variables have a power degree higher than one.

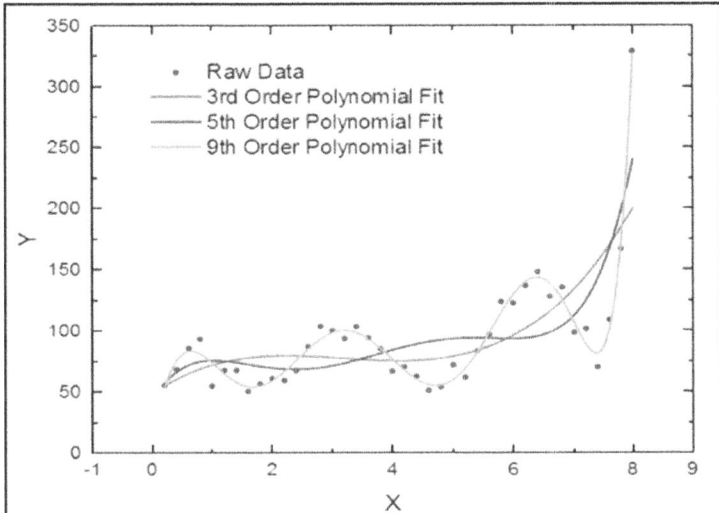

Figure 17.4: Polynomial regression

Transforming a regression to a polynomial regression can be useful to map non-linear relationship except that a high-power degree can lead to overfitting in some cases.

See also the following definitions: Linear regression and overfitting

Pooling

Pooling is a technique used in a convolutional neural network that compresses the input matrix in a lower dimension. Pooling means either taking the maximum or average value in the target area of an image. Pooling is useful for translational invariance in the input matrix.

See also the following definitions: Convolutional neural network and neural network

Population

A population represents the source from were a sample or a dataset was extracted. Usually, the size of a population is always bigger than the size of a dataset. We make a lot of assumptions about the population based on the dataset.

See also the following definitions: Dataset example

Positive class:

A positive class represents a class of output in binary classification. There are two classes positive and negative. Usually, positive represents the class we are testing for or the anomaly or true value. For example, "spam"/ "not spam" where "spam" represents the positive class.

See also the following definitions: Negative class and classification

Post-processing

Post-processing is all the transformation applied to a model prediction or output. It is usually used to adjust the result based on specific characteristics like for example for fairness. Post-processing can be defined as threshold applied directly to the output to be able to categorize it.

See also the following definitions: Predictive model and pre-processing

Precision and recall

Precision and recall are evaluation metrics used in binary classification in cases like anomaly detection for example. Precision represents how many positive cases are predicted correctly, while recall represents how many of the positive cases are predicted correctly. Precision and recall are considered complementary metrics and allow to deduce true positive compares to false positive and false negative. Precision and recall can be combined as one metric in F1 score.

See also the following definitions: Binary classification and mean average precision

Prediction

Prediction is the output of a trained machine learning model. After training a model with training data, we will use the trained model to predict new outcome. We evaluate a machine learning model on how well it is capable to produce prediction that is close to reality.

See also the following definitions: Predictive model and test set

Predictive model

A predictive model represents a trained machine learning model ready to score new data. It is usually used to describe machine learning models that are used to predict unknown values like supervised machine learning.

See also the following definitions: Prediction and training set

Predictor variable

A predictor variable represents a variable that is used as input to machine learning model. A predictor variable is the variable that will support the prediction of the target variable. Usually an input variable becomes a predictor if it is chosen as final variable for training. In some cases, we can name it as the independent variable.

See also the following definitions: Dependent variable

Pre-processing

Pre-processing represents a step-in data transformation and data cleansing where the raw data is manipulated to be fine-tuned and ready for machine learning algorithms. Pre-processing is a key step in machine learning as it helps increase model performance and diminishes noise.

See also the following definitions: Post-processing and predictive model

Pre-trained model

A pre-trained model is a machine learning model that has been trained prior to the actual project. This pre-trained model is then applied to the actual project. A pre-trained model is usually used for a deep neural network where we transfer the weights of the pre-trained model to the actual model and then train the model on the new data. This process is usually called transfer learning.

See also the following definitions: Deep learning and transfer learning

Principal Component Analysis (PCA)

PCA is an approach in dimensionality reduction and factor analysis. It is used either in data transformation prior to applying the machine learning model or used for data analysis. PCA works by transforming potentially correlated variables by applying an orthogonal transformation which output a set of uncorrelated variables. Note that PCA is sensitive to outliers.

See also the following definitions: Dimensionality reduction and factor analysis

Prior belief

Prior belief represents all the assumptions made on data, such as distribution assumptions, correlation assumptions, data collection process assumption, and so on.

See also the following definitions: Hypothesis and induction

Probability density

The probability density function represents the probability that a variable X is close to a real number x. If the probability density around a point x is large, so the random variable X is likely to be close to x.

See also the following definitions: Variable

Proxy label

Proxy label represents a label that helps estimate a target label indirectly. For example, we want to know if there is a car present in every picture in the dataset, but we don't have label to identify cars. However, we have a label containing if there is a road on the picture. Note that a proxy label is not perfect as it doesn't perfectly match with the true or target label, but can be useful to deal with absent labels.

See also the following definitions: Ground truth and dependent variable

P-value

P-value stands for probability value and it helps determine if a null hypothesis is significant. It represents the probability, as the null hypothesis is considered as true, to obtain extreme values. A small p-value will favor the alternative hypothesis meaning that the null hypothesis can be rejected more easily, at the opposite a large p-value will favor the null hypothesis meaning that it's harder to reject it.

See also the following definitions: Normal distribution

Python

Python is an interpreted, multi-paradigm and multiplatform programming language. It promotes structured, functional and object-oriented imperative programming. Python is the most popular programming language in data science, because it has an active community, it's easy to use, fast, and it gives access to useful libraries.

See also the following definitions: R, Anaconda, Jupyter Notebook, Scala, and Go

PyTorch

PyTorch is an open-source library developed for machine learning and more specifically deep learning for Python. It is based on Torch that has been developed by Facebook. PyTorch is considered to be more intuitive than other deep learning libraries like Tensorflow.

See also the following definitions: Tensorflow, Torch, and Caffe

CHAPTER 18
Q

Q-function

"In statistics, the Q function is the tail distribution function of the standard normal distribution. In other words, it is the probability that a normal (Gaussian) random variable will get a value greater than the standard deviations." Source: https://en.wikipedia.org/wiki/Q-function

In reinforcement learning, it specifies how good it is for an agent to perform a particular action in a state with a policy.

See also the following definitions: Normal distribution, reinforcement learning, agent, and action,

Q-learning

Q-learning is machine learning algorithm in the family of reinforcement learning. It is very popular in virtual environments such as video games. It is considered model-free learning as it derives an optimal policy directly from the interaction with the environment without building a model, it involves predicting the value function of a certain policy without having a concrete model of the environment and this is done using Monte Carlo technic. The Q function is approximated using Bellman equation. Q-learning has a period of exploitation and a period of exploration based on a random variable, this helps the model discover new patterns and avoid getting stuck in some situations.

See also the following definitions: Reinforcement learning, agent, action, and Q-function

Quadratic loss

Quadratic loss is a loss function also known as mean squared error. For more details see the mean squared error definition.

Quantile

Quantile is a technique to separate a feature into buckets that contains the same amount of example. For example, the 50th quantile of the median separates the feature into equal size buckets and the median value represents the middle of the values.

See also the following definitions: Decile, descriptive statistics, and quartile

Quantile loss

Quantile loss is useful in regression where we are interested in the uncertainty of our predictions as quantile loss provides an interval for prediction instead of point prediction. A regression with quantile loss gives prediction intervals even for residuals with changing variance or non-normal distribution.

See also the following definitions: Predictive model, machine learning, and loss function

Quartile:

A quartile falls under the family of quantiles and it separates a series into four equal parts. The first quartile denoted Q1 is the middle number between the minimum and the median. The four quartiles are denoted Q1, Q2, Q3, and Q4.

See also the following definitions: Quantile, decile, and descriptive statistics

Question answering (NLP)

Question answering is a field in natural language processing in computer science that focuses on answering human questions asked in natural language. Usually the computer builds an answer by questioning a structured or unstructured database this is called knowledge based.

See also the following definitions: Natural language processing

CHAPTER 19
R

R

R is a programming language and a free software for statistics and data science supported by the R Foundation for Statistical Computing. It is part of the GNU3 package list and is written in C (language), Fortran, and R. The R language is widely used by statisticians, data miners, and data scientists for the development of statistical software and data analysis.

See also the following definitions: Python, Anaconda, Jupyter Notebook, Scala, Java, and Go

Radial basis function network

Radial Basis Function Network (RBFN) is a neural network that contains a radial basis function as the activation function it is considered as a non-linear classifier. A neural of RBFN will store a prototype of input value and then compare it to new inputs and measure the similarity between them, then it will classify based on the similarity. The architecture of a radial basis function network looks like the following:

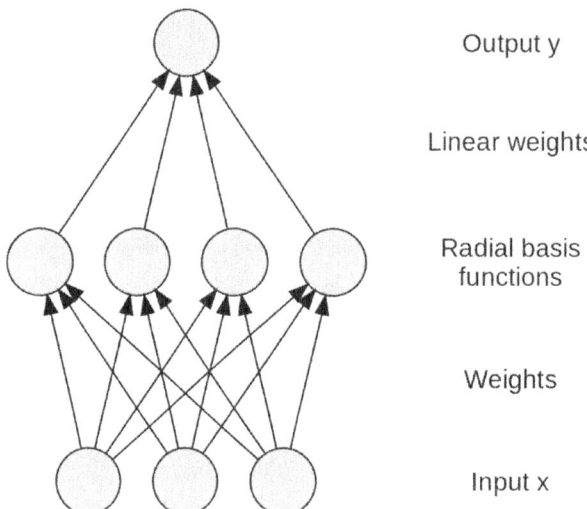

Figure 19.1: Radial basis function network
(Source image: https://fr.wikipedia.org/wiki/Fichier:Radial_funktion_network.svg)

The radial basis function network can be used for time series prediction and classification problems.

See also the following definitions: Neural network and activation function

Random-Access Memory (RAM)

Random-Access Memory (RAM) is the computer memory in which information processed by a computer device can be stored and then erased. It is a useful concept in data science as data transformation and data manipulation requires using RAM, so a data scientist has to know how much RAM memory is required to perform any data manipulation.

See also the following definitions: GPU, CPU, and device

Random forest

Random forest is an ensemble learning technique that falls under bagging techniques. It is one of the most popular machine learning algorithms and can be used for regression or classification. The building blocks of a random forest are decision trees, the model builds several decision trees based on a sample of features from training data then the result is aggregated. The decision trees created are called weak learners and the sampling from training data is done with replacement. We can visually represent random forest as follows:

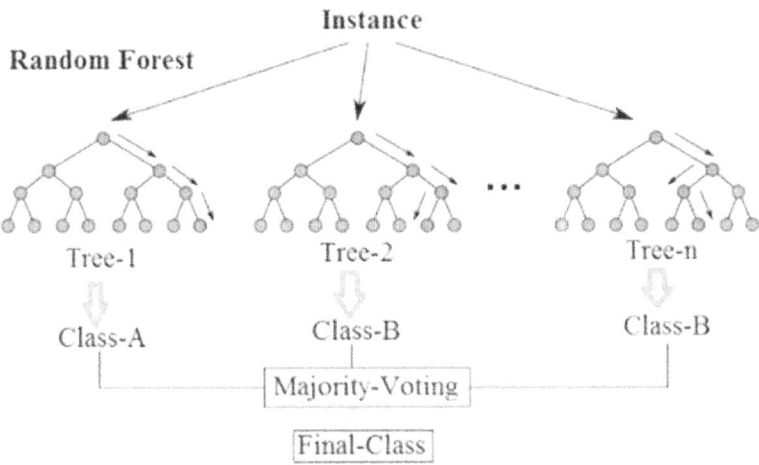

Figure 19.2: Random forest visual representation
(Source image: https://commons.wikimedia.org/wiki/File:Random_forest_diagram_complete.png)

What makes random forest so powerful is the force of the group of uncorrelated decision trees compared to an individual model.

See also the following definitions: Bagging, XGBoost, and decision tree

Random initialization

Random initialization is a technique in a neural network to initialize weights prior to training. This is useful as the first iteration needs to have weights with some values to perform weights updates. Usually, the weights are given a small value close to zero and randomly selected. It is also possible to initialize all weights to zero; this is called zero initialization. Random initialization is the most common way to initialize weights and is known to provide good results.

See also the following definitions: Weights, Xavier initialization, and neural network

Random policy

A random policy is a policy in reinforcement learning that can take any possible action randomly. So, each action in a random policy has the same probability.

See also the following definitions: Reinforcement learning and action

Random search

Random search is hyperparameter tuning technique or a technique that helps find optimal parameters. This technique is based on defining a range of possible hyperparameters and then training the model on random combination of hyperparameters, using an evaluation metric it finds the best or optimal combination.

See also the following definitions: Hyperparameter and grid search

Range

A range is defined as the spread of a series so it helps find how large a series is and it is the difference between the maximum value and the minimum value in the series. For example, a series that contains the following values: 1, 2, 4, 6, 7, 9, has the following range 9 minus 1 which is 8.

See also the following definitions: Descriptive statistics

Rank

A rank defines the position of a value in an order series. So, ranking is the capacity to order a series and find the rank of each value.

Rater

Rater is another word to describe an annotator. For more details see the definition of an annotator.

Recommendation engine

A recommendation engine is a system that is capable of recommending items or goods to customers or individuals. Recommendation engines are popular in e-commerce where they help create upsell and cross-sell opportunities. There are different types of recommendation engines. Some of them are based on only filter and business rules and others are based on mathematical or machine learning models like content-based filtering, user-user collaborative filtering or item-item collaborative filtering.

See also the following definitions: Association rules and item matrix

Reconstruction entropy

Reconstruction entropy consists in neural network to reconstruct the input based on an objective function that punishes the neural network when the result is far from the input. The input is usually summed with noise to avoid overfitting and learn different features.

See also the following definitions: Neural network, deep learning, and loss function

Rectified linear unit

Rectified linear unit or ReLU is an activation function in a deep neural network. It is well known for adding non-linearities to the model and is one of the most popular activation functions due to its robustness. It has the following formula:

$$f(x) = \max(0, x)$$

ReLU is also appreciated as it has a simple mathematical formula, meaning that is has a short computing time. This helps lighten the deep neural network.

See also the following definitions: Activation function, ELU, and softmax

Recurrent neural network

A recurrent neural network is type of neural network that works as a loop. Each sequence in the hidden layer feeds the neuron on its right. The information is then merged with the input. This process is useful to take into consideration the previous or past information within a neural network. The recurrent neural network is very popular for machine translation, natural language processing, speech recognition, image recognition. One popular type of recurrent neural networks is LSTM or long short-term memory.

See also the following definitions: LSTM, GRU, and neural network

Recursive neural network

A recursive neural network is a hierarchical structure of a neural network without "time aspect to the input sequence. The input is processed hierarchically in a tree form." Source: https://towardsdatascience.com/understanding-the-difference-between-ai-ml-and-dl-cceb63252a6c

See also the following definitions: Neural network

Regression

Regression is one of the most popular supervised machine learning types. The output in regression is always a real value like an amount or quantity. There are different types of regression such as linear regression, lasso regression, and ridge regression.

See also the following definitions: Logistic regression and machine learning

Regression spline

Regression spline is one of the most popular non-linear regression. It creates multiple polynomial models based on the separation of training data into multiple bins. The separation or bins are called knots. The knots are considered hyperparameters and can be modified depending on the case.

See also the following definitions: Regression, machine learning, and hyperparameter

Regularization

Regularization is a popular technique to avoid overfitting in machine learning. It adds an additional penalty term to the cost function; with this penalty the coefficients cannot get extreme values. It can be used in regression such as ridge regression or lasso regression but also in a neural network.

See also the following definitions: Overfitting and loss function

Reinforcement learning

Reinforcement learning is a type of machine learning where an agent interacts with an environment, the agent learns from the interaction with the environment. A popular application for reinforcement learning is self-driving cars or gaming.

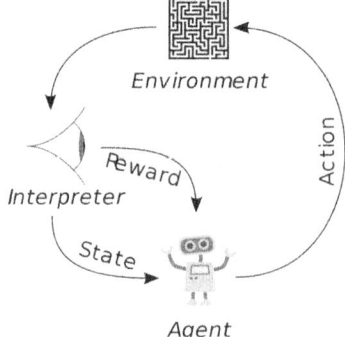

Figure 19.3: Reinforcement learning mechanism
(Source image: https://fr.wikipedia.org/wiki/Fichier:Reinforcement_learning_diagram.svg)

In reinforcement learning it is not required to have labeled data as opposed to supervised learning.

See also the following definitions: Action, Agent, and Q-learning

Relationship extraction

Relationship extraction is a technique in natural language processing where it extracts the semantic relation which occurs between two or more entities. For example, "Montréal is in Canada", the relationship between the entity Montréal and the entity Canada is stated by "is in".

See also the following definitions: Natural language processing

Relative entropy

Relative divergence also known as KL divergence is metric. For more details see the KL divergence definition.

Rectified linear unit (ReLU)

Rectified linear unit (ReLU) is an activation function in a neural network. For more details see the rectified linear unit definition.

Replay buffer

In reinforcement learning, a replay buffer corresponds to the memory used by the agent to store state transition.

See also the following definitions: Agent and reinforcement learning

Representation

Representation is the process of transforming raw data into a feature. Representation includes the process of feature engineering; it can be one hot encoding, feature creating, binning, and so on.

See also the following definitions: One hot encoding and feature engineering

Representation learning

Representation learning or feature learning is a technique in machine learning where it is not necessary to manually perform feature engineering, as the algorithm is capable to extract features from raw data and perform a specific task. Representation learning is present in k-means, PCA, deep neural networks.

See also the following definitions: Feature engineering and deep learning

Residual

Residual represents the difference between the actual value and the predicted value. Calculating the residual is important to understand the model, but it is also important for the model during the training to enhance its results performance.

See also the following definitions: Loss function

ResNet

ResNet stands for residual networks used essentially for computer vision tasks. It was the winner of ImageNet contest in 2015. ResNet was a revolution at this time as it was the only type of neural network that allowed to train a very deep neural network (more than 150 layers) without vanishing gradient issues. ResNet introduced some unique concepts such as skip connection which allows to stake a convolutional layer and add the input to the output of the convolutional block. There different architecture of ResNet such as ResNet50, ResNet152, and so on.

See also the following definitions: ImageNet, convolutional neural network, and AlexNet

Response variable

Response variable, also named dependent variable or target variable, is the variable that we are looking to predict. It is the variable of interest and it depends on other variables (independent variables).

See also the following definitions: Dependent variable and machine learning

Restricted Boltzmann Machine (RBM)

Restricted Boltzmann machine are stochastic and generative neural networks that can learn representation from raw data. It is a two-layer algorithm that will learn the probability distribution over the input. RBM has application in dimensionality reduction, classification, regression, recommendation system, feature learning, and so on.

See also the following definitions: Neural network

Reward

The reward represents the consideration in reinforcement learning when an agent takes an action in the environment. The reward is a key concept as it helps guide the agent about how well it is performing a task and helps improve the model overall.

See also the following definitions: Agent, action, and reinforcement learning

Ridge regression

Ridge regression is a regression technique used in the case data contains multicollinearity. Ridge regression works by adding bias to the estimates of the regression and it reduces the error and the variance. Ridge regression will perform L2 regularization on the objective function.

See also the following definitions: L2 regularization and regression

Ridge regularization

Ridge regularization is also known as L2 regularization. For more details see the L2 regularization definition.

Risk

The risk represents the output values from the loss function of a machine learning model. The objective is to minimize the risk.

Root Mean Square Propagation (RMSProp)

Root Mean Square Propagation (RMSProp) is deep neural network optimizer, which is similar to a gradient descent with momentum. With RMSProp it is not necessary to define a learning rate as it is automatically done and it adjusts for each parameter.

See also the following definitions: Optimizer, Adam Optimization, and Momentum

Recurrent Neural Network (RNN)

Recurrent Neural Network (RNN) is a type of neural network. For more details see the recurrent neural network definition.

Robotic Process Automation (RPA)

Robotic Process Automation (RPA) is a type of business process automation where the robotic software tries to copy the user interaction with the GUI. It is useful to avoid repetitive tasks and faster business processes. There is a lot of application such as processing transaction, data manipulation, triggering responses.

ROC-AUC

ROC-AUC is a visual tool for evaluation of classification problems. For more details see the Area Under the ROC Curve (AUC) definition.

Root Mean Squared Error (RMSE)

RMSE or root mean squared error represents the standard deviation of the difference between the actual value and predicted value. It helps measure how the residual is spread. It is an evaluation metric for regression problems. And it has the following formula:

$$RMSE = \sqrt{\frac{\sum_{i=1}^{n}(y_i - \hat{y}_i)^2}{n}}$$

Where y_i represents the predicted values, and $\hat{y}_i$ represents the actual values.

See also the following definitions: Root Mean Squared Logarithmic Error

Root Mean Squared Logarithmic Error (RMSLE)

Root Mean Squared Logarithmic Error (RMSLE) represents the standard deviation of the difference between the logarithm of the actual value and predicted value. It helps measure how the residual is spread. It is an evaluation metric for regression problems. Compared to root mean squared error, RMSLE deals better with the outlier thanks to the logarithm. And it has the following formula:

$$RMSE = \sqrt{\frac{\sum_{i=1}^{n}(\log(y_i + 1) - \log(\hat{y}_i + 1))^2}{n}}$$

Where y_i represents the predicted values, and $\hat{y}_i$ represents the actual values.

See also the following definitions: Root Mean Squared Error (RMSE)

Rotational invariance

Rotational invariance means that a function value doesn't change if we apply a rotation to the arguments. This is the mathematical definition, in data science rotational invariance is used to define a type of machine learning algorithm that is not affected when an image input is being rotated around himself.

See also the following definitions: Machine learning

R-squared/Adjusted R-squared

R-squared is a metric for regression problems that helps find the level to which the input variables are capable of explaining the variation of the output variable or target variable. For example, if R-squared is 70%, this means that 70% of the variations of the output variable are explained by the input variables. The limit of R-squared is that it doesn't matter how much input variables are being added to the model, the R-squared will be the same or increase. Whereas adjusted R-squared penalize adding input variable that doesn't explain the output variable.

See also the following definitions: Evaluation metrics and machine learning

CHAPTER 20
S

Sampling

Sampling is a technique which randomly selects a certain number of observations from a larger population. Sampling is a technique that helps study a larger population without having to analyze the entire population. In data science, sampling can be used for multiple reasons. For instance, instead of using all dataset and applying a machine learning model, it is easier to sample the dataset and then perform machine learning.

See also the following definitions: Stratified sampling and subsampling

Sampling bias

Sampling bias is a situation when the observations in a dataset didn't have the same chance of being selected, as some observations have higher or lower probability of being selected. So, the sample is not representative of the population.

See also the following definitions: Automation bias, bias, bias-variance trade-off, coverage bias, and implicit bias

SAS

SAS is statistical software that can mine, manipulate, and predict data from different sources. SAS contains a programming language called SAS language that can be used to perform various analysis but also contains graphical user interface that can be used by non-technical people.

See also the following definitions: Python, R, and SPSS

Scala

Scala is a multi-paradigm programming language designed to express common programming patterns in a concise, elegant, and confident way. It subtly integrates features of functional and object-oriented languages. The current implementation runs on the Java virtual machine and is compatible with existing Java applications.

See also the following definitions: Python, R, SAS, and SPSS

Scalar

In linear algebra, the real numbers which multiply the vectors in a vector space are called scalars. This scalar multiplication, which multiplies a vector by a number to produce a vector, corresponds to the external law of vector space.

Scaling

Scaling is a feature engineering technique that helps makes features to have the same value range. For example, if a feature has a range from 0 to 100 and we would like to bring it to a range from 0 to 1, we can scale that feature by dividing by 100.

See also the following definitions: Normalization

Scikit-learn

Scikit-learn is a free Python library for machine learning. It includes functions for estimating random forests, logistic regressions, classification algorithms, and support vector machines. It is designed to harmonize with other free Python libraries, notably NumPy and SciPy.

See also the following definitions: Python

Scoring

Scoring is the ability to predict a value from a built machine learning model. Scoring can also refer to a recommendation system that gives a ranking to each item generated.

See also the following definitions: Predictive model and machine learning

Seasonality

In time series, seasonality are patterns that repeat itself through the time at regular path such as weekly, monthly, and quarterly. Seasonality is usually considered as very predictable. It can be caused by various factors such as the weather, holidays, and so on.

See also the following definitions: ARIMA and Time series

Selection bias

In a statistical study, the term selection bias designates a systematic error made when selecting the subjects to be studied. This term brings together all the biases that can lead to the fact that the subjects actually observed during a survey do not constitute a representative group of the populations supposed to be studied and therefore do not make it possible to answer the questions asked in the protocol. Selection bias occurs during sampling, when selecting a representative sample of the population studied.

See also the following definitions: Sampling bias, automation bias, bias, bias-variance trade-off, coverage bias, and implicit bias

Self-supervised learning

Self-supervised learning is a new field between supervised learning and unsupervised learning where the data is automatically labeled, so it doesn't require a human annotator. In self-supervised learning, the algorithm will learn meaningful features from the unlabeled data.

See also the following definitions: Unsupervised learning and supervised learning

Semi-supervised learning

Semi-supervised learning is an approach in machine learning between unsupervised learning and supervised learning. As it takes a small sample of labeled data with a large amount of unlabeled data for training. Semi-supervised learning can be used in various domain, but it is very popular for document classification as the data is abundant and doesn't contain much labels.

See also the following definitions: Self-supervised learning, unsupervised learning, and supervised learning

Sensitivity

Sensitivity is measure in a binary classification problem that helps measure the proportion of actual positives that were classified as positive. Sensitivity is also called true positive rate. Another complementary measure exists called specificity and it helps measure the proportion of actual negatives that were classified as negative.

See also the following definitions: Positive class, negative class, and classification

Sentiment analysis

Sentiment analysis is a technique that helps identify human emotions (positive, negative, neutral, and so on.) in a text based on natural language processing. It is used by businesses to be able to better understand customer feedback and identify issues related to products or services.

See also the following definitions: Natural language processing

Sequence to sequence

Sequence to sequence is the ability to train a model to convert as input a sequence from one area (for example a sentence in French) to an output in another area (for example a sentence in English). Sequence to sequence is very popular in machine translation in free form question answering.

See also the following definitions: Natural Language Processing

Serialization

Serialization or data serialization is the process of sharing structured data in a format that allows data recovery to the original structure. Data serialization helps reduce data size which helps sharing and storing data easily.

See also the following definitions: Database and data engineering

Shape of a tensor

The shape of a tensor represents the number of elements in each dimension of the tensor. The shape is a list of integers.

See also the following definitions: Tensor

Siamese neural network

A Siamese neural network or twin neural network is type of artificial neural network that contains two or more identical neural network with the same weights each subnetwork takes one input. Usually, a Siamese network is used for binary classification, image classification, numerical data or text data.

See also the following definitions: Neural network

Sigmoid function

Sigmoid function is a type of activation function in a deep neural network. Graphically, its shape looks like an S-shape. Sigmoid function is being used as it is defined between 0 and 1, which makes it suitable for probabilities output.

See also the following definitions: Activation function, deep learning, and softmax

Signal processing

In data science, signal processing is the ability to exploit all signal data such as IoT, time series from devices, and so on. And be able to extract meaningful knowledge. For example, it is possible to use machine learning to create a predictive model that is capable of classifying a signal coming from IoT data.

See also the following definitions: Predictive model, Machine learning

Silhouette coefficient

In clustering, the silhouette coefficient is a measure of the quality of a partition of a set of data. For each point, its silhouette coefficient is the difference between the average distance with the points of the same group as it and the average distance with the points of the other neighboring groups. If this difference is negative, the point is, on average, closer to the neighboring group than to its own; it is therefore poorly classified. Conversely, if this difference is positive, the point is on average closer to its group than to the neighboring group; it is therefore well classified.

See also the following definitions: Classification

Similarity learning

Similarity learning, also called distance, makes it possible to measure the degree of kinship of two elements of the same set. It is used in the field of learning in classification or regression applications.

See also the following definitions: Evaluation metrics, classification, and regression

Single shot object detector

A single shot object detector is an artificial intelligence module that can detect multiple objects in one shot in an image. YOLO or You Only Look Once is the most popular single shot object detector. A single shot object detector usually has only two components: a single shot head and a backbone model. The backbone is always a pretrained model for image classification and the head is one or more convolutional layers added at the end of the backbone.

See also the following definitions: YOLO and deep learning

Singularity

Technological singularity or singularity is the hypothesis according to which the invention of artificial intelligence would trigger a runaway of technological growth which would induce unpredictable changes on human society. It is a hypothetical concept where machine intelligence surpasses by far human intelligence and capabilities. For more details see the superintelligence definition.

See also the following definitions: Artificial super intelligence

Skewness

In probability theory and statistics, the skewness coefficient corresponds to a measure of the asymmetry of the distribution of a real random variable. This is the first of the form parameters, with kurtosis. In general terms, the asymmetry of a distribution is positive if the right tail is longer or larger, and negative if the left tail is longer or larger.

See also the following definitions: Kurtosis and descriptive statistics

Skipgram

As the jargon of any language is enormous and can't be named by human, we require unsupervised learning strategies that can become familiar with the setting of any word all alone. Skipgram is one of the unsupervised learning strategies used to locate the most related words for a given word. It tries to predict the source context words given a target word.

See also the following definitions: Unsupervised learning

Smooth mean absolute error:

Smooth mean absolute error or Huber loss is regression loss function which is less sensitive to an outlier than mean square error. It has the following formula:

$$L(y, f(x)) = \begin{cases} \frac{1}{2}(y - f(x))^2 & for \ |y - f(x)| \leq \delta \\ \delta|y - f(x)| - \frac{1}{2}\delta^2 & otherwise \end{cases}$$

See also the following definitions: Loss function, mean square error, and mean absolute error

SMOTE

SMOTE or Synthetic Minority Over-Sampling is an oversampling technique that is used in the case one class in a classification technique is over dominating another class. SMOTE will create synthetic data from the minority class and this will help balance the classes.

See also the following definitions: Upsampling, downsampling, and sampling

Softmax

Softmax is an activation function in a deep neural network. Its mathematical behavior helps turn logits outputs into probabilities, so that's why it is used as the last layer in a deep neural network for classification problems.

See also the following definitions: Activation function, ReLU, and ELU

Sparse feature

A sparse feature is a feature with numerous missing values. To deal with sparse feature it is possible to replace the missing values with median, delete the observations with missing values or drop the feature.

See also the following definitions: Imputation and sparsity

Sparse representation

A sparse representation is a representation of a tensor where all elements are non-zero. For example, in word embedding, a sparse representation is opposed to a dense representation, and the vector of words will only contain the values of the words in the sentence, while a dense representation might contain millions of elements each of corresponding to a word in the English vocabulary.

See also the following definitions: Natural Language Processing

Sparse vector

A sparse vector is a vector containing mostly zeroes; it is usually associated with sparse feature. For more details see the sparse feature definition.

Sparsity

Sparsity represents the ratio of the number of zero elements in a vector divided by the total number of elements in the vector. For example, a sparsity of 99% means that 99% of elements in the vector contain zeros. Sparsity can be used in machine learning to describe a feature or model parameters.

See also the following definitions: Sparse feature

Spatial pooling

Spatial pooling is a technique used in a convolutional neural network that compresses the input matrix in a lower dimension. For more details see the pooling definition.

See also the following definitions: Convolutional neural network

Spatial-temporal reasoning

Spatial-temporal reasoning is a field in artificial intelligence where the goal is to develop a system capable of navigating and understanding time and space with the ability to manipulate objects and solve problems. It has several applications in natural language processing, geographic information systems, document interpretation, and so on.

See also the following definitions: Artificial intelligence

Specificity

Specificity is a measure in binary classification problem that helps measure the proportion of actual negative that were classified as negative. Sensitivity is also called true negative rate. Another complementary measure exists called sensitivity and it helps measure the proportion of actual positive that were classified as positive.

See also the following definitions: Sensitivity, positive class, and negative class

Speech recognition

Speech recognition is a computer science technique which allows human voice picked up by a microphone to be analyzed and transcribed into text in the form of machine-readable text. Speech recognition, speech synthesis, speaker identification or speaker verification are some of the techniques for speech recognition. Nowadays, speech recognition is largely based on deep neural network models.

See also the following definitions: Artificial narrow intelligence (ANI)

Speech segmentation

Speech segmentation is a process in natural language processing where it identifies the limits between words, sentences, and topics in a natural language. This technique can be used to process documents from news and articles, process documents from law or medical records.

See also the following definitions: Natural language processing

Splitting data

Splitting data is the ability to separate the main dataset in a machine learning exercise into two or more datasets. One of the datasets is called training data and the other one is called test data. This split is helpful to evaluate the model performance and avoid overfitting. If the metric on training data is high and the metric on test data is low, it means that there is probably overfitting. A dataset can also be split in training data, validation data and test data.

See also the following definitions: Training set, test set, and validation set

SPSS

SPSS is a statistical and data mining software. With its visual interface it helps build all kinds of statistical models and interacts visually with the data. SPSS can be used for data visualization, data manipulation, data modeling, and so on.

See also the following definitions: SAS and Watson Studio

Structured Query Language (SQL)

Structured Query Language (SQL) is a standardized computer language used to exploit relational databases. The data manipulation language part of SQL allows you to search, add, modify or delete data in relational databases.

See also the following definitions: Database and NoSQL

Squared hinge loss

Squared hinge loss is a loss function used for binary classification problems. Squared hinge loss is just the square of the output of the hinge loss. It punishes large error more than hinge loss whereas small error is less punished. It has the following formula:

$$L(y, \hat{y}) = \sum_{i=0}^{N} (\max(0, 1 - y \cdot \hat{y})^2)$$

See also the following definitions: Loss function and cross entropy

Squared loss

Squared loss represents the total amount of squared error in a classification or regression problem. In case we would like to have the accuracy, we divide by the number of observations, which corresponds to the mean squared error.

See also the following definitions: Regression and classification

Stacking

Stacking is an ensemble machine learning algorithm. It uses a meta algorithm to learn how to combine results from multiple models into one more accurate result. Stacking model will work generally by splitting the training data into two folds, the first fold is used to train the weak learners. Then predictions are made on the weak learners using the second fold, the prediction on the second fold and the second fold itself is used for training the meta algorithm. There are other ensemble models such as bagging or boosting.

See also the following definitions: Ensemble learning algorithm, bagging, and boosting

Standard deviation

In mathematics, standard deviation is a measure of the dispersion of the values of a statistical sample or a probability distribution. It is defined as the square root of the variance or as the quadratic mean of the deviations from the mean. In data science, standard deviation is used for data exploration, and in some machine learning models.

See also the following definitions: Descriptive statistics, mean, and variance

Standard error

Standard error is the standard deviation of the sampling distribution of a sample statistic. The term also refers to an estimate of the standard deviation, derived from a particular sample used to compute the estimate.

See also the following definitions: Standard deviation

Standardization

Standardization is the ability to rescale data with a mean of 0 and a standard deviation of 1. Whereas normalization means rescaling data in a range of values from 0 to 1. Usually, standardization is preferred over normalization.

See also the following definitions: Normalization

Stata

Stata is statistical and econometric software widely used by economists and epidemiologists. It is developed by StataCorp, a company based in College Station, Texas. It is used by statisticians but it is not so popular in data science.

See also the following definitions: SAS and SPSS

State

In reinforcement learning, a state is a parameter that describes the current situation and it is used by the agent to select an action.

See also the following definitions: Agent, action, and reinforcement learning

State-action value function

State-action value function is also called Q function, for more details see Q function definition.

Static model

A static model is a machine learning model that is trained offline. It is opposed to a model that is dynamic.

See also the following definitions: Dynamic model

Stationary

Stationary corresponds to a property of a time series that the mean and the variance doesn't change over time. A stationary time series is necessary to apply some statistical model such as ARMA.

See also the following definitions: ARIMA and Time series

Statistical inference

Statistical inference is the set of techniques used to induce the characteristics of a general group (the population) from a particular group (the sample), by providing a measure of the certainty of the prediction: the probability of error.

See also the following definitions: Generalization

Statistics

Statistics is the discipline that studies phenomena through the collection of data, their processing, their analysis, the interpretation of results and their presentation in order to make these data understandable by all. It is a science, a method and a set of techniques.

See also the following definitions: Descriptive statistics and machine learning

STD decomposition:

Seasonal and trend decomposition is a statistical technique that decomposes a time series into multiple series that represents a pattern. The image represents STD decomposition:

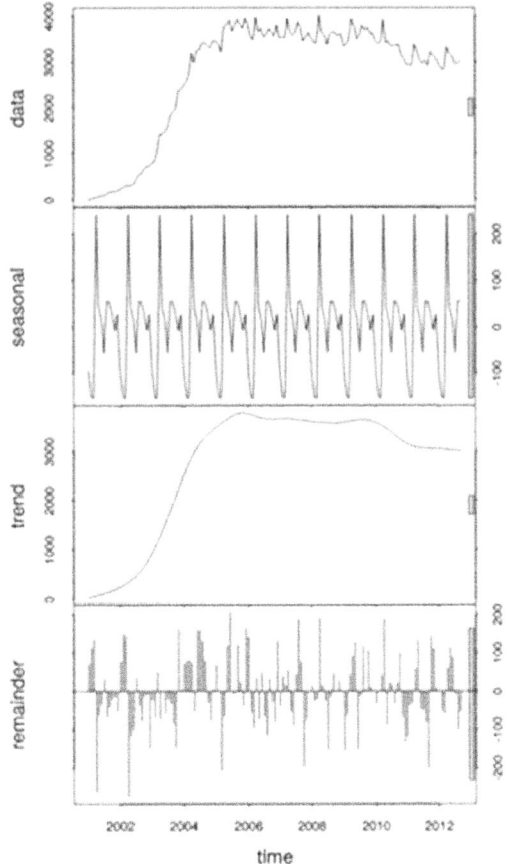

Figure 20.1: STD Decomposition
(Source image: https://commons.wikimedia.org/wiki/File:Mae.timeseries_decomposition.itwiki.svg)

For example, a time series can be decomposed into a trend, a cycle, seasonality and a noise.

See also the following definitions: ARIMA, time series, and stationary

Stochastic gradient descent

Stochastic gradient descent or SGD is a type of gradient descent algorithm to minimize the cost function. SGD will randomly pick one of the samples in the training data for each iteration, this technic reduces the computing time and is effective in case the training data is very large.

See also the following definitions: Gradient descent and neural network

Stratified sampling

Stratified sampling is a form of statistical representation that shows how a characteristic or variable behaves in a population by making evident the change of said variable in subpopulations or strata into which it has been divided. It consists of the previous division of the study population into groups or classes that are assumed to be homogeneous with respect to the characteristic to be studied and that do not overlap.

See also the following definitions: Sampling

Stride

A stride is a parameter for a convolutional neural network that acts as a filter for the compression of images. Modifying the stride will modify the way the filter moves over the image (1 as a stride means that the filter will move over the image 1 pixel at a time).

See also the following definitions: Convolutional neural network

Strong AI

It is an artificial intelligence that can perform the full range of human intelligence; it is also referred to as General AI. For more details see the Artificial General Intelligence definition.

See also the following definitions: Artificial Narrow Intelligence (ANI)

Strong classifier

An ensemble model, like boosting algorithm, is composed of weak learners and strong learners or strong classifiers. The strong classifier plays the role of regrouping the results of the weak classifiers into one accurate result.

See also the following definitions: Weak learner and ensemble model

Structural SIMilarity (SSIM)

Structural SIMilarity (SSIM) measures the similarity between two images. It helps compare the original image with the quality of a compressed image. The idea of SSIM is to measure the global similarity of structure between the two images, rather than a pixel-to-pixel difference.

See also the following definitions: Computer vision

Structured data

Structured data corresponds to data that have a clearly defined data type and can be searched easily. It usually resides in relational databases (RDBMS). Structured data is usually opposed to unstructured data.

See also the following definitions: Unstructured data

Subsampling

Subsampling is the result of two samplings; the first sampling is from the population and the second sampling is from the sample. It can be used in data preparation but also in machine learning when the data is too large.

See also the following definitions: Sampling and stratified sampling

Supervised learning

Supervised learning is the ability to train a model based on input data with its corresponding label. So, the model uses labels as references to compare its own result. Each time the model got an answer wrong it will adjust its parameters based on the difference between the true label and the predicted label.

See also the following definitions: Unsupervised learning

Support vector machine (SVM)

Support vector machine (SVM) is a machine learning algorithm popular for regression and classification. SVM is using a loss function called hinge loss.

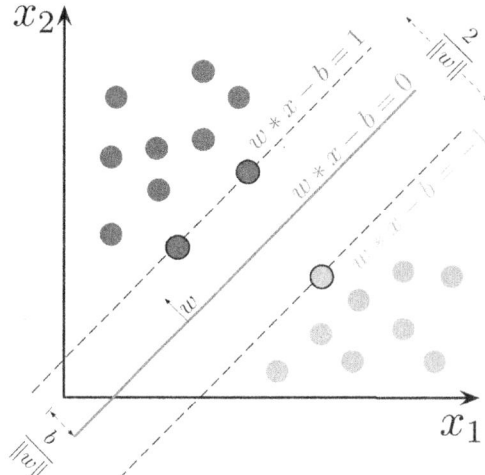

Figure 20.2: A representation of Support vector machine in a 2-dimension plane (Source image: https://en.wikipedia.org/wiki/File:SVM_margin.png)

SVM is a non-parametric technic as it is based on the kernel function. Kernels are useful to map features into higher dimensions.

See also the following definitions: Machine learning and supervised learning

SVM

For more details see support vector machine definition.

Synthetic feature

A synthetic feature represents a feature that is not available initially in the input data but has been created during data preparation. Usually, a synthetic feature can be from bucketing a continuous feature, multiplication of a feature by another or by itself, and so on.

See also the following definitions: Data preparation

CHAPTER 21
T

Tanh

Tanh is an activation function in a neural network. An activation function is positioned at the end of the neuron and is applied to the sum of the weights of the input. Tanh function is non-linear and is used in the case of classification with two classes.

See also the following definitions: Activation function, Softmax, ReLU, and ELU

Target variable

The target variable or dependent variable is the output variable of a machine learning model, as it represents the variable that needs to be predicted. The other kind of variable is a predictor or independent variables that are used to predict the target variable.

See also the following definitions: Dependent variable and supervised learning

T-distribution

In probability theory and statistics, Student's t-distribution is a probability law, involving the quotient between a variable according to a reduced centered normal law and the square root of a variable distributed according to the law of χ2. It is notably used for Student tests, the construction of confidence intervals and in Bayesian inference.

See also the following definitions: Bernoulli distribution, binomial distribution, chi-squared distribution, Gaussian distribution, exponential family distribution, normal distribution, and Poisson distribution

Tensor

A tensor is a generalization of a matrix of N-dimensional space. A rank 2 or 2-dimensional tensor is a matrix, a rank 1 or 1-dimensional tensor is a vector. A 3-dimensional tensor can be represented as follow:

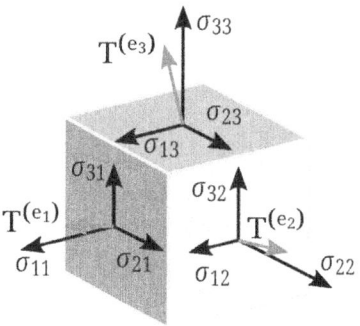

Figure 21.1: A 3-dimensional tensor
(Source image: https://commons.wikimedia.org/wiki/File:Components_stress_tensor.svg)

A matrix is only a simple array of numbers that can be used to represent abstract objects, while a tensor is an abstract object whose coordinates change when moving from one representation in a given base to that in another base.

See also the following definitions: Vector

Tensorflow

TensorFlow is an open-source machine learning tool developed by Google. The source code was opened on November 9, 2015, by Google and released under the Apache license. It is based on the DistBelief infrastructure, initiated by Google in

2011, and has an interface for Python and Julia. TensorFlow is one of the most used AI tools in machine learning, especially for a deep neural network.

See also the following definitions: Caffe, Pytorch, and Torch

Test set

A test set is a sample from the main dataset that is left behind to be used to verify if the machine learning model performs well after the training. See also the following definitions training set and validation set.

See also the following definitions: Training set, test set, and validation set

Text-to-speech:

Text-to-speech is a technology based on deep neural networks mainly that can convert text to voice.

See also the following definitions: Speech recognition

Theano

Theano is a Python deep learning software library developed by Mila - Quebec Institute of Artificial Intelligence, a research team from McGill University and the University of Montreal.

See also the following definitions: Caffe, Tensorflow, Pytorch, and Torch

Time series analysis

Time series analysis is a sub-field in statistics that focuses on temporal data. Time series analysis can be used for example to forecast the sales of items for a retailer month by month. Time series analysis is not only limited to forecasting but can also be used to analyze temporal data such as STD decomposition, and so on.

See also the following definitions: ARIMA and STD decomposition

Tokenization:

Tokenization is a task in natural language processing. It is used to separate words and sentences into tokens that are the building blocks in NLP. Tokenization can be performed on the word level, sentence level, and sub-word level.

See also the following definitions: Natural language processing

Topic modeling

In machine learning and in natural language processing, topic modeling is a probabilistic model for determining abstract subjects or themes in a document. And it falls under unsupervised machine learning models. It has several applications such as analyzing customers' reviews, and so on.

See also the following definitions: Natural language processing

Torch

Torch is a deep learning framework that has an underlying C/CUDA implementation that is not active anymore. It has been replaced by PyTorch since 2018.

See also the following definitions: Caffe, Tensorflow, Pytorch, and Torch

Tensor Processing Unit (TPU)

A **Tensor Processing Unit (TPU)** is an application-specific integrated circuit (ASIC), developed by Google specifically to accelerate artificial intelligence systems by neural networks. It has been developed specifically for Tensorflow.

See also the following definitions: GPU, CPU, and device

Training

Training is a phase in machine learning where an algorithm tries to learn patterns from data. Training is the central phase where data is ingested by the machine learning model. Without the training phase, we cannot call an algorithm a machine learning algorithm.

See also the following definitions: Scoring and machine learning

Training set

In machine learning, a dataset is usually split between a training set and a test set. The training set is the set used during the training phase. For more details see test set or validation set definition.

See also the following definitions: Test set and validation set

Translational invariance

Translational invariance is the ability of a machine learning model to ignore the translation of an image or its content. Meaning that if a dog in an image is being moved to the top corner or being rotated the model still recognize a dog in the image. In deep learning, a convolutional neural network has the ability to be translational invariance.

See also the following definitions: Rotational invariance

Transfer learning

Transfer learning is a popular technique a in neural network, where we transfer or copy weights of a trained model to another new model and start the training of the new model with the weights of the other model. This technic shows an enhancement in the training performance. Transfer learning works better when the underlying problems of the two models are close, for example, a model that recognizes animals in general with a problem that recognizes dogs specifically.

See also the following definitions: Neural network, deep learning, and pre-trained model

Transformer

Transformer is a deep learning technique that is popular for natural language processing tasks. It doesn't contain any recurrent neural network, but only attention-mechanism in encoder-decoder architecture. Transformer shows a real improvement in solving some type of tasks in NLP.

See also the following definitions: Attention mechanism, deep learning, and natural language processing

Trend analysis

Trend analysis is the practice of gathering information in order to spot trends in that information. Although trend analysis is generally used to predict future events, it could be used to estimate uncertain past events.

See also the following definitions: Time series analysis, descriptive statistics, and predictive model

Triplet loss

Triplet loss is a loss function in a deep neural network, used specifically in similarity learning.

See also the following definitions: Loss function and deep learning

True negative

In binary classification, a true negative is a value that has been predicted as negative and the true value is negative. For example, an IoT device where we want to predict is the device is malfunctioning or not. If the value predicted is not malfunctioning and the true value is not malfunctioning then we have a true negative.

See also the following definitions: True positive, precision, and recall

True positive

In binary classification, a true positive is a value that has been predicted as positive and the true value is positive. For example, an IoT device where we want to predict is the device is malfunctioning or not. If the value predicted is malfunctioning and the true value is malfunctioning then we have a true positive.

See also the following definitions: True negative, Precision and recall

Truncated SVD

In mathematics, the linear algebra process of decomposition into singular values (SVD) of a matrix is an important tool for the factorization of real or complex rectangular matrices. Its applications range from signal processing to recommendation systems. In recommendation systems, it is used for collaborative filtering, as it reduces the number of features in a data set by reducing the dimensions.

See also the following definitions: Recommendation engine, item matrix, and factorization matrix

T-test

In statistics, the Student test, or t-test, is a set of parametric statistical tests where the calculated test statistic follows Student's law when the null hypothesis is true. It is used to compare the mean of the two groups and see if there is a statistical difference between the two of them.

See also the following definitions: Hypothesis, Chi-square test, T-Test, and Z-test

Turing test

The Turing test is a proposal for an artificial intelligence test based on the ability of a machine to imitate human conversation. As described by *Alan Turing* in 1950 in his publication Computing Machinery and Intelligence, this test involves putting a human in a blind verbal confrontation with a computer and another human. If the person initiating the conversation is unable to say which of the other parties is a computer, the computer software can be considered to have successfully passed the test. This implies that the computer and the human will try to have a human semantic appearance.

See also the following definitions: Artificial intelligence

Type I error

In statistical hypothesis testing, type I error also known as false positive occurs when the null hypothesis is incorrectly rejected whereas the null hypothesis is true. The probability that a type I error occurs is associated with the value of the p-value. To reduce the risk of a type I error, it is possible to lower the p-value.

See also the following definitions: False positive and false negative

Type II error

In statistical hypothesis testing, type I error also known as false negative occurs when the null hypothesis is incorrectly not rejected whereas the null hypothesis is false. The probability that a type I error occurs is associated with the value of Beta. To reduce the risk of a type II error, it is possible to increase the sample size.

See also the following definitions: False positive and false negative

Chapter 22
U

Underfitting

An underfitting model is a model that is not capable to capture the underlying pattern in training data. The model performs poorly on test data, so it is not capable to generalize based on training data. Underfitting can be caused by multiple problems such as a model trained on the wrong features, a model trained for an insufficient amount of epoch, and so on.

See also the following definitions: Overfitting

Univariate analysis

Univariate analysis is the simplest form of statistical data analysis, where it analyzes only one variable. Univariate analysis includes descriptive statistics such as mean, mode, median, maximum, minimum, and so on.

See also the following definitions: Data analysis and descriptive statistics

Universal function approximation theorem

In the theory of artificial neural networks, the universal approximation theorem supports the fact that a feed-forward propagation network with one hidden layer that has a finite number of neurons, known as a multilayer perceptron, can estimate any continuous functions on subsets of Rn.

See also the following definitions: Multilayer perceptron, neural network, and hidden layer

Unlabeled data

Unlabeled data is a type of data that contains features but no label or tags for each observation. Unlabeled data are usually used as input in unsupervised learning or in semi-supervised learning. To use unlabeled data in supervised learning, it has to be labeled by an annotator.

See also the following definitions: Unsupervised learning

Unstructured data

Unstructured information or unstructured data is data that is represented or stored without a predefined format. They are typically made up of text or multimedia documents, but may also contain dates, numbers and facts. This absence of format leads to irregularities and ambiguities which can make it difficult to understand the data, unlike the case of data stored in spreadsheets or databases for example, which are structured information.

See also the following definitions: Structured data

Unsupervised learning

Unsupervised learning is a type of machine learning algorithm that uses unlabeled data as an input. Unsupervised learning is useful when there is no label in training data. A common type of unsupervised learning is a clustering algorithm where data is grouped together based on similar examples. PCA or principal component analysis is also a type of unsupervised learning that helps reduce the dimension of the data.

See also the following definitions: Supervised learning and machine learning

Upweighting

Upweighting is a technique that helps deal with an imbalanced target in a dataset. If the dataset contains a target that is separated into two classes one positive and one negative, but the negative class is more present than the negative class, then the dataset is imbalanced (i.e. 10 positive class for 2000 negative class). To avoid training on an imbalanced class we apply two things: first, downsampling the majority class then upweighting the majority which means adding a weight to each example in the majority class, the weight is equal to the downsampling factor.

See also the following definitions: SMOTE, sampling, and upsampling

User matrix

In recommendation systems, a user matrix is the result of matrix factorization and represents the latent factors about each user in the dataset. Item matrix is also a result of matrix factorization and represents the latent factors about each item. The user matrix has the same number of columns as the original matrix. For example, if the original matrix contains 100 columns representing 100 users, the user matrix will have 100 columns.

See also the following definitions: Item matrix and recommendation engine

CHAPTER 23
V

Validation set

A validation set is a holdout from the main dataset similar to the training set or test set. A validation set can be used during hyperparameter tuning to help find optimal parameters. A validation set can also be used to avoid overfitting.

See also the following definitions: Training set and test set

Vanishing gradient problem

The vanishing gradient problem is a problem posed, in a deep neural network, by the very rapid decrease in the values of the gradients during the backpropagation leading to the cancellation of the gradient and the stopping of learning.

See also the following definitions: Exploding gradient problem, and gradient descent

Variance

In statistics and probability theory, variance is a measure of the dispersion of values in a sample or in probability distribution. It expresses the mean of the squares of the deviations from the mean, also equal to the difference between the mean of the squares of the values of the variable and the square of the mean. Thus, the greater the deviation from the mean, the more it is preponderant in the total calculation of the variance which would therefore give a good idea of the dispersion of the values.

See also the following definitions: Standard deviation, mean, and descriptive statistics

Variational autoencoder

Variational autoencoder or VAE is a type of autoencoder in the family of deep neural network. VAE is used to generate new data such as the generative adversarial neural network. A VAE is an autoencoder whose training is regularized to make sure that the latent space has the right properties and to avoid overfitting. Like a standard autoencoder, VAE has an encoder and a decoder.

See also the following definitions: Deep learning and Generative Adversarial Neural Networks

VC dimension

In machine learning theory, the VC dimension or Vapnik-Chervonenkis dimension is a measure of the capabilities of a classification algorithm. It is defined as the cardinal of the largest set of points that the algorithm can pulverize. It is a central concept in Vapnik-Chervonenkis theory. It was defined by Vladimir Vapnik and Alexey Chervonenkis.

See also the following definitions: Classification

Vector

The notion of a vector is the foundation of a branch of mathematics called linear algebra. In this sense, a vector is an element of a vector space, which makes it possible to carry out operations of addition and multiplication by a scalar. An n-tuplet can constitute an example of a vector, provided that it belongs to a set provided with adequate operations.

See also the following definitions: Tensor

VGG

VGG is deep neural network architecture more specifically a convolutional neural network, that is used for image classification. It won, in 2014, the contest large scale visual recognition challenge. VGG includes 5 convolutional layers and 3 fully connected layers. The most popular form of VGG is VGG-16.

See also the following definitions: AlexNet, Deep learning, and ResNet

Chapter 24
W

Wasserstein loss

Wasserstein loss is a loss function used with a generative adversarial neural network or GAN. Wasserstein loss offers more stability to the training of GANs, as GANs can be challenging to train as it involves the training of a generator and a discriminator at the same time. Stable training requires an equilibrium between the two models. Wasserstein loss replaces the discriminator output with a score of the fakeness of the image or data instead of giving a probability of the generated image being fake or real.

See also the following definitions: Loss function and Generative Adversarial Neural Networks

Watson studio

Watson studio is a data science platform provided by IBM. Watson studio allows managing all aspects of a data science project within the same environment. Watson studio contains open-source tools such as Jupyter notebooks or RStudio as well as proprietary tools like SPSS or Watson machine learning.

See also the following definitions: Databricks, SPSS, SAS, and Jupyter Notebook

Weak classifier

Weak classifier is a classifier that performs just better than random classifier. There are used in algorithms such as random forest or XGboost. Grouped together, weak classifiers become a strong classifier can show high performance. In random forest, a weak classifier is called a stump.

See also the following definitions: Strong classifier and ensemble model

Weight decay

The weight decay method is a regularization technique used to limit overfitting in a neural network. It consists of adding a penalty to the error function which depends on the magnitude of the weights which connect the neurons. The following penalty is generally used:

$$\alpha \sum_i \omega_i$$

Where ω is the weight in the network and α is a positive coefficient which gives more or less importance to the penalty. The parameter α is generally very small, it tends towards zero.

See also the following definitions: Regularization, overfitting, and neural network

Weight sharing

Weight sharing is a type of model compression in a neural network, a technique to decrease the number of parameters and detecting better features.

See also the following definitions: Neural network

Weighted alternating least squares

Weighted alternating least squares or WALS is an algorithm used to build a recommender system. The alternating least squares method is an iterative matrix factorization method. In each attempt, either a row or a column factors is fixed and the other is computed, with respect to the other factor, by minimizing the loss function. The weighted type of the algorithm provides weights to unobserved entries or zero entries, as well as for non-zero entries in the matrix.

See also the following definitions: Recommendation engine and matrix factorization

Weighting

The weighting factor is a weight assigned to a data point that makes it heavier or lighter compared to other data points.

See also the following definitions: Sampling

Width

Width defines how large a neural network is, meaning what is the maximum number of nodes in a layer.

See also the following definitions: Neural network

Word embedding

The word embedding is a method of learning a representation of words used in particular in automatic language processing. This technique makes it possible to represent each word of a dictionary by a vector of real numbers. This new representation has the particularity that words appearing in similar contexts have corresponding vectors which are relatively close.

See also the following definitions: Natural language processing

Word segmentation

Word segmentation also called word tokenization, is a technic to divide strings of text written into separate words. Space is usually considered the best word separation possible.

See also the following definitions: Natural language processing and tokenization

Word2vec

In artificial intelligence and machine learning, Word2vec is a group of models used for lexical embedding. These models were developed by a research team at Google under the direction of *Tomas Mikolov*. These are two-layers artificial neural networks trained to reconstruct the linguistic context of words. The method is implemented in the Python Gensim library.

See also the following definitions: Embeddings and natural language processing

CHAPTER 25
X

Xavier initialization

Xavier initialization is a technic that is used to initialize weights in a neural network. Xavier initialization helps in starts training and avoiding neurons falling under saturation. It set weights to values randomly chosen from uniform distribution.

See also the following definitions: Random initialization, neural network, and weight

Xception

Xception is deep convolutional neural network architecture developed by Google. Xception showed a high performance as compared to VGG or ResNet. The Xception key is that it contains depth-wise separable conlutions.

See also the following definitions: Deep learning, VGG, and ResNet

XGboost

XGboost or extreme gradient boosting is an implementation of gradient boosting trees that outperformed all other machine learning models during the last few years. XGboost shows two major advantages: speed and performance. It can be used for classification and regression.

See also the following definitions: Random forest, boosting, and decision tree

CHAPTER 26
Y

You only look once (YOLO)

You only look once (YOLO) is a real time object detection framework. It is considered as the state of the art for object detection as it is fast and accurate.

See also the following definitions: Single shot object detector and deep learning

CHAPTER 27
Z

Zero shot learning

Zero shot learning is a problem configuration in machine learning where at the time of the test, a learner observes the samples of the classes that were not observed during the training and he must predict the category to which it belongs.

See also the following definitions: One shot learning and few shots learning

Z-test

In statistics, a z-test is a generic term designating any statistical test in which the test statistic follows a normal law under the null hypothesis.

See also the following definitions: ANOVA, chi-square test, and t-test

Index

A

A/A testing 20
A/B testing
  about 19, 20
  example 19
accuracy 20
action 21
activation function
  about 21, 182
  interaction, in reinforcement
      learning model 21
  selecting 22
  types 22
active learning
  about 22
  AdaBoost 23, 24
  AdaDelta 24
  AdaGrad 25
  Adam 25
  example 23
AdaBoost
  about 23
  working 24
AdaDelta 24, 25
AdaGrad
  about 24, 25
  mathematical formula 25
Adam
  about 25
  formula 26
Adaptive Gradient. *See* AdaGrad
adaptive learning rate 26
Adaptive Moment Estimation. *See* Adam
adjusted R-squared 223
affine layer 26, 121
agent 27
agglomerative clustering 27
AlexNet 27, 28
algorithm
  about 28
  example 28
amount of say
  formula 23
Anaconda 29
anchor boxes 29
annotation 30
annotator 30
ANOVA
  about 30
  example 30
Apache flume 120
Apache Hadoop 133
Apache Hive 138
Apache Oozie 192
Apache Spark 31
API deployment 93
Area under the Curve (AUC) 35
ARIMA
  about 31

equation 31
parameters 31
Artificial General Intelligence (AGI) 33
Artificial Intelligence (AI) 33
Artificial Narrow Intelligence (ANI) 33
Artificial Super Intelligence (ASI) 34
association learning
  association rules 34
attention mechanism
  about 34
  types 34
attribute 35
AUC-ROC 35
autocorrelation 36
autocorrelation function (ACF) 36
autocorrelation plot (ACF) 32
autoencoder 36, 37
automatic summarization
  about 37
  abstractive summarization 37
  extractive summarization 37
automatic text summarization 38
automation bias 38
autoregression 38
Auto Regressive Integrated Moving
    Average. See ARIMA
average pooling 38, 39
average precision 39
A/Z testing 20

B

backpropagation
  about 41
  bag of words 42
Backpropagation through time (BPTT) 42
bagging 42, 54
bagging algorithm 42
bar chart
  about 43
  example 43
base learner 44
baseline
  about 44
  visual representation 44
batch 44, 45
batch deployment 94

batch gradient descent 45
batch normalization 45
batch size 44
Bayesian inference 46
Bayesian statistics
  about 47
  working 47
Bayes' theorem
  about 46
  Bayesian inference 46
  Bayesian statistics 47
  example 46
  formula 46
Bellman equation 47, 48
Bernoulli distribution
  about 48
  simple representation 48
Bernoulli trial 53
bias 49
bias error 9
bias-variance trade-off 49
bidirectional recurrent neural
    network (BRNN) 49
big data 50
Big O notation
  about 50
  complexity 51
binarization 51
binary classification 51, 52
binary variables 52
binning 52, 56
binomial distribution
  about 52
  tree of probabilities 53
black box model 53
BLEU score 54
Boolean variable 99
boosting 43, 54
bootstrap aggregating 42
bootstrapping 55
bottleneck layer 55
bounding box 55
box plot 55, 56
bucketing 56
business analytics
  about 56
  versus, data science 57

business analytics levels
  cognitive analytics 57
  descriptive analytics 57
  diagnostic analytics 57
  predictive analytics 57
  prescriptive analytics 57
business intelligence
  about 57, 58
  versus, data science 58

C

Caffe 59
calibration
  about 59
  diagnosing 60
  using 59
candidate generation 60
candidate sampling 60
categorical cross-entropy
  about 60
  categorical variable 61
  formula 61
central processing unit (CPU) 79
centroid 61
centroid-based algorithm
  representation 61, 62
chainer 62
chain rule
  about 62
  example 62
channel 63
checkpoints 63
chi-squared distribution 63, 64
chi-square test 63
CIFAR-10 64
CIFAR dataset
  download link 64
classification 64, 65
classification accuracy
  about 20
  limits 20
classification threshold 65
classifier
  about 14, 65
  versus, model 14
clipping 66
cloud 66

cloud computing 66
clustering 66, 67
clusters 66
CNN
  about 67
  architecture 68
CNTK 68
co-adaptation 68
COCO 69
COCO dataset
  download link 69
coefficient of determination
  about 69
  formula 69
cognitive analytics 57
Cohen's kappa
  about 69
  fomula 69
collaborative filtering 70
complexity 71
computer vision 71
concordant-discordant ratio 72
confidence interval
  about 72
  example 73
  formula 72
confusion matrix
  about 73
  table 73
connectivity-based algorithm 73
continuous learning 74
continuous variable 75
contrastive divergence 75
convenience sampling 75
convergence 75
convex function 76
convolution
  about 76
  convolutional layer 76
  convulational neural network 77
  correlation 77
Convolutional Architecture for Fast Feature
        Embedding. *See* Caffe
convolutional layer 68
correlation
  about 15, 77
  formula 77

cosine similarity
  about 77
  formula 77
  geometric representation 77
cost function
  about 15, 78
  versus, loss function 15
covariance
  about 78
  formula 78
  versus, correlation 15, 16
coverage bias 78
cross-entropy 79
cross-entropy loss 163
cross validation 79
CUDA 80

D

dashboard
  about 81, 82
  example 81
data analysis 82
data annotations 30
data augmentation 82
database 85
databricks 85
data engineering 82
dataframe 85
data mining 83
data normalization
  about 17
  applying 17
data parallelism 83
data preparation 83
data sampling 7
data science 83, 84
data scientist
  good data scientist, becoming 6
dataset
  about 85
  missing data, handling 13
data transformation 7, 84
data wrangling 84
Davies-Bouldin index 86
DBSCAN 86
decile
  about 87

  table 87
decision boundary
  about 87, 88
  decision tree 88
  deduction 89
  deep belief network 89
  deep dream 90
decision tree 88, 89
decision tree split
  working 88
deduction 89
deep belief network (DBN)
  about 89
  architecture 89
deep dream
  about 90
  example 90
deep learning
  about 91
  architecture 91
  Deeplearning4j 92
  deep Q-network 92
  degree of freedom 92
  dense feature 92
  using, instead of traditional machine learning models 5, 6
Deeplearning4j 92
deep neural network
  architecture, building 2, 3
  input data, normalizing 4
  invention 16
deep Q-network 92
degree of freedom 92
dendrogram 73, 74
dense feature 92
dense layer 92
density-based algorithm 93
Density-Based Spatial Clustering of Applications with Noise. *See* DBSCAN
dependent variable
  about 93
  API deployment 93
depth 94
Depth-wise separable convolutional neural network. *See* DSCNN
descriptive analytics 57
descriptive statistics 94, 95

device 95
diagnostic analytics 57
dimensionality reduction 95, 116
dimension reduction 55
discounted cumulative gain 95
discrete variable 96
discriminative model 10, 96
discriminator 96
distributed computing
  using 7
divisive clustering
  about 96
  working 96, 97
downpour SDG
  about 97, 98
  schema 97
downsampling 98
Dplyr 98
DropConnect
  about 98
  Dropout regularization 99
  versus, Dropout 98
drop observations 13
Dropout 99
DSCNN 94
dummy variable 52, 99
Dunn index 99
dynamic model 100
Dynamic programming 100

E

early stopping 101
EDA (Exploratory Data Analysis) 101
embeddings 103
embedding space 102
ensemble learning algorithm 103
ensemble models 103
entropy 103
episode 104
epoch 104
epsilon greedy policy 104
Euclidean distance
  about 105
  formula 105
evaluation metrics
  about 6, 105
  example 106

experimentation 106
  types 6
expert system 106
exploding gradient problem 106
exploration
  versus, exploitation 107
exponential family distribution 107
Exponential Linear Unit (ELU)
  about 102
  formula 102
  representation 102
exponential loss 107
exponential smoothing
  about 108
  formula 108
Extract Transform and Load (ETL) 105
extrapolation 108
extreme gradient boosting 262
extreme values 109

F

F1 score
  about 111
  formula 111
face recognition
  about 111
  visual representation 112
facet 112
facet plotting
  example 112, 113
factor analysis 113, 114
false negative 114
false positive 114
feature 114
feature cross 115
feature engineering 115
feature hashing 115
feature learning 115, 116
feature reduction 116
feature selection 117
federated learning 117, 118
feedback loop 118
feedforward
  about 118
  graphical representation 119

few-shot learning 119
fine-tuning 119, 120
flume 120
F-measure 111
focal loss 120
forget gate 120
Frechet Inception Distance (FID) 121
frequentist inference 121
frequentist statistics 121
F-score 121
full softmax 121
fully connected layer. See affine layer

G

gain and lift charts
  about 123
  example 123, 124
Gated Recurrent Unit (GRU)
  about 124
  illustration 124
  reset gate 125
  update gate 125
Gaussian distribution 125
General AI 126
generalization
  about 126
  overfitting 126
  underfitting 126
generalization curve
  representation 126
generalized linear model (GLM)
  about 127
  using 127
generative adversarial neural network
    (GAN) 127
generative classification 128
generative model
  versus, discriminative model 10
generator 128
genetic algorithm 128
Ggplot2
  about 128, 129
  example 128
Gini coefficient 129
Gini index 129
GloVe 130
Go 130

good data scientist 6
goodness of fit
  about 130
  examples 130
GoogleNet 130
GPU (graphics processing unit) 131
gradient accumulation 131
gradient descent 131
greedy policy 131
Grid search 132
ground truth 132

H

Hadoop. See Apache Hadoop
hashing 133
heuristic technique 134
hidden layers 134
hidden Markov model
  about 134, 135
  example 135
hierarchical clustering 73, 135
highway layer
  about 136
  formula 136
highway network 136
hinge loss 136, 137
histogram 137
Hive. See Apache Hive
holdout sample 138
Holt-Winters forecasting 138
Huber loss 139
hyperparameter
  about 139
  tuning 139
hyperplane 139, 140
hypothesis 140

I

ImageNet 142, 143
ImageNet large scale visual recognition
    challenge (ILSVRC) 142
Image recognition
  about 142
  example 142
imbalanced dataset
  about 143

handling 11, 12
implicit bias
   about 143
   example 143
imputation
   about 143, 144
   example 143
inception 144
inception module 144
inception v1 130
independent and identically distributed
      (i.i.d) 145
Independent Component Analysis (ICA) 145
induction 145
inferential statistics 145
input gate 146
input gate, in LSTM cell
   visual representation 146
input layer
   about 146
   visual representation 146, 147
instance 147
instance-based learning 147
Integrated Development Environment
      (IDE) 141
International Conference on Machine Learning
      (ICML) 141
interpretability 147
Interquartile Range (IQR) 148, 149
Intersection over Union (IoU)
   about 148
   visual representation 148
item matrix 149
iteration 149

J

Jacobian 151
Julia 151
Jupyter notebook 152

K

Keras 153
kernel 153
kernel support vector machine (KSVM) 154
kernel trick
   about 13
   uses 13
KL divergence 154, 219
k-means 154
k-means cluster representation
   example 154
k-median 155
k-nearest neighbors (kNN) 155
Kolmogorov Smirnov (KS) chart 155
Kurtosis 156

L

L1 loss 157
L1 regularization
   about 157, 158
   versus, L2 regularization 9
L2 loss 158
L2 regularization 158
labeled data 159
lasso regression 159
latent variables 159
layer 159
Leaky ReLU 160
learning rate 160
least squares regression 160
LeNet 130
linear activation function 161
Linear Discriminant Analysis (LDA) 162
linear model
   about 162
   linear regression 162, 163
line chart 161
Log-Cosh loss
   about 163
   formula 163
logistic regression
   about 164
   equation 164
   logits 164
   log-odds 164
logits 164
log loss
   about 163
   formula 163
   Log-Cosh loss 163
Long Short-Term Memory (LSTM)
   about 146, 164
   loss curve 165

loss curve 165
loss function 15, 165
loss surface 166

M

machine learning
  about 167, 173
  origins 14
  problem, dealing with 17
  resources 16
machine learning algorithm
  fine tuning 1, 2
  selecting 8
  training faster 3, 4
machine learning project
  job, evaluating 4, 5
machine translation 167
magnet loss 168
Mahout 168
majority class 168
Management Information System (MIS) 173
Manhattan distance
  about 168
  equation 168
MapReduce 168
market basket analysis 169
market mix modeling 169
Markov chain
  about 169
  Markov decision process 169
  Markov property 169
Matplotlib 170
matrix factorization 170
maximum likelihood estimation 171
max pooling 170
mean
  about 18, 171
  mean absolute error 171
  mean reciprocal rank 171
  mean squared error 172
median
  about 18, 172
  using 18
memory-based algorithm 147
memory-based learning 172
mini-batch
  about 172

mini-batch gradient descent 173
minimax loss 173
minority class 173
missing data
  handling 13
ML. See machine learning
ML-as-a-service (MLaaS) 174
MLOps 174
MNIST 174
mode 174
model 14, 175
model accuracy
  versus, model performance 11
model capacity 175
model parallelism 175
model selection 175
model's performance
  evaluating 6

momentum
  about 175
  equation 175
Monte Carlo simulation 176
moving average 176
multi-agent reinforcement learning 176
multi-class classification 176
multilayer perceptron 177, 250
multinomial classification 177
multivariate analysis 177
multivariate regression 177
multivariate testing 20
MXNet 177

N

Naïve Bayes
  about 179
  called as naive 18
NaN 179
Nash equilibrium 179, 180
Natural Language Generation (NLG) 180
Natural Language Processing (NLP)
  about 180
  Natural Language Understanding (NLU) 181
  negative class 181
  negative log likelihood 181
Nesterov accelerated gradient 181

Neural Machine Translation (NMT)
  about 181
  neural network 182
Neural Turing Machine (NTM) 182
neuron 183
N-gram 183
node
  about 183
  noise 183
  noise contrastive estimation 184
no free lunch theorem 183
nominal variable 61, 184
nonlinear transform function 184
nonparametric learning algorithm 15
normal distribution 125, 184, 185
normalization 185
Normalized Discounted Cumulative Gain
       (NDCG) 185
NoSQL 186
notebook 186
Null
  about 186
  baseline accuracy 186
numerical data 187
Numpy 187
NVIDIA 187

O

object detection 189
objective 190
objective function 190
one hot encoding 190
one shot learning 191
one vs all 191
online inference 191
online learning 191
Oozie. *See* Apache Oozie
OpenCV (Open Computer Vision) 192
optimizer 192
ordinal variable 193
outlier 193
output gate 194
output layer 194
overfitting
  about 12, 195
  avoiding 12

P

Pandas 197
parallel processing 197
parameters 198
parameter update 198
parametric learning algorithm
  about 15
  versus, nonparametric learning algorithm 15
partial autocorrelation (PACF) plot 32
partial derivative 198
participation bias 198
partitioning 199
pattern recognition 199
Peak Signal-To-Noise Ratio (PSNR) 199
Pearson correlation 77
perceptron
  about 199
  representation 200
performance 200
perplexity 200
pie chart
  about 200
  representation 201
Pig 201
pipeline 201
Poisson distribution 202
polynomial regression 202, 203
pooling 203
population 203
positive class 204
POS tagging 198
post-processing 204
precision and recall 204
prediction 204
predictive analytics 57
predictive model 205
predictor variable 205
pre-processing 205
prescriptive analytics 57
pre-trained model 205
Principal Component Analysis (PCA) 116,
       117, 205, 206
prior belief 206
probability
  versus, likelihood 10
probability density 206

proxy label 206
p-value 206
Python 8, 207
PyTorch 207

Q

Q function 209
Q-learning 209, 210
Quadratic loss 210
Quantile 210
quantile loss 210
quartile 210
question answering, in NLP 211

R

R 8, 213
Radial Basis Function Network (RBFN)
  about 213
  architecture 213, 214
Random-Access Memory (RAM) 214
random forest
  about 214
  visual representation 214, 215
random initialization 215
random policy 215
random search 216
range 216
rank 216
rater 216
recommendation engine 216
reconstruction entropy 217
rectified linear unit (ReLU)
  about 217, 219
  formula 217
recurrent neural network (RNN) 42, 119, 217, 222
recursive neural network
  about 217
  regression 218
  regression spline 218
  regularization 218
reinforcement learning
  about 218
  action 21
relationship extraction 219
relative divergence 219

relative entropy 219
replay buffer 219
representation 219
representation learning 115, 220
residual 220
ResNet 220
response variable 220
Restricted Boltzmann Machine (RBM) 221
reward 221
Ridge regression 221
Ridge regularization 221
risk 221
Robotic Process Automation (RPA) 222
ROC-AUC 222
Root Mean Squared Error (RMSE)
  about 222
  formula 222
Root Mean Squared Logarithmic Error (RMSLE)
  about 223
  formula 223
Root Mean Square Propagation (RMSProp) 222
rotational invariance 223
R-squared 223

S

sampling 225
sampling bias 225
SARIMA (Seasonal ARIMA) 31
SAS 226
Scala 226
scalar 226
scaling 226
scikit-learn 226
scoring 227
seasonality 227
selection bias 227
self-supervised learning 227
semi-supervised learning
  about 228
  advantages 17
sensitivity 228
sentiment analysis 228
sequence to sequence 228
serialization 229
shape of a tensor 229

Siamese neural network 229
sigmoid function 229
signal processing 229
silhouette coefficient 230
similarity learning 230
single shot object detector 230
singularity 230
skewness 231
Skipgram 231
smooth absolute error loss 139
smooth mean absolute error
  about 231
  formula 231
Softmax 232
sparse feature 232
sparse representation 232
sparse vector 232
sparsity 232
spatial pooling 233
spatial-temporal reasoning 233
specificity 233
speech recognition 233
speech segmentation 233
splitting data 234
SPSS 234
squared hinge loss 234
  formula 234
squared loss 235
stacking 235
standard deviation 235
standard error 235
standardization
  about 17, 235
  applying 17
stata 236
state 236
state-action value function 236
static model 236
stationary 236
statistical inference 236
statistics 237
STD decomposition 237
stochastic gradient descent (SGD) 238
stratified sampling 238
stride 238
Strong AI 238
strong classifier 239

Structural SIMilarity (SSIM) 239
structured data 239
Structured Query Language (SQL) 234
stump 23, 258
subsampling 239
supervised learning 239
supervised machine learning
  versus, unsupervised machine learning 9
support vector machine (SVM) 240
synthetic feature 240
Synthetic Minority Over-Sampling (SMOTE)
    12, 231

T

Tanh 241
target variable 241
t-distribution 242
technological singularity 230
tensor 242
TensorFlow 242
Tensor Processing Unit (TPU) 244
test set 243
text-to-speech 243
Theano 243
time series analysis 243
tokenization 243
topic modeling 244
Torch 244
trade-off bias and variance 8
training
  about 244
  training set 244
transfer learning 245
transformer 245
translational invariance 245
trend analysis 245
triplet loss 246
true negative 246
true positive 246
truncated SVD 246
t-test 246
Turing test 247
type I error
  about 247
  versus, type II error 9, 10
type II error 247

U

underfitting 249
underfitting model 249
univariate analysis 249
universal function approximation theorem 250
unlabeled data 250
unstructured data 250
unsupervised learning 250
upweighting 251
user matrix 251

V

validation set 253
vanishing gradient problem 253
variance 254
variance error 9
variational autoencoder (VAE) 254
VC dimension 254
vector 254
VGG 255
VGG-16 255

W

Wasserstein loss 257
Watson studio 257
weak classifier 258
weak learner 103
weight decay 258
weighted alternating least squares (WALS) 258
weighting factor 259
weight sharing 258
width 259
Word2vec 259
word embedding 259
word segmentation 259
word tokenization 259

X

Xavier initialization 261
Xception 261
XGboost 262

Y

YOLO algorithm (You Only Look Once) 30, 263

Z

zero initialization 215
zero shot learning 265
z-test 265

Printed in Great Britain
by Amazon

86926223R00176